APPROACH
TO
STANDARD
ENGLISH

BY

J. BARCLAY, M.A.
and
D. H. KNOX, M.A.

ROBERT GIBSON & SONS GLASGOW, LTD

Publishers - - - - - - Glasgow

1957

First Impression	.	.	September	1942
Second Impression	.	.	. May	1943
Third Impression	.	.	December	1943
Fourth Impression	.	.	February	1945
Fifth Impression	.	.	. March	1946
Sixth Impression	.	.	October	1947
Seventh Impression	.	.	. May	1948
Eighth Impression	.	.	January	1949
Ninth Impression	.	.	September	1950
Tenth Impression	.	.	September	1951
Eleventh Impression		.	. June	1952
Twelfth Impression	.	.	. July	1953
Thirteenth Impression		.	February	1954
Fourteenth Impression		.	December	1954
Fifteenth Impression		.	December	1955
Sixteenth Impression		.	January	1957

PRINTED IN GREAT BRITAIN BY BELL AND BAIN, LTD., GLASGOW

PREFACE

" Approach to Standard English " has been prepared in response to the request of various teachers for a junior edition of "A Study of Standard English." It is suitable for use in at least the first two years of a Senior Secondary School curriculum, and for the complete course of a Junior Secondary School.

It has been our intention to present the essentials of formal training with due consideration of important modern developments in the teaching of English. As in "A Study of Standard English," no attempt has been made to prescribe a definite course of study, but it is hoped that the contents are sufficiently comprehensive to enable the most exacting teacher to find what he requires when devising his schemes of work. The Exercises have all been carefully tested in the classroom and have been found satisfactory.

We wish to express our indebtedness to the authors of "Modern English Usage" for their simplification —so far as such a complicated matter can be simplified—of the rules of spelling.

If we have inadvertently infringed any copyright, we offer our sincere apologies.

Note.—It is a matter of regret that Mr. G. B. Ballantyne, who collaborated with us in "A Study of Standard English," has been too much occupied with military duties to take an active part in the present work though his advice and help in the planning of the book have been of the utmost service.

J. B.
D. H. K.

ACKNOWLEDGMENTS

We value highly the permission to include copyright material and are happy to put on record our indebtedness for :—

"COURAGE," to Mrs. Galsworthy and Messrs. Wm. Heinemann, Ltd.

"SEA FEVER," reprinted from Collected Poems of John Masefield (Wm. Heinemann, Ltd.) by permission of the Author.

"THE ICE CART," from "Collected Poems, 1905–1925," by permission of Mr. Wilfred Gibson and Messrs. M'Millan & Co., Ltd.

"THE ROMAN ROAD," from "The Collected Poems of Thomas Hardy," by permission of the Trustees of the Hardy Estate and Messrs. M'Millan & Co., Ltd.

"THE SCARECROW," to Mr. Walter de la Mare and Messrs. Faber & Faber.

"THE THRUSH'S NEST," to Mr. John Clare and Messrs. J. M. Dent & Sons, Ltd.

Extract from "BRITISH HISTORY" by Rait, to Messrs. Thomas Nelson & Sons, Ltd.

Extract from "WIND IN THE WILLOWS," to Mr. Kenneth Grahame and Messrs. Methuen & Co., Ltd.

Extract from "HOW IT IS MADE," by Ellison Hawks, to Messrs Odhams Press, Ltd.

Extract from "SHERWOOD," to Mr. Alfred Noyes and Messrs. Wm. Blackwood & Sons, Ltd., publishers of "Collected Poems."

CONTENTS

CONTENTS

CHAPTER I

PARTICULAR ANALYSIS

A **Sentence** is a group of words expressing a complete thought.

A **Clause** is a group of words expressing a thought but forming part of a Sentence.

A **Phrase** is a group of words which expresses a distinct part of a thought.

EXERCISE I

Classify the following groups of words as Sentences, Clauses or Phrases :—

1. perched on a tree
2. the cattle have stampeded
3. which I gave you
4. the bride took
5. the hungry dog
6. the mutineers scuttled the ship
7. when I arrived home
8. the garden has been
9. the cat mewed piteously
10. give the prize to

EXERCISE II

Turn the following phrases into sentences by adding suitable words :—

1. after the ball was
2. caused him intense pain

3. the sexton tolled
4. ashore during the storm
5. shout of anger he attacked his foe
6. many hands make
7. in a whisper
8. how beautiful are
9. gathers no moss
10. Rome is the

In this chapter we are concerned with the Simple Sentence which may be classified as :—

1. **A Statement :** The house is near the station.

2. **A Question :** What are the wild waves saying ?

3. **An Exclamation :** What a piece of work is man !

4. **A Desire :** May the best man win.

5. **A Command :** Carry out the order without fail.

EXERCISE III

Classify each of the following sentences as **statement, question, exclamation, desire, command** :—

1. Tell the truth and nothing but the truth.
2. A man severe he was and stern to view.
3. Let their names be praised evermore.
4. Do you remember the last game.
5. How beautiful are the faces of old women.
6. Surely you will help us now.
7. May we never lack a friend.

8. Oft had I heard of Lucy Gray.
9. Must he then watch it rise no more.
10. What a wonderful life he has led.

EXERCISE IV

Change the following statements (1-5, into desires, commands; 6-10, into exclamations) :—

Examples :
{ You must obey orders without fail.
{ Obey orders without fail.

{ The captive was very pale.
{ How pale the captive was !

1. You had better leave the heavy luggage at the station.
2. Your answer is required without hesitation.
3. You must behave in an honourable fashion.
4. Silence is demanded during the ceremony.
5. My orders are that you remain in this room.
6. You are a very careless fellow.
7. The boy is bleeding very badly.
8. It is sad to see him so pale.
9. The moonlight sleeps very sweetly upon this bank.
10. There was a great fall there, my countrymen.

EXERCISE V

Make a sentence about each of the following in the form of :—

(a) Statement :
    Saturday morning ; a school chum ; a tyre puncture ; home lessons ; a cowboy story.

(b) Question :
    Skating ; the school magazine ; a film star ; football ; pocket money.

(*c*) Exclamation :

    War ; cricket ; a bonfire ; bullying ; ice cream.

(*d*) Desire :

    A picnic ; an escaped lion ; scoring a goal ; a chocolate ; a holiday.

(*e*) Command :

    Telling the truth ; crossing at traffic lights ; school sports ; helping at home ; playing the game.

The two principal and necessary parts of a Simple Sentence are the **Subject** and **Predicate**. These contain the different parts of the thought expressed in the sentence. The Subject names the thing, idea or person we are thinking about and may be a noun, pronoun or group of words doing the work of a noun. The Predicate tells what the Subject does or is and must always be or contain a Finite Verb.

The Subject of a Sentence is found by asking *who* ? or *what* ? is spoken about. The Predicate of a Sentence is found by asking *what happens* ? or *what is stated* ?

Examples :

1. *The dogs* are barking.
2. *The stranger* shook the heavy gate.
3. *The galley slaves, urged on by voice and lash,* rowed desperately away from the sinking ship.
4. Be silent.

Apply the tests given above and we find that the Subjects of 1, 2, 3 4 are : *The dogs, The Stranger, The galley slaves, urged on by voice and lash, You* (understood). The Predicates consist of the remaining parts of the sentence. This division of the sentence into Subject and Predicate is called **Particular Analysis**.

EXERCISE VI

Divide the following sentences into Subject and Predicate :—

Example :

The curfew tolls the knell of parting day.

SUBJECT	PREDICATE
The curfew	tolls the knell of parting day.

1. Who is the man in the blue suit ?
2. The great tower of the abbey loomed darkly above their heads.
3. To fear God and honour the king was his religion.
4. The horse, the friend of man, has been domesticated for many years.
5. The meteor flag of England shall yet terrific burn.
6. Bang went sixpence.
7. How lightly he enters to challenge his foe !
8. The gallant hound the wolf had slain.
9. Falstaff, a very fat man, is the cause of much mirth in the play.
10. What evil looks had I from old and young !

The Subject may consist of a Noun, a Pronoun, a Phrase or a Noun Clause, as italicised below. It generally precedes the Predicate, except in questions.

Examples :

1. The *wolf* howls.

2. *He* spoke to his friends.

3. $\begin{cases} \textit{Riding to the fair} \text{ was a great adventure.} \\ \textit{To err} \text{ is human.} \end{cases}$

4. *What he actually said* was of little importance.

EXERCISE VII

Write down the Subject in each of the following sentences and say what it is :—

1. My stars shine darkly over me.

2. The house with the crooked windows made them afraid.

3. What the eye cannot see may be very important at times.

4. What letters has the postman brought to-day ?

5. The King, Charles I, was condemned to death.

6. Riding at the ring was a favourite sport of the Middle Ages.

7. Where the bee sucks is the fairy's home.

8. Silver and gold have I none.

9. Blessed are the peace makers.

10. With spur and whip he urged on the tired horse.

EXERCISE VIII

Make up Subjects (noun, pronoun, phrase or clause) to complete the sense of the following phrases :—

1. .... make fine birds.
2. .... is of little interest to us.
3. How lovely are .... !
4. .... is the lady in the fur coat ?
5. Suddenly .... flashed in the intense darkness.
6. .... has no real influence on my actions.
7. What .... touched his body and not for justice ?
8. .... gives happiness to many.
9. .... should be taught in the lower classes.
10. Turning a corner .... collided with a car.

When the Subject consists of a group of words in which the essential noun or pronoun is qualified, the qualifying word or phrase is called the **Enlargement of the Subject.**

Examples :

1. *Handsome* men are slightly sunburnt.
2. Horses *with flowing manes* went galloping past.
3. The President, *Mr. Roosevelt*, defended liberty.
4. *The child's* answer pleased the company.

The Enlargement of the Subject may be

(1) *Adjective* ; (2) *Adjective Phrase* ; (3) *Noun in apposition* ; (4) *Noun in Possessive Case.*

EXERCISE IX

Write down the Enlargement of the Subject in the following sentences :—

1. The idle apprentice was discharged by his master.
2. The lady with the lamp was adored by the wounded soldiers.
3. The ship in the offing was recognised to be an enemy cruiser.
4. The sight of the cloak of Cæsar brought tears to their eyes.
5. John, the worst king of England, lost Normandy early in his reign.
6. Lashed to the helm, we drive our ships onwards.
7. The cry of women in a state of excitement startled Macbeth.
8. The bird's cage is more ornamental than useful.
9. The packing case, badly damaged by careless handling, has arrived at last.
10. Our distinguished visitor, Lady Jane Thomson, is delighted with the exhibition.

The Predicate and Its Parts

(a) The Object—Direct and Indirect

The Predicate, like the subject, may consist of a group of words which are described according to their function. When the action of the finite verb does not stop with the subject but requires some person or thing to be acted upon, the person or thing is called the **Direct Object**, and the verb is said to be **Transitive**. Verbs which do not require an object are said to be **Intransitive**. The Object is found by asking the question **Whom ? or What ?**

after the Verb and is the third most important part of the sentence.

Example :

The servant brushed the dusty *suit*.

The word " *suit* " answers the question, What ?

EXERCISE X

Pick out the finite verbs in the following sentences. Say whether they are transitive or intransitive. If transitive name the objects :—

1. The audience laughed heartily at the joke.
2. He gave his name to the man in charge.
3. He did not omit to charge for delivery.
4. He had no respect for the fighting qualities of the enemy.
5. The horse was purchased by a stranger.

EXERCISE XI

Insert suitable objects to complete the sense of the following :—

1. The gardener killed...............in the cabbage bed.
2. Too many cooks spoil..................
3. What..................had the injured man ?
4. Where have the children been picking.............. ?
5. The outlaws prepared...............for the travellers.

Verbs that denote giving, lending, promising, and similar actions may take two objects, one direct and the other the Indirect Object.

Example :

1. The directors granted the *workmen* an increase.

2. The doctor has promised *me* a complete cure.

" *Workmen* " and " *me* " tell to whom the " *increase* " is " *granted* " and to whom the " *cure* " is " *promised* " and are called the **Indirect Object**.

Note.—When the Indirect Object follows the Direct Object, it is replaced by an adverbial phrase introduced by " **to** " or " **for** " and is described in Analysis as the **Extension of the Predicate**.

Example :

The directors granted *the workmen* an increase.

The directors granted an increase *to the workmen*.

EXERCISE XII

(*a*) **Pick out the Indirect Objects and then replace by Adverbial Phrases :—**

1. Sing me a song.
2. The committee has bought the groundsman a new mower.
3. The teacher was telling the children a fairy tale.
4. Fetch me an interesting book from the library.
5. The surly porter refused the weary traveller shelter.

(*b*) **Insert Indirect Objects to complete the following sentences and then turn the Indirect Objects into Adverbial Phrases :—**

1. The boxer dealt...............a smashing blow.
2. The proud father bought...............a new football.
3. The foreman has sent.................more building material.

4. The sympathetic jury awarded.................compensation for the loss of her husband.

5. The great actor gave..................a thrill by his acting.

(b) The Complement.

Verbs which usually denote naming, choosing or appointing are called **Factitive Verbs** and may be so used that a single object does not complete the sense. Such verbs and the verb " *to be* " are called Verbs of Incomplete Predication and require a **Complement** to complete the sense. The Complement may be a noun, adjective or adjectival phrase, an infinitive or a clause.

Examples :

1. The Witan appointed Harold, *king*.
2. The insult made him *angry*.
3. They built the house *of concrete*.
4. The delay caused him *to fail*.
5. The excuse is *that he did not hear*.

The Complement answers the question " **What ?** " inserted after the verb or direct object, if any.

EXERCISE XIII

(a) **State the complements in the following sentences :—**

1. They elected him captain of the team.
2. Judged by his answers he is a bright lad.
3. The horse is the friend of man.
4. Wrong measurements made his calculations err.
5. The judge has pronounced him innocent.

2

(b) **Complete the sense of** the following by adding complements :—

(1) After the battle, the nobles crowned Henry, ...

(2) The citizens by their votes elected him..................

(3) ....are the uses of adversity.

(4) The umpire declared him...................

(5) Despite his age, the old man seems.................…

(c) Extension of the Predicate.

Just as adjectives or adjective phrases describe or qualify the noun-subject, so the action of the finite verb may be modified or made more definite by the addition of adverbs or adverbial phrases. These are called **Extensions of the Predicate** and may be **Extensions** of **Time, Place, Manner, Purpose** or **Reason** as they tell " when," " where," " how," " why."

Examples :

1. He arrived *early*.

2. The stranger stood *outside the cottage*.

3. Our soldiers attacked *with great daring*.

4. The old man had spoken with him *to keep him quiet*.

There is also an **Extension of the Predicate**, consisting of a **Noun Phrase** denoting exact duration or point of time, measurement, weight or value sometimes called the **Adverbial Object.**

Examples :

1. He waited *half an hour*.
2. He walked *twenty miles*.
3. The boxer weighed *fourteen stones*.
4. The diamond ring cost *fifty pounds*.

EXERCISE XIV

Write out and name the kind of Extension of the Predicate in the following sentences :—

1. They took a walk every morning and evening.
2. Full fathom five thy father lies.
3. He disappointed his friends by his lack of courage.
4. The regiment in one day marched thirty miles.
5. He fled out of the land of bondage.
6. The plucky winner was loudly cheered by the spectators.
7. He put on a heavy oilskin to face the storm.
8. Where did he come from ?
9. The air force having been destroyed, the army was soon defeated.
10. He was passing rich on forty pounds a year.

We are now ready to do **Particular Analysis** in full detail. Study the following examples :—

1. As a precaution, the vigilant sentry took the suspicious-looking stranger prisoner to his officer.
2. On the eve of the battle, the commander granted his soldiers freedom to depart.
3. Why, sir, have you disappeared so long from your native town ?

SUBJECT		PREDICATE				
NOUN OR EQUIVALENT	ENLARGEMENT	FINITE VERB	OBJECT	COMPLEMENT	EXTENSION	
1. Sentry	The vigilant	took	the suspicious stranger	prisoner	to his officer (Place) as a precaution (Reason)	
2. Commander	The	granted	freedom to depart (Direct) his men (Indirect)		on the eve of the battle (Time)	
3. You		have disappeared			why (Reason) so long (Time) from your native town (Place)	

Note.—Nominative of Address (Sentence 3, " sir ") is omitted in Analysis.

For **Particular** Analysis, test in the following order :—

1. Pick out the verb.
2. Put who ? or what ? before the verb : answer is the Subject.
3. Put whom ? or what ? after the verb : answer is the Object. Then put to whom ? : answer is Indirect Object.
4. If verb does not completely express the action, there is a complement.
5. Put " when," " where," " how," " why " after the verb : answers give Extensions of Time, Place, Manner, Purpose or Reason.
6. Arrange questions and poetic passages in the normal order before analysis.

EXERCISE XV

Make a Particular Analysis of the following sentences :—

1. He must practise carefully in his spare time.
2. The industrious workman was granted a week's holiday.
3. He gave his name to the official in charge.
4. The house was purchased at a low price by a stranger.
5. The jolly landlord bustled forward to welcome the guest.
6. He began a thorough search during the afternoon in the hidden valley.
7. What happy days we spent by the seaside that summer !
8. I decided in the first place to treat myself to a good lunch.

9. The game so nearly lost seemed now to be as good as won.

10. Has any one of the crew landed on this island before ?

11. Rome, the eternal city, was the centre of the Christian church in the West.

12. Then he called to him his standard bearer, his foster brother.

13. Before him, with a cautionary finger on his lips, stood his friend.

14. All alone, by the side of a pool
    A tall man sat on a three-legged stool.

15. Breathes there the man with soul so dead ?

16. Oft had I heard of Lucy Gray,
    That solitary child.

17. And furious every charger neighed,
    To join the dreadful revelry.

18. Dark as winter was the flow
    Of Iser rolling rapidly.

19. Nine fathom deep he had followed us
    From the land of mist of snow.

20. On either side the river lie
    Long fields of barley and of rye.

21. Twenty miles that day did we march through the driving snow.

22. It was no child's play tramping all day on snow-shoes.

23. The boy in the shop asked his employer for a holiday to go to the match.

24. At breakfast, Miss Smedley, the governess, behaved in a most mean and uncalled-for manner.

CHAPTER II

PARSING

All Parsing is done in three stages. You must consider first the function of the word to be parsed, that is, the work it does in the sentence and so determine what part of speech it is. Next describe the grammatical form of the word and finally state its relation to the other words in the sentence. Before you begin the actual parsing of a word, you must learn the rules of grammar which affect it as a part of speech.

There are eight **Parts of Speech** :

(1) **Noun.**	(5) **Adverb.**
(2) **Pronoun.**	(6) **Preposition.**
(3) **Adjective.**	(7) **Conjunction.**
(4) **Verb.**	(8) **Interjection.**

THE NOUN

A **Noun** is a word used as a name, *e.g.* airman, Churchill, ship, truth.

Nouns are divided into *Four* Kinds or **Classes** :

Proper.	**Abstract** (including Verbal).
Common.	**Collective.**

A **Proper Noun** is a word used as the name of a particular person, place or thing : George, Paris, Pyramids.

A **Common Noun** is a word used as the name of each member of a class : sailor, mountain, sheep.

An **Abstract Noun** is a word used as the name of a state, quality or condition which has no separate existence in itself : goodness, boyhood.

Note.—A **Verbal Noun** (a part of the verb ending in -ing) or the infinitive may be classified as a kind of Abstract Noun used as the name of an action : writing, thinking, to talk, to speak.

A **Collective Noun** is a word used as the name of a number or group of persons, animals or things taken together and spoken of as one : congregation, herd, senate.

Notes :—

(i) Proper Nouns may be used in the plural : the six Georges.

(ii) Certain Common Nouns become Proper Nouns when used to denote one important member of a class : the Bible, Parliament, the Prime Minister.

(iii) When the persons, animals or things in a Collective Noun are thought of as individuals, the noun is treated as a plural and sometimes called a *Noun of Multitude*.

(iv) Proper, Common and Collective Nouns are classified as Concrete. In Parsing, this is seldom stated.

EXERCISE I

1. **Write down ten Proper Nouns that are** (*a*) the names of persons you know, or (*b*) the names of persons in history, or (*c*) of cities, mountains, rivers, etc.

2. **Write down ten Common Nouns that are the names of** (*a*) well-known objects, or (*b*) of animals or plants.

3. **Write down ten Abstract Nouns from the following nouns, adjectives or verbs :** child, warm, laugh, wise, advise, hate, brave, obey, slave, marry.

4. **Write down ten Collective Nouns for the following :—** A number of cattle, of sailors, of trees, of ships, of books, of horse soldiers, of worshippers, of fish, of partridges, of rioters.

5. **Classify the following Nouns as Proper, Common, Abstract (Verbal), Collective :—**Flock, Indus, avalanche, sleeping, ermine, Vatican, to err, ability, crew, tennis, Troy, crusade, swarm, weasel, galloping, livelihood, Hercules, shark, explosive, jury.

GENDER

Genders in Grammar are four in number and correspond to sex in Nature.

1. Names of Males are of the **Masculine** Gender— man, lion.

2. Names of Females are of the **Feminine** Gender—girl, goose.

3. Names of Things without life are of the **Neuter** Gender—table, spade.

4. Names that can be used of Male or Female are of the **Common** Gender—child, fowl.

Gender is denoted in *three* ways :—

1. **By different words :**

Masc.	*Fem.*	*Masc.*	*Fem.*
Boy.	Girl.	Husband.	Wife.
Buck.	Doe.	Monk.	Nun.
Earl.	Countess.	Sir.	Madam.
Father.	Mother.	Uncle.	Aunt.
Hart.	Roe.	Wizard.	Witch.

2. **By a difference of word ending :**

Masc.	Fem.	Masc.	Fem.
Abbot.	Abbess.	Hero.	Heroine.
Conductor.	Conductress.	Negro.	Negress.
Duke.	Duchess.	Prince.	Princess.
Fox.	Vixen.	Songster.	Songstress.
Heir.	Heiress.	Viceroy.	Vicereine.

3. **By the use of a masculine or feminine noun or pronoun as prefix or suffix :**

Masc.	Fem.	Masc.	Fem.
Beggar-man.	Beggar-woman.	He-goat.	She-goat.
Bridegroom.	Bride.	Jack-ass.	Jenny-ass.
Cock-sparrow.	Hen-sparrow.	Man-servant.	
			Maid-servant.

Note.—By the figure of speech called Personification, things without life are sometimes spoken of as if alive and written with a capital : Peace, The Sun, Death.

EXERCISE II

(a) **Tell the Gender of the following Nouns :**—Nephew, coachman, history, egg, infant, class, niece, author, lesson, prince, companion, hind, Rome, ox, mummy, punster, day, Summer, drone, reindeer.

(b) **Give the masculine or feminine equivalent of the following Nouns:**—Princess, bull, gander, mare, lord, executor, duke, host, arbitress, governor, lad, belle, son, ewe, widower, tailor, tigress, sultana, viscount, she-bear.

NUMBER

A Noun may be **Singular** or **Plural** in Number according as it stands for only one person or thing or for more than one person or thing :

boy, book ; boys, books.

Formation of Plurals

1. **By adding -s to the** Singular : *cats, valleys.*
2. **By adding -es to the** Singular when a noun ends in a hissing sound (**-ch, -s, -x**) : *churches, asses, boxes.*
3. **By changing -y into -ies** when a noun ends in **-y** preceded by a consonant : *armies, babies.*
4. **By changing -f or -fe** preceded by a long vowel into **-ves** : *loaves, wolves (but chiefs, briefs, roofs, cliffs).*
5. **By adding -en to the** Singular : *oxen, children, brethren.*
6. **By changing the vowel** : *mice, teeth, men.*
7. **By pluralising the principal part** when the noun is a compound one : *sons-in-law, assistant-masters, men-o'-war.*

Notes.—

  (i) Some nouns have the same form for Singular and Plural—*deer, trout, grouse.*
 (ii) Some nouns have no singular—*ashes, wages, shears.*
(iii) The plurals of other Parts of Speech used as Nouns follow the ordinary rules : *ifs, buts.*
 (iv) Letters of the alphabet and figures generally form the plural by adding -'s : *4's, m's.*
  (v) Foreign Plurals often retain the foreign Plural endings : *addendum, addenda ; phenomenon, phenomena ; fungus, fungi (funguses).*

EXERCISE III

(*a*) **Tell the Number of** the following Nouns :—Samuel, dress, brethren, grouse, wives, halos, fish, solos, dwarf, shelves, axes, cherubim, trousers, mathematics, analysis, stamen, series, gallows, salmon, hail.

(*b*) **Write the plural of the following Nouns :**—Horse, knife, soliloquy, piano, James, 7, court-martial, beau, index, negro, radius, crisis, bandit, simile, crocus, studio, cactus, seraph, ruby, sheaf.

CASE

The **Case** of a Noun (or Pronoun) shows the relation in which it stands to some other word in a sentence. The Case is indicated by the position of the word in the sentence, the meaning of the sentence, and in the **Possessive Case** by the ending. There are *three* cases :

a. **Nominative.**

b. **Objective.**

c. **Possessive.**

The **Nominative Case** is used :

1. When the Noun (or Pronoun) is the subject of a clause or sentence.

    The *boy* stood on the burning deck.
    How lovely are the *leaves* in Autumn!

2. When the Noun (or Pronoun) is in apposition to, that is, is used to describe or explain the Subject (Nominative in Apposition).

    The king, your *father*, is disposed to sleep.

3. When the Noun (or Pronoun) represents the person or thing addressed (Nominative of Address or Vocative).

    O liberty! what crimes are committed in thy name!

4. When the Noun (or Pronoun) is used with a participle or participial phrase and is not connected with the main structure of the sentence (Nominative Absolute).

Note.—The participle may be omitted.

The sun *having set,* they returned home.

The match *over,* the players left the field.

5. When the Noun (or Pronoun) is used after a verb of Incomplete Predication (be, seem, become, etc.).

He is a well known *leader* of the people.

The lad soon became a trusted *servant.*

The Objective Case is used :

1. When the Noun (or Pronoun) is the **Direct Object** of a Transitive Verb, finite or infinite.

He defeated all his *opponents.*

He died to save his *friend.*

2. When the Noun (or Pronoun) is the **Indirect Object** of a Transitive Verb, finite or infinite.

He gave the *beggar* a shilling.

3. When the Noun (or Pronoun) is used after Passive Verbs of asking, promising or giving (**Retained Object**).

The guide was promised a handsome *reward* by the rescued party.

4. When the Noun (or Pronoun) is the complement of a Factitive Verb (**Factitive Object**).

They elected the popular speaker, *chairman.*

5. When a Noun (or Pronoun) is governed by a Preposition. (The Preposition " *to* " is understood after *like, unlike, near, opposite*).

He spoke wisely to the *people*.

Like his *brother*, he is full of wild schemes.

6. When a Noun follows an Intransitive Verb of kindred meaning (**Cognate Object**).

He ran a well judged *race*.

7. When a Noun is used adverbially to denote limitation of time, distance, weight, value (**Adverbial Object**).

He easily walked the remaining *ten miles*.

Note.—Rules 1-5 apply equally to the Personal Pronoun.

The **Possessive Case** is used to denote possession and is normally used of persons and animals. It is the only case which is inflected, that is, shows a change in the form of the Noun.

The **Possessive Case** is formed :

1. By adding —'s to the Singular Noun.

The *boy's* shoes.

2. By adding an apostrophe (') to Singular Nouns ending in —s or a hissing sound or plurals ending in —s.

for *goodness'* sake ; *birds'* feathers.

3. By adding —'s to the last part of Compound Nouns or Nouns consisting of more than one word.

His son-in-*law's* house ; William the *Conqueror's* reign.

4. **By adding —'s** to the last noun of two or more nouns possessing the same object or denoting the same person.

William and *Mary's* reign ; your brother *John's* wife.

EXERCISE IV

(a) **Write the Possessive Singular of the following Nouns :**
Robert, soldier, farmer, conscience, horse, monkey, teacher, frog, wasp, disciple, niece, hero, aunt, William the First, father-in-law, Joey the Clown, Socrates, Dickens, Jesus, Venus.

(b) **Write the Possessive Plural of the following Nouns :—**
Mistress, Nephew, man-servant, Miss Jones, bird, milliner, lady, brother-in-law, tortoise, grampus, kitten, commander-in-chief, hostage, airman, grocer, warehouseman, bee, Brown, Smith & Co., pony, sergeant.

(c) **Change the Possessive Forms in (a) and (b) into Objectives after the Preposition " of " inserting suitable nouns for the things possessed :—**
Example : Apostles' creed.

The creed of the apostles.

(d) **Write the following in Possessive Form :—**The song of the reaper ; the cry of the children ; the wings of a dove ; the bodyguard of the king ; the horses of the victors ; the novels of Scott ; the premises of Evans, Jones & Co. ; the friends of men ; the horn of the hunter ; the great deeds of Robert the Bruce ; for the sake of conscience ; the reign of George the Fifth ; the hands of the maidens ; the harp of the hero ; the ears of the asses ; the sting of the asp ; the scales of the fish ; the tears of a crocodile.

Scheme of Parsing for Nouns.

Noun : Class or kind, person, number, gender, case, reason for case.

Example : *John* gave *food* to the hungry *peasants*.

John : Noun, proper, 3rd pers. sing., masc., nom., subject of " gave."

food : Noun, common, 3rd pers., sing., neuter, object of " gave."

peasants : Noun, common, 3rd pers., plural, common, objective case, gov. by " to."

EXERCISE V

Parse the Nouns in the following sentences :—

1. The shipwrecked sailors escaped from the island.
2. The martyr died for conscience' sake.
3. The leader, a jolly sailor, was home on leave.
4. The morning being wet, the picnic was postponed.
5. The hermit lives a lonely life.
6. Mr. Bumble, the beadle, took Oliver by the hand.
7. The nation with joy acclaimed him leader.
8. O Death ! where is thy sting ?
9. The boy, despite his youth, showed great courage.
10. So light to the saddle the lady he swung.
11. The teacher taught the boy French.
12. Good King Wenceslas looked out on a winter morn.
13. Cycling provides good and healthy exercise.
14. Sweet are the uses of adversity.
15. He was granted an estate by his grateful countrymen.
16. Sleep the sleep that knows no waking.
17. Soldiers, you will not desert your leader.
18. Ten long years he waited for this chance.
19. Skipping will keep you fit without any other exercise.
20. He was offered promotion by his employer.

THE PRONOUN

Pronouns (Latin, *pro*, instead of) are words used instead of nouns and may be classified :

Personal.	**Demonstrative.**
Possessive.	**Interrogative.**
Reflexive.	**Indefinite.**
Emphatic.	**Numeral.**
Relative.	**Distributive.**

Note.—The Possessive, Reflexive and Emphatic Pronouns are derived from, and closely related to, the Personal Pronoun.

Personal Pronoun

Personal Pronouns are so called because they stand for the three persons :—

1. The person speaking ;
2. The person spoken to ;
3. The person spoken of.

Table of Personal Pronouns.

PERSON.	SINGULAR.		PLURAL.	
	Nom.	Obj.	Nom.	Obj.
1	I	me	We	us
2	Thou	thee	You	you
3	He She It	him her it	They	them

Examples:

1. *I* can speak freely to *you* because *he* is not here.
2. *We* must not discuss *them* with *you*.

Notes.—

(i) *We* may be used to denote one person. (*a*) The Royal *we*—*We* give *our* royal consent. (*b*) The Editorial *we*—*We* oppose the policy of the government.

(ii) *Thou* is now used only in poetry or in addressing God.

(iii) *It* may be used impersonally. (*a*) *It* is the queen. (*b*) *It* is raining to-day.

Possessive Pronoun

Possessive Pronouns are so called because they stand for a Possessor. The Possessive Pronouns are *mine*, *thine*, *his*, *her*, *ours*, *yours*, *theirs*, and were formerly the Possessive Case of the Personal Pronouns.

Note.—(1) The Possessive Pronouns *ours*, *yours*, *theirs* are **not** written with an apostrophe. (2) The other forms of the Possessive Case of the Personal Pronouns, *my*, *thy*, *his*, *her*, *its*, *our*, *your*, *their*, are now treated as **Possessive Adjectives** and are always used with a noun (" his " may be used with or without a noun).

(1) The book is his not yours.

(2) With luck, since ours is the first **innings,** theirs will be played in the twilight.

Reflexive Pronoun

Reflexive Pronouns are so called because they refer back or repeat the Subject in the Objective

Case. Reflexive Pronouns are formed by adding the noun -self to certain singular forms of the Personal Pronoun and -selves to the plural :—

Myself, *thyself*, *himself*, *itself*, *ourselves*, *yourselves*, *themselves*.

I injured *myself* during the struggle.

Emphatic Pronoun

Emphatic Pronouns are so called because they emphasise or strengthen the Noun or Pronoun they refer to. Emphatic Pronouns take the case of, and are usually immediately after, the noun or pronoun they refer to. They are formed in the same way as the Reflexive Pronouns.

Examples :

I met the very man *himself* yesterday.
For he *himself* has said it.

Relative Pronoun

Relative Pronouns are so called because they relate to some Noun or Pronoun already mentioned in the sentence and called the Antecedent (*ante*— before, *cedo*—I go). A Relative Pronoun agrees with its antecedent in person, number and gender. A Relative Pronoun generally introduces an adjective clause which restricts or defines the Antecedent.

The Relative Pronouns are *who* (*whom*, *whose*), *which*, *that*, *what*, *as*, *but*.

He knows the man *who* owns the dog.
Tell me *what* you require.

Notes.—

(i) *Who* refers to *persons* only ; *which* to *animals* or *things* ; *that*, *what* to *persons*, *animals* or *things*.

(ii) *Who* or *which* may introduce a clause which does not define or restrict the meaning but merely continues the sense without telling anything new about it. *What* and *that* always introduce a clause that defines.

The clown sang a song to the Duke, *who* rewarded him.

" Who " is equal to " and he."

(iii) *As* is only used after *such*, *same*.

This is the *same* story *as* he told you.

(iv) *But* is only used after a negative and is equal to *who . . . not.*

There is not a soul *but* misses him.

or, There is not a soul *who* does *not* miss him.

(v) The *Relative Pronoun* is often omitted when, if expressed, it would be in the *Objective Case*.

The explanation is one I cannot believe.

(vi) The Antecedent is often omitted before *what*. In parsing, the word " that " is understood. *What* is sometimes treated as equal to " *that which* " before parsing :

He explained clearly *what* he had done.

He explained clearly *that which* he had done.

Demonstrative Pronoun

Demonstrative Pronouns are so called because they point out the person or thing named. The Pronouns are *this*, *that* (*these*, *those*), *such*, *some*, *yon*, *yonder* (in poetry). When used before a Noun, they are called **Demonstrative Adjectives**.

This is no answer to the question.

Such are my opinions.

Interrogative Pronoun

Interrogative Pronouns are so called because they ask a question. They are *who? (whom? whose?) which? what? whether? Whose? which?* and *what?* are used before Nouns as Adjectives.

Which of you has done this?

What do you expect from such a man?

Indefinite Pronoun

Indefinite Pronouns are so called because they do not point out with precision the person or thing to which they refer. They are—*one, any, anything, anybody, aught, naught, certain, other, else, somebody, something, nobody, nothing, no one.*

Notes.—

(i) The Indefinite Pronouns may be used before nouns as Adjectives.

(ii) Indefinite Pronouns which refer to number or quantity are—all, few, little, less, enough, many, much, more, most, several, whole ; little, much, less, whole, all.

Numeral Pronoun

Numeral Pronouns are so called because they stand for a number : **Cardinal**—*one, two, three* ; or **Ordinal**—*first, second, third.*

Four of the soldiers escaped, but the *fifth* was captured.

Note.—The Numeral Pronoun may be used before a noun as an adjective.

Distributive Pronoun

Distributive Pronouns are so called because they stand for a Noun which denotes all the individuals of a class considered separately. They are—*each, each one, everyone, either, neither.*

Each has tried to injure the other.

Notes.—

(i) The Distributive Pronouns may be used before nouns as adjectives.

(ii) Each other (used only of two) and one another (used of more than two) may be parsed together and are sometimes called Reciprocal Pronouns.

(iii) Distributive Pronouns are followed by Singular verbs.

Scheme of Parsing for Pronouns.

Pronoun : Kind or Class, Person, Number, Gender, Case, reason for case.

Example.—*You yourself told me that.*

you : Pers. Pronoun, 2nd pers., sing., common, nom., subject of " told."

yourself : Emphatic Pronoun, 2nd pers., sing., common, nom. in appos. to " you."

me : Pers. Pronoun, 1st pers., sing., common, indirect object of " told."

that ; Dem. Pronoun, 3rd pers., sing., neut., object of " told."

EXERCISE VI

Parse the Pronouns in the following sentences:—

1. This island is mine.

2. He himself has said it.

3. The very trees themselves whisper that name.

4. What are you saying ?
5. Such as hunt the king's deer will be punished.
6. Who was the king, yet lives.
7. This is the same as that.
8. Mine is the honour, yours the shame.
9. Whatever you say, I cannot believe that.
10. Tell me what you mean by this.
11. Each lay in his narrow cell.
12. They greeted one another in jovial mood.
13. Some will listen, others will turn away.
14. Three he struck down but the fourth escaped.
15. He met a traveller who told him about it.
16. He extricated himself very cleverly from the difficulty.
17. What do they know of England ?
18. I know no lover of his country but will make him welcome.
19. I have been in the room itself.
20. Neither of the two wished the other to see him.

THE ADJECTIVE

Adjectives (*ad*, to ; *jacio*, I throw) are words " added to " a Noun to describe or limit the application of the Noun by qualifying its meaning.

There are **three classes of Adjectives** :—

1. **Adjectives of Quantity**.
2. **Demonstrative Adjectives**.
3. **Adjectives of Quality or Description**.

1. **Adjectives of Quantity** limit a Noun by expressing quantity or number, definitely or indefinitely—large, seven, several.

(a) **Definite Numerical Adjectives** state the exact number and include the indefinite article—one, five, twenty, a, an.

Note.—Dozen, hundred, thousand, million in the Plural may be used as Nouns : *Dozens* of eggs were smashed in the collision.

(b) **Indefinite Numerical Adjectives** state a number indefinitely—all, few, many, certain, several.

(c) **Indefinite Quantitative Adjectives** state a quantity indefinitely—little (less, least), much (more, most).

2. **Demonstrative Adjectives** limit a Noun by pointing out the things named : this, that, our, every.

(a) **Possessive Adjectives** point out by showing possession of the thing named—my, your, their.

(b) **Distributive Adjectives** point out by showing selection of thing named—every, neither, either.

(c) **Ordinal Numbers** point out by showing order—fifth, eleventh.

Note.—The articles, definite (the) and indefinite (a, an), are Demonstrative Adjectives.

(d) **Interrogative Adjectives** point out by asking a question about the thing named—*what ? which ? whose ?*

3. **Adjectives of Quality or Description** limit a noun by telling the quality or describing the thing named—good, clever, beautiful.

Adjectives of Quality may be derived from proper names or names of material—African, copper, paper.

Comparison of Adjectives

There are **Three Degrees of Comparison** according to whether you indicate the presence of a quality in a person or thing with or without reference to one or more members of the same class of persons or things.

The Degrees of Comparison are :—

1. Positive—small.
2. Comparative—smaller.
3. Superlative—smallest.

The **Positive Degree** of an Adjective expresses the quality of the thing named—wise, happy, beautiful.

The **Comparative Degree** of an Adjective expresses the quality of the thing named in a higher or lower degree with reference to one other member of the same class—wiser, happier, more beautiful.

The **Superlative Degree** of an Adjective expresses the quality of the thing named in the highest or lowest degree with reference to two or more members of the same class—wisest, happiest, most beautiful.

Formation of the Comparative and Superlative

1. To the Positive add *-er* to form the Comparative and *-est* to form the Superlative : small, small*er*, small*est*.

(a) If the Positive ends in *-e*, cut off the *-e* and add -er and -est to form the Comparative and Superlative.

(*b*) If the Positive ends in -y preceded by a *consonant* change the -y into -i before adding -er and -est—pretty, prettier, prettiest, but —gay, g*ay*er, g*ay*est.

Note.—When y is accented, add -er and -est— shy, shyer, shyest.

(*c*) If the Positive ends in a single consonant preceded by a short vowel, double the consonant before adding -er and -est—flat, fla*tt*er, fla*tt*est.

2. Adjectives of more than two syllables form their Comparatives and Superlatives by prefixing ' *more* ' or ' *less* ' and ' *most* ' or ' *least* ' to the Positive—*wonderful, more wonderful, most wonderful.*

Note.—Only Adjectives which have qualities capable of varying in amount have degrees of comparison. Adjectives denoting shape, direction, nationality, material, Demonstrative Adjectives and most Adjectives of Quantity, cannot be compared—Welsh, perpendicular, several.

Irregular Comparison of Adjectives

Positive.	*Comparative.*	*Superlative.*
good	better	best
bad	worse	worst
little	less, lesser	least
far	farther	farthest
[forth]	further	furthest
much, many	more	most
late	later, latter	latest, last
old	older, elder	oldest, eldest
[fore]	former	foremost, first
hind	hinder	hindmost
near	nearer	next, nearest

	upper	uppermost
		upmost
[in]	inner	inmost
[out]	outer, utter	outermost, utmost
top	—	topmost
very	—	veriest
head	—	headmost
south	—	southmost

EXERCISE VII

Compare (when possible) the following Adjectives :— Sad, young, perfect, silver, good, cruel, trustworthy, woollen, triangular, unkind, wet, genteel, annual, manly, ill, principal, straight, Spanish, gray, superior, shy, weekly, hostile, inseparable, middle.

Adjectives may be used *attributively*, that is, before a Noun, or *predicatively*, that is, as part of the Predicate though it refers to the Subject :—

The *white* gate (Attributive).

The gate is *white* (Predicative).

Scheme of Parsing for Adjectives

Adjective : Kind, degree (where adjective can be compared), word it describes, limits and qualifies.

Example :

The white house was *beautiful* in *his* eyes.

The : Adj., demons., qual. " house."
white : Adj., quality, positive, qual. " house."
beautiful : Adj., quality, positive, qual. " house."
his : Adj., poss., qual. " eyes."

EXERCISE VIII

Parse the Adjectives in the following sentences :—

1. Loud noises are distasteful to quiet people.
2. Good writing material is now scarce.
3. A many-coloured coat would seem strange to modern taste.
4. To err is human, to forgive divine.
5. The dining hall is very spacious.
6. The greatest damage was done during the early morning.
7. A strong force of colonial troops crossed the swollen river.
8. Three men were in the boat, two of them English.
9. This unique spectacle is most interesting.
10. Gay gilded scenes in shining prospect rise.
11. His actions were both thoughtful and sensible.
12. The allied troops won golden opinions from the conquered people.
13. His narrow escape made him alive to his danger.
14. He seems both foolish and obstinate.
15. Give every man thine ear but few thy voice.
16. These two poets lived near each other.

THE VERB

Verbum in Latin means a word. It is THE WORD —the most important word—of the sentence because by using it we are able to make a statement about the subject, usually a Noun or Pronoun. This statement may describe an action, a state or condition. When we make a statement about anything we are said to **predicate** something about **that thing.**

1. The policeman caught the thief. $\left\{\begin{array}{l}\text{Action predicated,}\\ \text{and passing from}\\ \text{policeman to thief.}\end{array}\right.$

2. The audience was attentive.
3. The released prisoner was happy. $\left.\begin{array}{l}\\ \\ \\ \\ \end{array}\right\}$ State or condition predicated.

4. The prisoner wept. $\left\{\begin{array}{l}\text{Action predicated}\\ \text{but not passing.}\end{array}\right.$

In Sentence 1 the action passes over from the subject (policeman) to the object (thief). When action passes in this manner the verb is said to be **Transitive** (from Latin *trans*—across, and *ire*— to go).

In Sentences 2 and 3 no action is denoted by the verbs which help merely to describe a state or condition. In Sentence 4 no action is passing to an object.

When a verb merely describes a state or condition or an action that is not passed over to an object it is said to be **Intransitive**.

Accordingly, it will be seen that *a Transitive Verb is one that can take an object.*

Transitive verbs may be used intransitively, as :—

Transitive Use.	*Intransitive Use.*
The heat thawed the ice.	The ice thawed.
He broke the test-tube.	The test-tube broke.
We eat plenty of vegetables.	We eat to live.

Intransitive Verbs may be used transitively, as :—

Intransitive Use.	*Transitive Use.*
Plants grow under favourable conditions.	He grew the usual vegetables in his garden.
The scaffolding gave.	He gave a donation.

EXERCISE IX

Use the following verbs transitively and intransitively in sentences :—To walk, run, float, fly, keep, gather, lengthen, widen, stop, lift.

Direct and Indirect Object

1. He gave *me sixpence.*
2. He awarded *him* the *prize.*

In these sentences we apparently have two objects. In 1, we have *me* and *sixpence*, in 2, *him* and *prize.*

The thing given is the **direct object**—in 1, *sixpence*, in 2, *prize.* The person or other animal named is the **indirect object**—in 1, *me*, and in 2, *him.*

Verbs of Incomplete Predication

When we say, " Rain falls," " Time flies," there is complete sense in the statements. But if we say, " I was," " She seems," " He became," the sense is incomplete. We require to add something to complete the sense. That which is added we call the **Complement**. Thus, in—

I was *happy*,   She seems *angry*,   He became *premier*,

happy, *angry* and *premier* are the complements of these statements.

Verbs that require a complement to complete their sense or predication (such as, to be, become, seem) are called Verbs of **Incomplete Predication**. Such complements are usually Nouns, Adjectives or Pronouns.

Principal (Notional) and Auxiliary Verbs

A **Principal** or **Notional** verb is so called because it contains the principal idea or notion to be stated, as :—

1. He *had* a fine house.
2. He *had* departed before I arrived.

In Sentence 1, *had* means possessed—the verb had contains the principal idea.

In Sentence 2, departed contains the principal idea ; *had* helps to convey the idea of the time of departing, so had is used here as **an Auxiliary Verb**. Auxiliary Verbs are helping verbs (Latin, *auxilium*—help), that is, they help principal verbs in their conjugation.

The auxiliary verbs are :—*be, shall, will, have, may, do*.

It should be noted that an auxiliary verb may sometimes be used as a principal verb, as :—

As Auxiliary.	*As Principal.*
Study that you *may* succeed.	You *may* depart now.
The world *is* rotating.	God *is* (= exists).
I *shall* write soon.	You *shall* obey.

Note.—Certain transitive verbs in the passive **require** a noun (in the nominative case) to complete their meaning, as :—He was made *manager*. She was appointed *secretary*. Such verbs are called **factitive** verbs (L. *facio*—I make).

Impersonal Verbs

These verbs take *it* for their subject, **as :**— It *behoves*, it *repents* (me), it *irks*, *methinks* (it seems to me), it *shames*, it *rains*.

VOICE

Consider these statements :—

1. The dog *killed* the rabbit.   Active.
2. The rabbit *was killed* by the dog.   Passive.

The verb *killed* (in 1) is said to be in the **Active Voice** (Lat. *activus*—doing) because it indicates from its form that the subject of the sentence is the doer of the action expressed by the verb.

The verb *was killed* (in 2) is said to be in the **Passive Voice** (Lat. *patior*—I suffer, or endure) because it indicates from its form that the subject of the sentence is *acted upon*, that is, that it suffers from, or is the object of, some action.

In order to convert a sentence in the active voice into the passive voice, note that the *object* of the active-voice sentence (rabbit) becomes the subject of the passive-voice sentence, and the *subject* of the active-voice sentence (dog) appears in the passive-voice sentence as an adverbial phrase (by the dog).

Accordingly, *when a verb is used intransitively it has no passive voice.*

Can you change "His wound hurt" into the passive voice?

Notes.—Verbs that have two objects in the active voice (*i.e.* one direct; one indirect) retain *one* object in the passive voice form, as :—

Mr. Brown taught him Latin. Active.

He was taught *Latin* by Mr. Brown. Passive.

Latin is an example of the **retained object.**

A **cognate object** is one in which the sense it conveys is already included in the verb used, as :—

He fought the good *fight.*

Some verbs are active in form but passive in meaning, as :—

A house to let (to be let).

EXERCISE X

Convert the following sentences from the active to the passive voice:—

1. The policeman caught the prisoner.
2. The spider killed the fly.
3. He read the story.
4. His father said it.
5. The foreman gave the worker his pay.
6. He sent me a letter.

EXERCISE XI

Convert the following sentences from the passive to the active voice:—

1. The book was given me by him.
2. The piano was played by the guest.
3. The milk was given to the cat by the lodger.
4. His fault was forgiven him by his father.

4

FINITE AND INFINITE (Infinitive) VERBS

If we consider the verb *to sing*, it conveys the idea of a certain action but it tells us nothing about when the action occurred or who performed it—whether it concerned one person or more, whether it happened in the past, is happening, or will happen. Accordingly, " *to sing* " tells us nothing about who did the action (*i.e.* about its **Person** and **Number**) or when the action was done (**Tense**). Because in these respects the verb *to sing* is unlimited, it is termed **infinite** or **infinitive** (Latin *in*—not, *finitus*—limited) and has **no subject**.

Remember that the **finite** verb *takes a subject* ; a verb in the **infinitive** mood *cannot take a subject*.

Examples of the **Finite Verb** :—

1. An assertion : Two and two make four. How hot it is !
2. Question : How are you ?
3. Command : Shut (you) that door.
4. Wish (Optative) : May the best man win.
5. Supposition : Were he king, he would command support.

MOOD

There are three moods of the finite verb illustrated in these sentences :—

1. Indicative Mood. { He walked into the shop. An assertion or statement. Did he walk into the shop ? A question.
2. Imperative Mood. } Walk (you) into the shop. A command.

3. Subjunctive } If you walk into the shop, you
   Mood. } will get it. A condition.

Mood *is the manner or mode of the verb in which the action or state is regarded by the speaker or writer.*

The **Indicative** mood is used most frequently as in this mood we make statements and ask questions.

The **Imperative** mood is used to express a command.

(Note that the subject is frequently omitted and has to be supplied in parsing and analysis.)

The **Subjunctive** mood is used to express *doubt, hesitation, condition,* or *a wish,* as :—

> I inquired if he *were* quite recovered.
> If I *be* not mistaken, he should succeed.
> If he *were promoted,* he would be pleased.
> Long *live* the King.

Note.—The distinctive forms of the verb in the sub-junctive mood are not used frequently nowadays ; the indicative forms usually replace them (*e.g. be* is replaced by am, *were* by was).

EXERCISE XII

Give the mood of the verbs in the following sentences:—

1. If I am correct, he must be wrong.
2. Go to the Ant, thou Sluggard, consider her ways and be wise.
3. Drink to me only with thine eyes.
4. Shut the door.
5. If that be true, the position is intolerable.
6. If he were king, it would be a different matter.
7. Thy will be done.

8. Run upstairs and fetch the key.
9. May the best man win.
10. If I am not grossly mistaken, the general reply would be in the negative.

TENSE

Tense [derived from Old French *tens* (Fr. temps), Latin *tempus*] is that form of the verb that indicates (*a*) the **time**, and (*b*) **state**, *i.e.* the completeness or incompleteness of the action, as :—

(*a*) **Time :**

All time can be measured under past, present and future. All tense forms must belong to one of these divisions but there are distinctions possible within these divisions, as :—I write, I am writing, I do write. These are all present tenses.

> *I write* is usually called the **present indefinite** and is the simplest form of the present tense.
>
> *I am writing* is the **present continuous** form.
>
> *I do write* is the **emphatic** form of the present tense.

The **state** of the action refers to whether the action is completed or incomplete.

> *I have written* is usually called the **present perfect** form.
>
> *I was writing* is usually termed the **past continuous** form.

Accordingly, **the state of the action**, whether it is completed (**perfect**) or incomplete (**continuous or imperfect**) may be indicated in the tense form.

	Indicative		Subjunctive	
	Active	Passive	Active	Passive
Pres. Indefinite	ask	am asked	ask	be asked
Continuous	am asking	am being asked	be asking	am being asked
Emphatic	I do ask			
Past Indefinite	asked	was asked	asked	were asked
Continuous	was asking	was being asked	were asking	were being asked
Fut. Indefinite	shall ask	shall be asked		
Continuous	shall be asking			
Pres. Perfect	have asked	have been asked	have asked	have been asked
Perfect Continuous	have been asking		have been asking	

	Indicative		Subjunctive	
	Active	Passive	Active	Passive
Past Perfect	had asked	had been asked	had asked	had been asked
Perfect Continuous	had been asking		had been asking	
Fut. Perfect	shall have asked	shall have been asked		
Perfect Continuous	shall have been asking			
Fut. in the Past — Indefinite	should ask	should be asked		
Continuous	should be asking			
Perfect	should have asked	should have been asked		
Continuous	should have been asking			

Notes.—

1. Present Tense.

(*a*) *I write.* (*b*) *I am writing.* (*c*) *I have written.*

If we consider the meaning conveyed by these three statements, we find that (*a*) the action is confined to the present, or I am accustomed to write (perhaps to earn a living) : accordingly, we call this tense **indefinite.**

In (*b*) the action is continuing and we term the tense **continuous.**

In (*c*) the meaning conveyed is that the act of **writing** is *just now* completed, so we call the tense **present perfect.**

It is similarly so with other tenses—the past and the future may be indefinite, continuous or perfect.

2. Future in the past tenses are apt to be difficult to understand but if you study the following it may help.

He tells me he will arrive in good time (Future indefinite).

If this sentence is turned into the past tense—as if it were reported—we have, *He told me he would arrive in good time, i.e.* the act of arriving is future to the telling —it will not take place until after the time of the telling.

3. Past tenses may be (*a*) *perfect* (sometimes called *past perfect* or *pluperfect*) or (*b*) *perfect continuous.*

(*a*) The *past perfect* is used when some action was completed, or supposed to be completed, before another action began, as :—

He had missed his train when I met him.

(*b*) The *past perfect continuous* tense denotes an action that was continuing in the past before another action began, as :—

He had been walking up and down the platform before I met him.

4. *Perfect forms* of tenses always use the auxiliary verb *have*.

Continuous forms of tenses always use the auxiliary verb *to be*.

Future tenses are formed by combining shall and will with the infinitive mood.

SEQUENCE OF TENSES

(See also under Direct and Indirect Speech)

Rule 1.—A present or future tense in the principal clause is followed by *any* tense in the dependent clause, as :—

He reports that he *is making* good progress.

He reports that he *was making* good progress.

He reports that he *had made* good progress.

He will say that he *is making* good progress.

He will say that he *has made* good progress.

He has reported that he *has made* good progress.

He has reported that he *is making* good progress.

Rule 2.—A past tense in the principal clause must be followed by a past tense in the dependent clause, as :—

He reported that he *had made* good progress.

He reported that he *would make* good progress.

He reported that he *should make* good progress.

He said that he thought he *would make* good progress.

NUMBER AND PERSON

A verb must agree with its subject in **Number** and **Person**, as :—

1. I am happy.
2. We are happy.

In sentence 1, the subject is singular and we must make the verb singular to correspond and be in agreement with it.

In sentence 2, the subject is plural and we must make the verb plural to correspond and be in agreement with it.

Number, therefore, is the form of the verb which indicates whether we are speaking of one thing or of more than one thing. We write :—

I go.
Thou goest.
He (she, it) goes.
We go.
You go.
They go.

It will be noticed that we alter the conjugation of the verb according as the subject is the person speaking: as:—*I, we*; first person: the person spoken to, as:—*thou, you*; second person: or the person spoken about, as:—*he, she, it, they*; third person.

Notes.—

1. **Strong and Weak Verbs.**—Verbs are divided into strong and weak verbs according to how they form their past tense.

(a) Verbs of the **strong** conjugation form their past tense or past participle by a change of the *internal* vowel. These are Old English verbs, as :—*swim*, swam, swum.

(b) Verbs of the **weak** conjugation form their past tense or past participle by adding -*d*, -*ed*, or -*t* to the present form, as :—walk, walked, dream, dreamt.

All new verbs admitted into our language are weak.

(c) Verbs which have the same form for all three parts are usually weak, e.g., *burst, cast, cost, cut, hit, hurt, let, put, set, shed, shut, spread, thrust.*

2. When asked to give the principal parts of a verb give (a) the *pres. indicative*, (b) *past indicative*, (c) *past participle*, as :—forget, forgot, forgotten.

List of Weak Verbs

Present.	Past.	Past Participle.	Present.	Past.	Past Participle.
Bend	bent	bent	Gild	{ gilded { gilt	{ gilded { gilt
Bleed	bled	bled	Have	had	had
Build	built	built	Keep	kept	kept
Creep	crept	crept	Lay	laid	laid
Dream	{ dreamt { dreamed	{ dreamt { dreamed	Leap	{ leaped { leapt	{ leaped { leapt
Feel	felt	felt	Sleep	slept	slept

List of Strong Verbs

Present.	Past.	Past Participle.	Present.	Past.	Past Participle.
Abide	abode	abode	See	saw	seen
Awake	awoke	awoke	Shrink	shrank	shrunk
Bid	{ bade { bid	{ bidden { bid	Sit	sat	sat
			Slide	slid	slid
Chide	chid	{ chidden { chid	Speak	spoke	spoken
Cling	clung	clung	Spit	spat	{ spat { spit
Drive	drove	driven	Steal	stole	stolen
Eat	ate	eaten	Stride	strode	stridden
Freeze	froze	frozen	Strive	strove	striven
Go	(went)	gone	Take	took	taken
Hang	hung	{ hanged (weak) { hung	Thrive	throve	thriven
			Wear	wore	worn
Know	knew	known	Wring	wrung	wrung

EXERCISE XIII

Give the chief parts of the following verbs :—To clothe, deal, hear, knit, lay, lie, lend, leap, mean, sell, teach, tell, think, weep, wet, work, awake, begin, bind, bite, choose, cling, draw, fling, forbid, forsake, grind, know, ring, run, sit, slay, slink, stick, sting, swear, take, tear, wear, weave, win, write.

THE VERB INFINITE (Infinitive Mood)

As already noted, the **Verb Infinite** consists of such forms of the verb as denote actions or states without reference to person or number.

These forms are :—

1. The **Infinitive mood.**
2. The **Gerund.**
3. The **Participles.**

1. The **Infinitive** mood is used

(*a*) as a **Noun,** as :—

To err is human. *To err* is equivalent to a noun and is the subject of the sentence.

I want *to see* you. *To see* is equivalent to the object of want.

I desire nothing except *to be left* to my own devices. *To be left* is object after the preposition except.

(*b*) as an **Adverb of reason or purpose,** as:—

I came *to see* you. *To see* is equivalent to an adverb modifying came.

(*c*) as a **Complement,** as :—

I must *see* you. *See* completes the sense.

Notes.—

1. There are four forms of the infinitive, viz.,

	Active.	*Passive.*
Present.	to sing.	to be sung.
Perfect.	to have sung.	to have been sung.

2. When a verb is named, we use the present infinitive form retaining the *to*, as :—*to dance, to sing.*

In constructions often the *to* is omitted, as :—*He let me do it. You must go.*

When purpose is intended the *to* is **not** omitted, as :— *He came to see me. This task is to be completed.*

3. Avoid the **split-infinitive**, as :—*He asked me to quickly run to the station*, should be *to run quickly*, etc.

EXERCISE XIV

How is the verb in the infinitive mood here used? :—

1. He travelled *to see* the world.
2. *To walk* in the country is healthy recreation.
3. Let me *come.*
4. *To have succeeded* is a great tribute to his patience.
5. You heard me *go.*
6. That made him *smile.*
7. He bid him *halt.*
8. He does nothing except *complain.*
9. *To stand* still is useless.
10. He lived *to eat.*

2. The Gerund.

A gerund is a noun formed from a verb and ends in **-ing**. If the verb used is intransitive, the gerund has mainly the function of a noun. If the verb used is transitive, the gerund may have a following object and therefore retains the function of a verb, as :—

Living is a difficult business these days.

Here *living* is equivalent to *to live*—it is a *noun equivalent*.

He had no difficulty in *spending* his money.

Here the gerund is preceded by a preposition, *in*, and is followed by an object, *money*.

When the gerund is preceded by either of the articles (*a* or *the*) or a possessive adjective and followed by a preposition, it is a verbal noun, as :—

His *reading* the book was annoying (gerund).

His *reading* of the book was unpleasant (verbal noun).

The following examples illustrate the uses of the gerund form :—

1. *Swimming* is an excellent exercise (used as subject).

2. He enjoys *swimming* in the sea (used as object).

3. His hobby was *swimming* (used as complement).

4. He was keen on *swimming* (used as object after preposition.)

5. He was expert at *teaching* English (takes object ; verb function stronger).

6. He was pleased at *being taught* English (as in 5).

7. He collects *spinning*-tops (*i.e.* tops for spinning ; verb function stronger).

Note.—There are *four* forms of the gerund :—

	Active.	Passive.
Present.	singing.	being sung.
Perfect.	having sung.	having been sung.

The Participles

As gerunds resemble nouns in their function, **so** do participles resemble **adjectives** in theirs. Participles resemble adjectives in that they limit the meaning of nouns ; they have the function of verbs in that

(a) they help verbs to form their tenses ; and
(b) they take objects if the verb used is transitive, as :—

Possessing a cheerful disposition, he was always welcome.

The present participle *possessing* refers to he and does the work of an adjective.

The *auctioned* goods were found to be very inferior.

The past participle *auctioned* refers to goods and does the work of an adjective.

He was *having* his dinner when I entered.

Here the present participle *having* is helping the verb to form its past indefinite tense.

I saw the man *leading* a pony.

Here the present participle *leading* refers to man and takes an object, pony.

The **present participle**, ending in **-ing**, has four forms :—

	Active.	*Passive.*
Present.	acting.	being acted.
Perfect.	having acted.	having been acted.

The **past participle** forms end in *-en, -n,* or *-ed, -d,* or *-t,* in accordance with whether the verb is strong or weak.

EXERCISE XV

In the following verbs ending in -ing, state whether it is (*a*) a present participle, (*b*) a gerund, (*c*) part of a tense form :—

1. *Pressing* on he arrived at his destination.

2. He delighted in *correcting* people.

3. The *collecting* of this salvage will be difficult.

4. *Spending* too much time in pleasure is *ruining* his health.

5. He was *taking* part in too many disputes.

6. He received a present of a *rocking*-horse.

7. *Hurrying* is not going to remedy matters.

8. He was *singing* loudly when I passed.

9. Her *singing* of Schubert's song was delightful.

Parsing Table for the Verb

	Kind.	Voice.	Mood.	Tense.	
Verbs : Weak Strong	Transitive Intransitive Auxiliary	Active Passive	Indicative Imperative Subjunctive Infinitive	Present Past Future	See under Tense (p. 53) for particular forms.

Also give Person and Number and remember that a verb agrees with its subject.

N.B.—Never give person or number for an infinitive form.

THE ADVERB

Adverbs modify words ; that is, they add something to the meaning but limit the application of the words. Adverbs may modify any part of speech except a noun, or pronoun, or interjection, but generally modify Verbs, Adjectives or other Adverbs or adverbial equivalents (Adverbial Phrases or Adverbial Clauses).

> The train rushed *swiftly* through the station.
> This is a *most* beautiful day.
> He thinks *too* much.
> He placed the point of his pencil *exactly* on the spot.
> The ambush occurred *just* where the road wound upwards.

Adverbs are generally formed from Adjectives by adding -ly—quick, *quickly*, wonderful, *wonderfully*.

(*a*) Many adjectives ending in -ly have the same form for the adverb—*daily, early, lovely, only, contrary*.

(*b*) Some adverbs have the same form as the adjective—*fast, hard, little, long, much, previous, contrary*.

Classification of Adverbs

There are **five** main classes of Adverbs :—

(1) Adverbs of **Time**—indicating time of action— **when** ?

(2) Adverbs of **Place**—indicating place of action —**where** ?

(3) Adverbs of **Manner**—indicating **manner** of action—**how** ?

(4) Adverbs of **Degree**—indicating intensity of action—**how far** ?

(5) Adverbs of **Reason**—indicating cause of action—**why** ?

Notes.—

(i) Adverbs which not only modify a word but also link the sense of clauses are sometimes called Conjunctive Adverbs (Time, Place, Reason)—*for, however, then, therefore*.

They were prepared to resist ; *however*, there was no need.

(ii) Adverbs of Degree may include what are sometimes called Adverbs of Affirmation, Negation, Emphasis, Comparison and Number. Adverbs of Degree commonly modify Adjectives or other Adverbs :—

He was *not* attracted by the offer.

(iii) Adverbs of Time, Place, Manner, Reason may be used to ask a question and treated as Interrogative Adverbs :—

Why did you do this ?
How did it happen ?

Examples :

Time :—*soon, late, now, immediately*.

Place :—*here* (*hither, hence*), *there* (*thither, thence*), *near, above, by, anywhere*.

Manner :—nearly all adverbs ending in -ly, and *thus, well, ill, firstly, only*.

Degree :—*very, too, so, as, about, seldom, often, certainly, probably, even*.

Reason :—*why, wherefore, therefore*.

5

Position of Adverbs

Adverbs must be placed beside the word they modify.

(1) The adverb is placed before Adjectives, Prepositions or other Adverbs :—

He was *too* happy to speak.

(2) The Adverb is placed after an Intransitive Verb, or the Direct Object of a Transitive Verb :—

She sang *sweetly*.

The ships of the enemy returned our fire *feebly*.

Exceptions—seldom, often, never, always.

He *seldom* spoke to them.

(3) The Adverb is placed between the Auxiliary and Participle in compound tenses of the verb, but *not* between " to " and the Infinitive.

I have *often* heard him speak of you.

Comparison of Adverbs

All Adverbs, except those which have the same form as the corresponding Adjective, form the Comparative and Superlative by adding " more " and " most " to the Positive :—

quickly, more quickly, most quickly.

Irregular Comparison of Adverbs

Positive.	Comparative.	Superlative.
far	farther	farthest
(furth)	further	furthest
ill, badly	worse	worst
well	better	best
much	more	most
long	longer	longest
early	earlier	earliest
late	later	latest
little	less	least
fast	faster	fastest

Scheme of Parsing for Adverbs

Adverb : Kind, degree (if adverb can be compared), word it modifies.

Example : He *now* moved *very speedily forward*.

now : Adv., time, mod. " moved."
very : Adv., degree, mod. " speedily."
speedily : Adv., manner, positive, mod. " moved."
forward : Adv., place, mod. " moved."

EXERCISE XVI

Parse the Adverbs in the following sentences :—

1. The children ran quickly.
2. The bus moved quite slowly.
3. John works more steadily than his friend.
4. It was too good to be true.
5. Always try to speak plainly.
6. Again and yet again our guns replied.
7. Still they gazed wonderingly at the strange figure.
8. You are still in error ; however, you may go.

9. Only now and then we heard from him for many years.

10. Whence came Niall of Succoth so hurriedly ?

11. Merrily, merrily, shall I live now.

12. Yonder looms faintly the island.

13. He fell off backwards ; however, he picked himself up unhurt.

14. If he confesses even now, his offence will be fully pardoned.

15. Seldom have so many depended so much on so few.

16. He was already sufficiently experienced to deal sensibly with most of his difficulties.

17. I have no reason to be afraid for I have never injured him.

18. Slowly and sadly we laid him to rest.

19. He talks rather well, but he often behaves foolishly.

20. I could have better spared a better man.

PREPOSITION

Prepositions are words which express the relation between a thing, or an action, or a quality or attribute and some other thing : that is, between a noun, verb or adjective and a noun or pronoun.

1. The **dog** *in* the **film** is very clever.

2. I **arranged** the papers *on* the **table**.

3. He is **popular** *among* his **classmates**.

The Preposition governs the noun or pronoun in the Objective Case and generally comes before it. When the word governed by the Preposition is a Relative Pronoun expressed or omitted, it may come after.

The boy described the men whom he was talking *to*.

The agent you wrote *to* last week called to-day.

Prepositions may be simple words—to, from, at, in, by, with, about, or certain participles—considering, respecting, regarding, having.

Note.—What are sometimes called Compound Prepositions—*out of, up to*, may be treated as composed of an Adverb and a Preposition.

Scheme of Parsing for Prepositions

Preposition : Word it governs.

Example : He went *to* the fair.

'to : Prep., gov. fair.

EXERCISE XVII

Pick out the Preposition, name the word it governs, and name the Part of Speech to which it expresses the relation :—

1. The face at the window alarmed him.
2. I have not looked at it since yesterday.
3. Barring accidents, he will be here in time.
4. What is the opinion of the guide respecting equipment ?
5. He is eager in all his work.
6. From scenes like these auld Scotia's grandeur springs.
7. He came up to the field on the following day.
8. Out of pity I decided to help him.
9. He looks at life through rose-coloured spectacles.
10. In every way his information concerning the facts of the case is reliable.

THE CONJUNCTION

Conjunctions are words that join words, phrases or clauses together :—

  (*a*) William *and* Mary ruled the land.

  (*b*) By sheer energy *and* iron determination he built up a sound business.

  (*c*) I was very much annoyed *and* I did not hide my feelings.

Conjunctions which join clauses are of two classes :—

1. **Co-ordinating conjunctions** are those which join clauses of equal importance—*and, or, else, but, still, yet, however, for, then, therefore.*

2. **Subordinating Conjunctions** are those which join clauses where one is dependent upon the other—*that, after, before, since, till, while, as, lest, if, because, although, then.*

Notes.—

  (i) Correlative conjunctions are co-ordinating.

     They are : *either—or* ; *neither—nor* ; *not only—but also.*

  (ii) Adverbial conjunctions are subordinating.

     They are : *where, when, why, how.*

Scheme of Parsing for Conjunctions

Conjunction : Kind (Co-ord. or Subord.), words, phrases or clauses it joins.

EXERCISE XVIII

Parse the Conjunctions in the following sentences :—

1. He and his brother are in the team.
2. I shall obey but it is against my will.
3. With much thought and great pains I have prepared a speech.
4. He has been here since you gave him his instructions
5. Whether the team will win is another question.
6. The play will go on if the audience is willing.
7. You will see either him or the second in command.
8. The stranger asked eagerly when the ship was due to sail.
9. He is taller than any of his subjects by the breadth of a nail.
10. The helmet shone as he rode down to Camelot.

EXERCISE XIX

(a) **Point out the Adverbs, Prepositions and Conjunctions in the following sentences :—**

1. I waited two hours after he left.
2. None but the brave deserves the fair.
3. He will come before the game begins.
4. Though he has deserted me, send his treasure after him.
5. He fell off the platform and lay stretched out on the line.
6. He enjoyed the concert despite his complaints, just as I expected.
7. I hoped that he would come in out of the rain.
8. The sooner it's over, the sooner to sleep.
9. Nothing, as you know, could be fairer than that.

10. Either you obey or you take the consequences.

11. Through his folly all of us must lie low for some time.

12. Come unto these yellow sands where the waves come rippling in.

13. As he stood close by, the roar of the crowd nearly deafened him more than once.

14. Since when has my father ceased to give orders here ?

15. Except for a few bruises, he came away none the worse.

16. We fell out, my wife and I.

17. Out of the night came the wild haunting cry of the seabirds.

18. It matters naught how strait the way.

19. He has paid for his folly, for he has suffered much in the last year or two.

20. I can see he really likes you as much as, if not more than, I hoped.

(b) **Say whether the words italicised in the following sentences are Prepositions or Adverbs :—**

1. We saw the barrage-balloon going *up*.

2. He climbed *up* the ladder.

3. They then walked *round* the field.

4. Above the air-field planes were to be seen flying *round*.

5. After the game was *over*, we were perfectly happy.

6. The cow jumped *over* the moon.

7. If you wish information, enquire *within*.

8. *Within* the room all was dark.

9. He was so exhausted that he fell *behind*.

10. Look *behind* the picture for the spring.

THE INTERJECTION

Interjections (*inter*—between, *jacio*—I throw) are sounds thrown into a sentence to call the attention of the person addressed or to express an emotion such as joy, sorrow or surprise. They are not part of the structure of the sentence but may help to complete the sense—*alas! hurrah! pshaw! hear! hear!*

Note.—Hark! hush! are sentences consisting of a verb in the imperative mood with the pronoun " you " understood.

Scheme of Parsing

Parsing among young classes tends so often to become a mere matter of memorising certain terms that in order to encourage an intelligent approach, the following stages are suggested.

First Year—Scheme of Parsing as shown in ordinary type.

Second Year—Add details given in italics.

Third Year—Add details given in bold type.

Noun : **Kind, person,** *number*, *gender*, **case,**
{ subject of.
{ governed by.

Pronoun : kind, *person*, *number*, *gender*, **case,**
{ subject of.
{ governed by.

Adjective : kind, degree, { limiting.
{ qualifying.

Verb : **strong or weak (neuter)**, trans. or intrans., **voice**, *mood*, tense ; *person*, *number*, agreeing with its subject.

Infinitive : tense, voice, simple or gerundial, case,
{ subject of.
{ governed by.

(*a*) **Participle :** *trans. or intrans.*, tense, voice, object
(if any), word it { limits.
{ qualifies.

(*b*) **Gerund :** *trans. or intrans.*, tense, voice, case,
{ subject of.
{ governed by.

Adverb : kind, degree, word it modifies.

Preposition : word it governs.

Conjunction : kind (co-ord. or subord.), words,
phrases or clauses it joins.

Remember that in English a word may be any
part of speech. What it is depends on what it does.
To discover what a word does, make a Particular
Analysis of the sentence in which it is used. Do
this always before you parse a word.

Example of Parsing

Presently one of the Doones, catching sight of her,
informed the others.

Presently : Adv. of time, mod. " informed."

one :   Pron., Indef., *3rd pers.*, *sing.*, *masc.*, nom.
subject of " informed."

of :   Prep., gov. " Doones."

the :   Adj., demons., { limit.
{ qual. " Doones."

Doones : Noun, **proper**, 3rd pers., *plur.*, *masc.*,
obj. gov. by " of."

catching : Participle, *trans.*, pres., **active**, object
                " sight," $\begin{cases} \text{limit.} \\ \text{qual. " one."} \end{cases}$

sight : Noun, **common**, **3rd pers.**, *sing.*, *neut.*, obj.
              gov. by " catching."

of : Prep., gov. " her."

her : Pron., pers., *3rd pers.*, *sing.*, *fem.*, obj. gov.
              by " of."

informed : Verb. **weak**, trans., **active**, *indic.*, past,
              3rd pers., *sing.*, agreeing with " one."

the : Adj., demons., $\begin{cases} \text{limit.} \\ \text{qual. " others."} \end{cases}$

others : Pron., indef., *3rd pers. plur.*, *masc.*, obj.
              gov. by " informed."

EXERCISE XX

Parse the words in the following sentences :—

1. I am monarch of all I survey.
2. This is not true so far as I am concerned.
3. They are both fond of the new pet.
4. The minstrel was infirm and old.
5. Napoleon appointed his brother, Joseph, King of Spain.
6. None of the boys was present at the school display.
7. Many a brave soldier has breathed his last since the war began.
8. I come to bury Caesar, not to praise him.
9. Having finished a long day's work, the ploughman collects his spades, his mattocks and his hoes.
10. The audience applauded his singing of the song with great enthusiasm.

11. To run a long race successfully, more than speed is needed.

12. Be good, sweet maid, and let who will be clever.

13. Each of the captives was occupied with his own sad thoughts.

14. There is a very good farm to let in the next parish.

15. Though he slay me, yet will I trust him.

16. Tell my mother I shall come by and by.

17. What thou would'st highly, that would'st thou holily.

18. What work have these men done to-day, sir ?

19. Then rose from sea to sky the wild farewell.

20. By his own industry and the negligence of others, he very soon became the manager of the business.

21. For of such is the Kingdom of Heaven.

22. No one knows what will happen, but all fear the worst.

23. So runs my dream but what am I ?
    An infant crying in the night
    And with no language but a cry.

24. Of the vast hosts of the Persians, many thousands perished in this great battle.

25. Last night a fine wooer came down the glen seeking the fair maid there.

26. Full many a gem of purest ray serene
    The dark unfathomed caves of ocean bear.

27. None but the brave deserves the fair.

28. By sailing down the broad river, they escaped the perils of the deadly jungle.

29. Like many another martyr, he, too, has died for righteousness' sake.

30. Yet once more, o ye laurels, and once more,
    Ye myrtles brown, with ivy never-sere,
    I come to pluck your berries harsh and crude.

CHAPTER III
GENERAL ANALYSIS

Particular Analysis is the process of breaking up a Simple Sentence which contains only one Subject and one Predicate. There are, however, sentences which contain two or more connected thoughts, each of which is expressed in a Clause consisting of a Subject and Predicate. That part of Grammar which deals with the division of sentences into clauses and with the relations of clauses to one another is called **General Analysis** and is applied to the following sentences:—

1. Compound.
2. Complex.
3. Compound-Complex.

COMPOUND SENTENCE

The **Compound Sentence** consists of *two or more simple sentences or principal clauses joined by Co-ordinating Conjunctions*. The number of *Clauses* in a Compound Sentence depends on the number of Predicates expressed or understood.

Compound Sentences are divided into *four classes* and named according to the kind of conjunction used:—

(1) **Copulative** (*clauses of similar meaning*), **as:**
　　He *went* to the fair and there *sold* the horse.

(2) **Adversative** (*clauses contrasted in meaning*), **as:**
　　He *asked* permission to visit the **prisoner but the guards** *refused*.

(3) **Alternative** (*one clause excludes the other*), as:
Either you *are* early or my watch *is* slow.

(4) **Illative** (*one clause implies the other*), as:
The Nabob *was* never *contradicted* hence he never *learned* to control himself.

EXERCISE I

(*a*) **Analyse the following sentences into clauses and give the conjunctions or joining words (stated or implied).**

1. He received his prize and returned to his place.
2. Help may come, but I have given up hope.
3. I cannot see the steps clearly nor the dark path beyond them.
4. Either the man is a villain, or else he is very unsuspicious.
5. He was a keen soldier, therefore he made a good officer.

(*b*) **Combine the following simple sentences to form compound sentences making use, where suitable, of the conjunctions and, but, or, nor, hence, for, therefore, either . . . or, neither . . . nor.**

1. Draw up your chair. It is a cold night.
2. The new dog is a good watch dog. He is very fierce.
3. Oliver did not hide the purse. He did not attempt to escape.
4. The general was noted for his kindness. The captives hoped for mercy.
5. You are an innocent man. You are the victim of a plot.

COMPLEX SENTENCE

The **Complex Sentence** consists of *one principal clause and one or more subordinate clauses* : that is, it contains a main thought which is connected with one or more subordinate thoughts.

A Subordinate Clause may do the work of :

I. A **Noun** as Subject, Object or Complement : **Noun Clause.**

II. An **Adjective** : **Adjective or Adjectival Clause.**

III. An **Adverb** : **Adverbial Clause.**

NOUN CLAUSE

A **Noun Clause**, like the Simple Sentence, may be a Statement, Question, Exclamation, Desire or Command, but is dependent on the Principal Clause.

Examples :

1. He declared *that he was willing to fight for his native land* : **Dependent Statement.**

2. Tell me *where you have been all day* : **Dependent Question.**

3. See *what a rent the envious Casca made* ! : **Dependent Exclamation.**

4. He desired *that he might be led between the pillars* : **Dependent Desire.**

5. The captain commanded *that the prisoners should be released* : **Dependent Command.**

The Noun Clause may be the Subject or the Object of a Principal Clause, Nominative in Apposition to the Subject, or Objective in Apposition to the Object, Complement to the Predicate, governed by a Preposition.

Examples :

1. *What I have spoken* is the truth : **Subject.**
2. He asked me *what I wanted* : **Object.**
3. His excuse that *no one had wakened him* was received with scorn : **Nominative in Apposition.**
4. He made reply *that he was ill* : **Objective in Apposition.**
5. That is not *what was said* : **Complement.**
6. For *what we are about to receive* may we be truly thankful : **Governed by Preposition.**

EXERCISE II

(a) **Use the following Noun Clauses as subjects of Sentences :—**

1. How it came about..................
2. Where the attack will take place..................
3. When the order will come..................
4. What you have told me..................
5. That a pig can fly..................

(b) **Use the following Noun Clauses as Objects or Complements of Sentences :—**

1. ....what many men desire.
2. ....to what you have told me.
3. ....how much it cost you.
4. ....when the ships will come.
5. ....if he was going.

EXERCISE III

Pick out the Noun Clauses and state what work each clause performs :—

1. I saw clearly that he did not mean to return.

2. That he was anxious to go was apparent to all.

3. I am not sure where he is living now.

4. To his surprise his father asked why he wished to leave school.

5. I cannot but remember such things were.

6. This letter refers to what you heard yesterday.

7. Who is to be the victim will be decided by lot.

8. It is hard to realise that salt is a luxury to many tribes.

9. There is no doubt that he is the guilty party.

10. The reality was very different from what he had expected.

EXERCISE IV

Substitute equivalent Noun Clauses for the Nouns in italics. State the function of each clause :—

1. I know the *culprit*.

2. The best *runner* will be the winner.

3. His *dishonesty* was soon known to everybody.

4. The search party looked in vain for his *hiding place*.

5. By his *statement* he encouraged his friends.

6. The real *value* of the book is not fully understood.

7. There is no malice in his *remarks*.

8. A newspaper keeps its readers in touch with *affairs*.

9. The *future* is still unknown.

10. They enquired among his friends for his *address*.

ADJECTIVE CLAUSE

An **Adjective Clause** does the work of an Adjective or Adjective Phrase and may qualify the Subject, Object or Complement of another Clause which need not be a Principal Clause. The noun or pronoun qualified is known as the **Antecedent**.

6

Examples :

They welcomed the *exiled* fugitives : **Adjective**.

They welcomed the fugitives *in exile* : **Adjective Phrase**.

They welcomed the fugitives *who were in exile* :

Adjective Clause.

The Adjective Clause is introduced by

(a) Relative Pronouns : *who, which, that, what.*

(b) Conjunctive or Relative Adverbs : *when, where, why, whither, whence.*

(c) *As* after *same, such* in another clause and *but* after a question or negative statement.

The Antecedent is always expressed before Conjunctive Adverbs and omitted before *what*. A Relative Pronoun may be omitted if it is not the subject of the clause.

Examples :

1. This is the cat *that* killed the **rat**.
2. I am monarch of all I survey.
3. Show me the cottage *where* the poet was born.
4. He displayed a jewel such *as* I had never seen before.
5. What man is there *but* will fight for his country ?
6. There is not a person *but* admires him.

EXERCISE V

Pick out the Adjective Clauses and give the Relative Pronouns and the Antecedents :—

1. We are unable to trace the man about whom you enquired.

2. He named the hour when the ceremony was to take place.

3. I dare do all that may become a man.

4. He who fights and runs away
Will live to fight another day.

5. There is not a blade of grass but reminds me of her.

6. This is the house where the great man lived.

7. Such a work as you describe is not to be obtained easily.

8. I know a bank whereon the wild thyme blows.

9. The reason why he slew the hound is not very clear.

10. The girl, whose hat had blown away, tried in vain to catch it.

EXERCISE VI

(a) **Substitute equivalent Clauses for the word or phrase italicised :—**

1. A warlike nation will not have a *peaceful* history.

2. This is the scene *of the accident*.

3. I cannot foresee the day *of our meeting*.

4. He is beloved by his *friends*.

5. *Tall* men cannot stand erect in buses.

(b) **Insert suitable Relative Pronouns and name the Antecdents, if given in the following :—**

1. The cups................cheer, but not inebriate.

2. ....the gods love, die young.

3. There is not a villager................knows the legend.

4. Such a man................you describe is difficult to understand.

5. The time will come................you will be glad to benefit by his work.

ADVERBIAL CLAUSE

An **Adverbial Clause** does the work of an **Adverb** and may modify a *Verb*, an *Adjective* or an *Adverb* in another Clause. It is introduced by a Subordinating Conjunction and is classified according to the kind of Conjunction.

Examples :

1. **Time** : His father died *when he was still very young.*

   Conjunctions : *When, before, after, while, since, till, until, as, as soon as, whenever.*

2. **Place** : The stone fell *where he was standing.*

   Conjunctions : *Whither, whence, where.*

3. **Manner** : He behaves *as we expect him to do.*

   Conjunction : *As.*

4. **Degree** or **Comparison** : This novel is just as interesting *as his last one was.*

   Conjunctions : *Than, as* (after " *as,*" " *such,*" " *same,*" in another clause).

5. **Reason** : *Since we cannot avoid it,* let us face it.

   Conjunctions : *Because, for, as, since.*

6. **Condition** : Test it for yourself *if you do not believe it.*

   Conjunctions : *If, unless, whether . . . or, in case, provided that, so long as, but.*

7. **Concession** : *Though he was willing to help,* no one would employ him.

   Conjunctions : *Though, although, even if, whatever, however.*

8. **Consequence** or **Result** : He suffered so much *that even his enemies were sorry for him.*

   Conjunctions : *So . . . that.*

9. **Purpose** : He worked hard *so that he might succeed.*

Conjunctions : *That, so that, in order that, lest.*

An Adverbial Clause of Time answers the questions : **When ? How long ? How often ?**

An Adverbial Clause of Place answers the questions : **Where ? Whither ? Whence ?**

An Adverbial Clause of Manner answers the question : **How ?**

An Adverbial Clause of Degree or Comparison answers the questions : **How much ? To what extent ?**

An Adverbial Clause of Reason answers the question : **Why ?**

An Adverbial Clause of Condition answers the question : **On what condition ?**

An Adverbial Clause of Concession answers the question : **In spite of what ?**

An Adverbial Clause of Consequence answers the question : **With what result ?**

An Adverbial Clause of Purpose answers the question : **For what purpose ?**

Note.—Clauses introduced by *when* and *where* may be Noun Clauses, if they answer the question, " *What ?* " ; or Adjective Clauses, if they have an Antecedent expressed.

EXERCISE VII

Pick out the Adverbial Clauses and the Subordinating Conjunctions. Name the clauses and the words modified :—

1. Where the tree falls, let it lie.

2. The giant was as tall as the great pine trees.

3. Though they managed to win the match, the victory was a narrow one.

4. There is no better training than this school offers.

5. He never took the road through the woods again lest he might be disappointed.

6. Unless ye repent, ye shall all likewise perish.

7. As soon as the sergeant fell, a wonderful change came over the men.

8. He hit out at the bowling as he had been advised.

9. Since he was a stranger to the town, he passed a solitary evening.

10. He will be thoroughly disguised so that he may escape capture.

EXERCISE VIII

Insert suitable Conjunctions and name the kinds of clauses :—

1. I never loved the snow................Maurice died.

2. ....the truth were known, ne would be punished.

3. He left the company early..............he was worn out.

4. He is not such a good runner..............his brother is.

5. The cavalry charged at such a speed................the gunners were taken by surprise.

6. He died.................we might live.

7. ....she sang beautifully, she did not win the prize.

8. They are much more capable of paying................. we are.

9. They hunted carefully.................the treasure had once been.

10. She will have her own way.................you may say,

EXERCISE IX

Turn the Adverbs or Adverb Phrases into equivalent Adverb Clauses and name the kinds :—

1. He cannot be present *on account of his illness*.
2. He is buried *among his ancestors*.
3. He always behaves *according to his beliefs*.
4. *In spite of many temptations*, he remains true to his country.
5. Stevenson went to Samoa *to preserve his health*.
6. *Instead of the cultivated garden*, there was now waste land.
7. *Without my consent*, he cannot join the society.
8. *Having given a promise*, we expect him to keep it.
9. He came *at my request*.
10. *By steady work* he has become very capable.

EXERCISE X

Complete the following sentences by adding Adverbial Clauses on the lines suggested :—

1. Show me the treasure.................. **(Time.)**
2. The natives concealed themselves............... **(Place.)**
3. The gunners kept careful watch......... **(Reason.)**
4. They made special preparations............ **(Purpose.)**
5. I was not interested in the story................. **(Concession.)**
6. The explorer had penetrated farther................. **(Comparison.)**
7. He was not so successful................. **(Degree.)**
8. The sound of the bells was so clear................. **(Manner.)**
9. The potato crop was so bad................. **(Consequence.)**

EXERCISE XI

Construct Complex Sentences on the following lines :- -

1. Prin. Cl.— Adj. Cl.
2. Prin. Cl.— Adv. Cl. of Time.
3. Prin. Cl.—Noun Cl.
4. Prin. Cl.—Adv. Cl. of Place—Adj. Cl.
5. Noun Cl.—Prin. Cl.—Adj. Cl.
6. Prin. Cl.—Noun Cl.—Adv. Cl. of Reason.
7. Adv. Cl. of Condition—Adj. Cl.—Prin. Cl.
8. Adj. Cl.— Prin. Cl.—Adv. Cl. of Manner.
9. Adv. Cl. of Concession—Prin. Cl.
10. Prin. Cl.—Adv. Cl. of Degree.

COMPOUND-COMPLEX SENTENCE

A **Compound-Complex** Sentence is one that contains *two or more Principal Clauses and one or more Subordinate Clauses*.

Examples :

1. The Greeks already knew the ill tidings and were prepared, as during the night a deserter from the Persian camp had warned them that an attempt would be made to outflank them.

2. Till noon we quietly sailed on,
   Yet never a breeze did breathe :
   Slowly and smoothly went the ship,
   Moved onward from beneath.

Examples of General Analysis

1. **Compound Sentence :**

She waved him an adieu from the window and stood there for a moment, looking after him.

2. Complex Sentence :

He rode by his General's side as they hastened after the troops of the General's brigade, which preceded them at a rapid march since they had to reach camp before dusk.

3. Compound-Complex Sentence :

There was a violent commotion in the sea where the moon's rays were concentrated, and I had just decided that I must arouse the captain, when it suddenly ceased.

(1)

No.	Clause	Kind	Relation.
A	She waved him an adieu from the window . .	Prin.	Independent.
B	And stood there for a moment, looking after him	Prin.	Co-ord. with A.
	Compound Sentence		

(2)

No.	Clause	Kind	Relation
A	He rode by his General's side	Prin.	Independent.
a_1	As they hastened after the troops of the General's brigade . . .	Adv. (Time)	Mod. " rode."
a_2	Which preceded them at a rapid march . .	Adj.	Qual. " brigade."
a_3	Since they had to reach camp before dusk .	Adv. (Reason)	Mod. " preceded."
	Complex Sentence		

(3)

No.	Clause	Kind	Relation
A	There was a violent commotion in the sea .	Prin.	Independent.
a_1	Where the moon's rays were concentrated .	Adj.	Qual. " sea."
B	And I had just decided .	Prin.	Co-ord. with A.
b_1	That I must arouse the captain . . .	} Noun. {	Objective by " had decided."
b_2	When it suddenly ceased .	{ Adv. } (Time). }	Mod. " had decided."

Compound-Complex Sentence

EXERCISE XII

Make a General Analysis of the following Sentences :—

1. My hand touched and clung to a rope, which immediately towed me towards the boat.

2. Had it not been for this impediment, I really believe he would have beaten us altogether.

3. It was a letter which he had written at daybreak before he took leave of Amelia.

4. You know that he is very poor and he will lose every shilling if he does not take care.

5. He was not the dogged Scrooge he had been ; and though the Spirit's eyes were clear and kind, he did not like to meet them.

6. Again the spectre raised a cry, and shook its chain and wrung its shadowy hands.

7. I remember it was with extreme difficulty, that I could make him understand the meaning of the word.

8. By degrees, he became more calm, and besought, in a low and broken voice, that he might be rescued from his present dangers.

9. Mr. Brownlow led the way into another room, and there heard from Rose a full narration of her interview with Nancy which occasioned him no little surprise.

10. Though I swam very well, I could not deliver myself from the waves to draw breath, till that wave, having spent itself, went back, and left me upon the land.

11. When the settled season began to come in, as the thought of my design returned with the fair weather, I was preparing daily for the voyage.

12. Probably the same motives which induced Cedric to open his hall to the Jew, would have made him insist on his attendants receiving Isaac with more courtesy.

13. If you will be guided by my counsel, you will give up this wild-goose chase, and try your hand at some other game.

14. The houses where the Europeans live are shut off from the native quarter by a barricaded fence of barbed wire which completely encloses the buildings in a square and therein dwell the families of the British population.

15. He hoped that they would be too tired to follow up the pursuit but the enemy now knew where he was located and left no stone unturned to run him down.

16. A good many years ago I was told an anecdote of the well-known judge, which, as I have never heard it repeated, is probably not generally known.

17. Such was the case with a woman who, wishing to cross a ferry when there was a pretty strong wind blowing, asked the ferryman if he thought it was quite safe

18. The strange thing is that everyone who wishes to be considered respectable keeps a little of this money, and is horrified at the suggestion that it should be used for ordinary purchases.

19. This place of concealment she sought by the advice of a Glencoe man who came on her suddenly and, touched by her anxiety, told her that she was in no further danger.

20. Though, his temper being naturally jovial, he at last got over it he grew careless of himself and never dressed afterwards in the modern fashion.

21. Once, at a splendid dinner-party the guests suddenly missed Garrick, and could not imagine what was become of him, till they heard the peals of laughter of a young negro boy.

22. I cannot find the place
Where his paw is in the snare.

23. And now it is an angel's song
That makes the heavens be mute.

24. They smote their strong way through the drench
and drift,
Till the keen hour had chafed itself to death.

25. So thick a haze o'erspreads the sky
They cannot see the sun on high ;
The wind hath blown a gale all day
At evening it hath died away.

26. They took the son and bound him,
Neck and heel in a thong,
And a lad took him and swung him
And flung him far and strong,
And the sea swallowed his body.

27. He long lived the pride of that country-side
And, at last, in the odour of sanctity died ;
When, as words were too faint his merits to paint,
The Conclave determined to make him a Saint !

28. She has heard a whisper say,
    A curse is on her if she stay
      To look down to Camelot.

29. Ill fares the land, to hast'ning ills a prey
    Where wealth accumulates and men decay :
    Princes and lords may flourish, or may fade,
    A breath can make them, as a breath has made.

30. When Spring, with dewy fingers cold,
    Returns to deck their hallow'd mould
    She there shall dress a sweeter sod
    Than Fancy's feet have ever trod.

31. It may be we shall touch the Happy Isles,
    And see the great Achilles, whom we knew.

32. Like phantoms, to the iron porch, they glide ;
    Where lay the Porter, in uneasy sprawl
    With a huge empty flagon by his side.

33. Though my hopes may have fail'd, yet they are not
        forgot ;
    Though cold is my heart, still it lingers with you.

34. My heart leaps up when I behold
    A rainbow in the sky :
    So was it when my life began
    So is it now I am a man.

35. What is this life if, full of care,
    We have no time to stand and stare ?

36. If I should die, think only this of me :
    That there's some corner of a foreign field
    That is for ever England.

37. If such there breathe, go, mark him well
    For him no Minstrel raptures swell.

38. I will hold my home in the high wood,
    Within a walk of the sea,
    And the men that were boys, when I was a boy
    Shall sit and drink with me.

39. We travel the dusty road, till the light of day is dim,
    And sunset shows us spires away on the world's rim.

40. It is the generous Spirit, who, when brought
    Among the tasks of real life, hath wrought
    Upon the plan that pleased his boyish thought.

41. I am content with what I have
    Little be it, or much ;
    And, Lord, contentment still I crave,
    Because Thou savest such.

CHAPTER IV

Section A

THE DICTIONARY—AND HOW TO USE IT

The indispensable book for the student of English is a Dictionary of the English language. Buy the best dictionary you can afford and use it. Whenever you are doing any English work, have your dictionary by your side : acquire the dictionary habit as early as you can.

A good dictionary supplies a great deal of information about the words in our language. Some of this information you may think unnecessary but the deeper you go into the study of our language, the more you will realize the necessity for giving this information.

Observe that :—

1. The words of a dictionary are all arranged in *alphabetical order*, e.g. a word such as *Aaronic* will be found before words beginning with ab, such as *abate*, or ac, such as *achieve*.

Key words are usually found at the top of the pages. These words guide you to which words are in the different columns. Practice will soon make you expert in finding your word quickly ; but in order to do so, *you must be absolutely certain of the order of the letters in our alphabet.*

2. A good dictionary provides us with :—

> (a) **the correct spelling** (or spellings) of each word.

(*b*) **the correct pronunciation** of each word.

Words of several syllables are usually divided into their pronounced syllables by means of short dashes (*e.g.* monˈ-u-ment, psychic, sī-kik). The accented syllable or syllables is or are usually denoted by a downward short stroke (ˈ), the accent mark. The syllables are usually spelled as they are sounded, *i.e. phonetically*. The vowel sounds are usually indicated either by a list giving examples of the various vowels at the beginning of the dictionary or by key vowels illustrated in short words at the top of every page. In *Chambers's Dictionary* those key words are :—fāte ; fär; mē; hèr; mīne; mōte; mūte; moon.

(*c*) **the part of speech** which words usually are, *e.g.* happy, adj.

(*d*) **the various meanings** which words convey, *e.g.* impinge, v.(erb) t.(ransitive) (with, on, upon, against), to strike or fall against ; to touch upon.

(*e*) **the derivation** of the words, *i.e.* the language or languages from which the words come, *e.g.* Gardyloo, n.(oun), the old warning cry of housewives in Edinburgh before throwing their slops out of the window into the street. (Pseudo-French (that is, false or spurious French) gare de l'eau, should be gare l'eau, " beware of the water.") (*Chambers's Dictionary.*)

In addition to the above, many dictionaries also give :—a list of Prefixes and Suffixes, etymology of

Names and Places, a list of Abbreviations, Correct Ceremonious Forms of Address, Pronouncing Vocabulary of Scripture Proper Names, the more Common English Christian Names (with their origin and meaning), Words and Phrases from Latin, Greek, and Modern Foreign Languages and Tables of Weights and Measures.

NOTE.—

1. When searching for the meaning of a word, do not be content to take the first meaning you come to. Some words have a great many meanings and most words several. If the word whose meaning you are searching for is in a passage, substitute the meaning you have selected for the original word and see if it satisfies the sense, *i.e. prove* that the meaning you have selected is that intended by the writer.

2. As well as paying attention to the meaning of the word, have a look also at its derivation. Whether you study Latin or Greek or not, you will soon acquire a serviceable knowledge of some Latin and Greek roots that are very helpful in guessing the meanings of other words from these roots.

EXERCISE I

Make a list of the following words in correct alphabetical order :—

1. dissect, disunite, displace, divorce, district, display, diversity, disquiet, distract, ditty.

2. phrase, physique, phœnix, phonograph, phlegm, physiognomy, phosphorus, photograph, physics, phonetic.

3. instruct, instal, instead, inspire, insolubly, instinct, inspect, instance, insipid, insole, instant, insist.

7

Section B

DISTINCTION OF THE MEANINGS OF WORDS

The English vocabulary is very rich ; it has a great many words that closely resemble each other in meaning. Words which closely resemble each other in meaning are called **Synonyms**. For example, *to begin, to commence, to start, to invent, to discover, to innovate* have all something in common in meaning but notice that we *cannot use them interchangeably* ; this proves that synonyms are *not identical* in meaning.

A boy *begins* his career.

A race *starts*.

A concert *commences*.

To invent means to devise something for the first time.

To discover means to uncover, *i.e.* to find something which already existed. We can say, for example, that Columbus discovered America but it would obviously be wrong to say that Columbus invented America, because Columbus did not devise America.

Read good literature and take note of how the authors use their words and you will through time realise the correct usage of words.

EXERCISE I

Distinguish the meanings of the following :—

practice : practise   dying : dyeing

adapt : adopt : adept   meddle : medal

annoy : aggravate   metal : mettle

council : counsel
affect : effect
assent : ascent
lose : loose
new : novel
between : among
compliment : complement
cast : caste
individual : person
passed : past
troupe : troop
chord : cord
famous : notorious
satire : satyr
affluence : influence
human : humane
duel : dual
bier : beer
aisle : isle
brooch : broach

pedal : peddle
desert : dessert
surplice : surplus
glacier : glazier
rapt : wrapt
waste : waist
hole : whole
skull : scull
meter : metre
current : currant
yolk : yoke
wreck : wreak
rain : rein : reign
ingenious : ingenuous
physic : physique
eligible : legible
marshal : martial
cymbal : symbol
vacation : vocation

EXERCISE II

Give one word to express the meaning of each of these phrases :—

1. A person who helps to detect crime.
2.   ,,   ,,   is interested in ancient relics.
3.   ,,   ,,   owes money.
4.   ,,   ,,   to whom money is due.
5. A place where grain is stored.
6.   ,,   ,,   weapons of war are stored.
7.   ,,   ,,   birds are kept alive in captivity.
8.   ,,   ,,   fish   ,,   ,,   ,,
9.   ,,   ,,   shares are bought and sold.
10.   ,,   ,,   bees are kept.

PROVERBIAL AND IDIOMATIC PHRASES

Idiom is the form of expression that is characteristic of the native speakers of a language. Each language has its own peculiar expressions which could not be translated word for word into another language without the result being condemned as, *e.g.* not English or not French. Many proverbs are idiomatic in this sense. We have a proverb, " Set a thief to catch a thief," whereas the French equivalent expression is *à bon chat bon rat* (to a good cat a good rat). Many of these proverbial and idiomatic expressions, and many that owe their origin to the Bible, English, classical or other literature, to history, sports or metaphor, are common in our speech and writing and their meaning should be learned if not already known.

EXERCISE III

(*a*) **Give the meaning of each of the following.**

(*b*) **Use each correctly in a sentence, so as to bring out its meaning.**

(*c*) **Where possible, give the origin of the expression.**

1. To shut the door when the horse is stolen.
2. The exception proves the rule.
3. To carry coals to Newcastle.
4. To go against the grain.
5. To lead some one up the garden path.
6. To sponge on someone.
7. Handsome is as handsome does.
8. Charity begins at home.
9. Least said soonest mended.
10. You may as well be hung for a sheep as a lamb.

11. A bolt from the blue.

12. Misfortunes never come singly.

13. Beggars cannot be choosers.

14. One good turn deserves another.

15. Let sleeping dogs lie.

16. A rolling stone gathers no moss

17. To run the gauntlet.

18. To send to Coventry.

19. Honesty is the best policy.

20. To look a gift horse in the mouth.

21. A dark horse.

22. To let the cat out of the bag.

23. To play with fire.

24. To catch a Tartar.

25. When in Rome, do as the Romans do.

26. A burnt child dreads the fire.

27. Fine feathers make fine birds.

28. Where ignorance is bliss, 'tis folly to be wise.

29. To eat humble pie.

30. Poetic justice.

31. Poetic licence.

32. A free-lance journalist.

33. To blow your own trumpet.

34. Waste not, want not.

35. To strike the colours.

36. Nothing venture, nothing win.

37. Easy come, easy go.

38. Birds of a feather flock together.

39. It takes two to make a quarrel.

40. Where there's smoke, there's fire.

41. When the night's darkest, the dawn is nearest.

42. Spare the rod and spoil the child.
43. Prevention is better than cure.
44. Enough is as good as a feast.
45. A new broom sweeps clean.
46. To turn the tables on some one.
47. Out of sight, out of mind.
48. What is sauce for the goose is sauce for the gander.
49. A drowning man will clutch at a straw.
50. An Indian summer.
51. A Vicar of Bray.
52. To hit below the belt.
53. To gain on the swings what you lose on the round-abouts.
54. To kill the goose that lays the golden eggs.
55. To count one's chickens before they are hatched.
56. To be a dog in a manger.

CHAPTER V

SPELLING

To be able to spell correctly is essential in composition. English spelling is difficult on account of these facts :—

(1) The alphabet, composed of twenty-six letters, has to represent many more sounds than there are letters. For example, c may sound hard (like k) in such words as *cat*, *cad* ; soft as in such words as *ceremony*, *cist*.

(2) Our vowels also vary in the sounds they represent—compare *sow*, *sow* (verb) ; *break*, *speak*.

(3) English spelling often depends on the spelling of the word or words in the language or languages from which the English word is derived, *e.g.* dou*b*t (Latin *dubitare*), where the b is a survival of the original spelling in Latin.

Attention to the following points should help your spelling :—

(1) When in doubt about the spelling of a word, consult a dictionary (always have one handy).

(2) Learn by heart the rules of spelling (see below).

(3) Be careful in your pronunciation—to speak about gram*a*phone or sir*ee*ns will not help you to be an accurate speller.

(4) Try to find out and remember the derivations of words as these are often helpful.

(5) Above all, try to imprint in your mind the *appearance* of the correct spelling of the word. We can often tell from the appearance of a word whether it is correctly spelled or not.

RULES

1. **i precedes e except after c. This rule applies only to syllables with the vowel sound ē.**

    Examples :—chief ; yield ; believe.

    N.B.—In such words as deign, neighbour, leisure, feign, inveigle, the vowel sound is not ē.
    Exceptions :—weird ; seize.
    But after c we have:—receive; deceive; conceit.

2. **Final e when mute (i.e. unpronounced) is dropped before a suffix beginning with a vowel, but *not* before a suffix beginning with a consonant.**

    Examples :

    (1) before a suffix beginning with a vowel : squeeze, squeezing ; rise, rising ; excite, excitable ; move, movable.

    (2) before a suffix beginning with a consonant : judge, judgement ; like, likely ; change, changeling.

    Exceptions :—

    (*a*) the e is retained even before a vowel if there is need to preserve the soft sound of c or g, as in :—
      hinge, hingeing ; singe, singeing ; courage, courageous ; trace, traceable ; change, changeable ; peace, peaceable.

    (*b*) truly, duly, wholly, ninth.

3. **When a suffix, beginning with a vowel, is added to words ending in a single consonant preceded by a single vowel, double the consonant if the words are :—**

(*a*) **monosyllables,** or

(*b*) **if they have their accent on the final syllable.**

(*c*) **If the final syllable is *not* accented, keep the consonant single.**

(*d*) **A final l is *doubled* whether the final syllable is accented or not.**

Examples :—

(*a*) Words ending in single consonant preceded by single vowel + suffix beginning with a vowel.

Monosyllables : sad, sadder ; rot, rotted ; fit, fitted ; pat, patted.

(*b*) Words ending in single consonant preceded by single vowel and accented in last syllable + suffix beginning with a vowel : begin, beginning ; regret, regretted ; instil, instilled ; permit, permitted ; model, modelling ; commit, committal.

(*c*) Words ending in single consonant preceded by single vowel and *not* accented in last syllable : limit, limited ; vomit, vomited ; inhabit, inhabited ; inspirit, inspirited ; morbid, morbidity.

(*d*) Words ending in single l preceded by a single vowel + suffix beginning with a vowel : travel, travelled ; control, controlled ; jewel, jewelled ; marvel, marvellous ; instal, installation.

Exception :—paralleled.

FORMING PLURALS

4. (a) **Words ending in o preceded by a consonant usually form the plural by adding *es* to the singular.**

Examples :—cargo, cargoes ; banjo, banjoes ; hero, heroes ; potato, potatoes ; negro, negroes ; motto, mottoes.

Exceptions :—piano, pianos ; canto, cantos ; commando, commandos ; archipelago, archipelagos.

(b) **Words ending in o preceded by a vowel usually from the plural by adding *s* to the singular.**

Examples :—folio, folios ; bamboo, bamboos ; cameo, cameos ; embryo, embryos.

5. **Words ending in y.**

(a) If preceded by a *consonant* use ies for plural.

Examples :—enemy, enemies ; lily, lilies ; fly, flies ; ally, allies ; penny, pennies ; pony, ponies.

(b) if preceded by a *vowel* add s to the singular.

Examples :—monkey, monkeys ; journey, journeys ; valley, valleys.

(c) if preceded by a consonant change y to ie to form comparative and superlative degrees.

Examples :—dry, drier, driest ; happy, happier, happiest ; ruddy, ruddier, ruddiest.

6. Words with prefixes pro-, suc- and ex- take the -eed form, *e.g.* proceed, succeed, exceed. But pre- takes the -ede form, *e.g.* precede.

Notes : (1) proceed, but procedure.
(2) precede, accede, concede, recede, secede, intercede, **but** super*sede*.

The following words are frequently misspelt. Weak spellers should commit them to memory.

A

Abbreviate	aghast	appalling
accelerate	allege	apparition
accidentally	allegiance	apparel
accommodate	all right	appreciate
accompaniment	allotted	arctic
accumulate	allotment	argument
accurate	almond	arithmetic
accustomed	already	artillery
achieve	ambassador	artisan
acknowledge	amenity	ascendancy
acquaintance	amiable	ascertain
acquiesce	analyst	ascetic
acquire	anniversary	assassinate
addition	annotate	asthma
address	announce	assurance
adjourn	annoy	atmosphere
aeroplane	anonymous	attach
aggravate	apologise	autumn
agreeable	apostle	**awkward**
aggrieved	appal	

B

Baggage
bailie
balloon
banquet
barricade
bayonet
beginning
behaviour

believe
beneficial
benefited
bereave
besiege
billiards
blissful
bouquet

Britain
Britannia
Briton
Brittany
buccaneer
buoyant
burglar
business

C

Cæsar
calendar
calibre
campaign
cannibal
caricature
carriage
casualty
catarrh
caterpillar
cauliflower
ceiling
celibacy
cemetery
census
centenary

century
changeable
character
chasm
chauffeur
chestnut
chief
chimney
chronicle
chrysanthemum
coalesce
college
colonel
colonnade
commemorate
committee

comparative
complementary
complimentary
concurrence
confectionery
conscious
coolly
corollary
correspondingly
corroborate
courageous
crescent
cruelly
cyclic

D

Dearth
decease
deceive
deferred
definite
deign
delineate
demeanour

dependent
depth
descendant
develop
diarrhœa
diary
dilemma
diocese

diphtheria
disappear
disappoint
disastrous
discernible
discipline
discreet
diseased

disguise
dispel
dissatisfied
dissipate
dissuade

distil
doggerel
donkey
doughty
draught

drought
drunkenness
dynasty

E

Earnest
eccentricity
ecstasy
effervescence
effigy
eighth
embarrass
emissary

encyclopædia
ennoble
enrolment
enthusiasm
etiquette
exaggerate
excel
excite

exhilarate
existence
expense
expressible
extravagance
exuberant

F

Fallacious
familiar
fascinate
February

feign
fiery
foully
friend

fuchsia
fulfil
furlough

G

Galloping
gardener
garrison
gauge
genealogy
giraffe
glacier

gnarled
gnaw
goal
goddess
good-bye
government
grammar

grandeur
grievance
guardian
guer(r)illa
guillotine
gymnasium

H

Handkerchief
harangue
harass
heinous
hindrance

honorary
honourable
Huguenot
humorous
humour

humorist
hundredth
hypocrisy

I

Icicle	indestructible	inoculate
illegible	indictment	intelligent
illiterate	indispensable	intricacy
immediately	inferred	intrigue
immovable	inflammable	inveigh
incorrigible	initiative	irreparable
incredible	innocent	irresistible
independent	innocuous	isosceles

J

Jeopardy	jostle	juvenile

K

Keenness	knowledge	knuckle
knoll		

L

Labyrinth	libellous	livelihood
lacquer	lieutenant	longitude
laundry	likable	loose
legitimate	literally	lose
leisure	literature	

M

Machinations	marriageable	mischievous
machinery	mathematics	misspell
mackerel	mattress	moustache
manageable	Mediterranean	murmur
manœuvre	miscellaneous	

N

Naphtha	neigh	niece
necessarily	neighbour	noticeable
negligible	negotiate	nuisance

O

Occasionally	offered	opponent
occurred	omission	oscillate
occurrence	omitted	overreach

P

Panegyric	physician	prejudice
paraffin	pianos	principal
parallel	picnic	principle
paralysis	picnicking	procedure
parasite	piece	privilege
Parliament	pigeon	professor
parricide	pleurisy	pronunciation
pastime	porridge	propeller
pavilion	Portuguese	prophecy
peaceable	possession	prophesy
perceive	precipice	pulley
perseverance	presence	pursue
persuade	preferred	putrefy

Q

Qualms	quarrelling	quiet
quarrel	queue	quite

R

Raisin	reminiscence	retrieve
Receive	renegade	rheumatism
receptacle	repetition	rhinoceros
reconnaissance	requital	rhyme
reference	representative	rhythm
referred	reprieve	righteous
rehearsal	reservoir	roguery
reliable	resistance	rumour
relieve	responsible	
religious	restaurant	

S

Salable
salmon
saltpetre
sacrilegious
saucer
sceptic
scintillate
scissors
scythe
secrecy
separate

shriek
siege
sieve
skein
skilful
sleight
soliloquy
soluble
sorcery
squalor
steadfast

stony
strategy
stupefy
subtle
suddenness
superannuation
supersede
subterranean
symmetry
symptom
synonymous

T

Tariff
temporarily
testament
thousandth

tobacco
toboggan
traceable
tragedy

tranquillity
transferred
traveller

U

Umbrella
unanimous
unconscious
unconscionable

uncontrollable
underrate
undoubtedly
unique

until
unwieldy

V

Vaccinate
vacillate
variegated
vegetable

veil
vengeance
vicious
vicissitude

villain
vinegar

W

Waif
Wednesday
weird

wharf
wholesome
withhold

woollen
worshipped
wreck

Y

Yacht

yield

yodel

EXERCISES

1. *a*. Supply the missing vowels :—

   acad—my, choc—late, acr—bat, sem—lina, rel—tive, respons—ble, oct—gon, hypocr—sy, persever—nce, independ—nt, med—cine, ben—factor, mir—cle, pen—trate, indispens—ble.

   b. Supply the missing consonants :—
   solem—, coun—ellor, pre—udice, panto—ime, accep—, a—knowledge, autum—, meton—my, ecsta—y.

   c. Write the present participles of the following verbs :—
   sit, cycle, hope, singe, dye, admit, notice, pity, gauge, change, hinge.

   d. Form nouns with the -tion or -sion termination from these verbs :—
   persuade, pretend, recognize, negotiate, resume, divert, substitute, publish, depreciate, instal, represent.

2. Some of the following words are represented by phonetic spelling from a dictionary ; re-write in ordinary spelling :—

   I was surprised that the kas'l kood not ak-kom' mod-āt the kong'gre-gā-shun that assembled there last Wenz'dā to lis'n to the in-dit'-ment. I still felt the āk kauz'd by my kof and by my stū-pen'dus efforts in kawk'ing my skif.

8

CHAPTER VI

PUNCTUATION

The use of stops of various kinds helps us to read and understand what is written, provided the stops are correctly inserted. When words are spoken, various pauses are observed by the speaker ; some punctuation marks correspond to these natural pauses.

It should be realised that all writers do not use the same principles of punctuation, especially in the use of the comma. However, there is fairly general agreement on the use of the punctuation marks detailed below.

Note that sometimes punctuation marks are essential for an understanding of the writer's meaning. For instance,

John said the teacher was at fault.

Punctuation can give this sentence different meanings. It might mean,

" John," said the teacher, " was at fault," or John said, " The teacher was at fault."

The **Period** or full stop (.) is used :—

(1) to mark the end of a complete sentence, except when it is in the form of an exclamation or a question.

Even to so humble a post he was found **unequal.**

(2) to indicate abbreviations. (If the abbreviation contains the initial and last letters of the word, the period is optional.)

B.C., J. Smith, Esq., M.A., Bart. or Bart

The **Comma** (,) indicates the shortest punctuation pause. It is used :—

(1) between two or more words that are the same part of speech ; or between two or more clauses of the same kind :—

   (a) He was unreliable, unsteady, incapable and assuredly not to be trusted.

   (b) The Swale, the Ure, the Nidd, the Wharfe flow into the Yorkshire Ouse.

   (c) When he was poor, when he was ill, when he was an outcast, he never uttered a word of complaint.

(2) before and after a parenthetical word, phrase or clause :—

   (a) Let us, however, consider the matter closed.

   (b) I am, subject to your approval, about to apply for that post.

   (c) The disappointment, as you can well understand, has been very great.

(3) between nouns or pronouns in apposition, and after the Nominative of address :—

   (a) Elizabeth, daughter of James the First, married the Elector of the Palatinate.

   (b) Rejoice, O Delos, with thine olives green.

(4) after an adverbial clause when it precedes the clause it modifies ; or after an adverbial phrase at the beginning of a sentence :—

(a) While supper was being prepared, he enlarged upon the happiness of the neighbouring shire.

(b) Upon our arrival at the inn, my companion fetched the jolly landlord.

(5) between clauses in a compound sentence where each clause is fully expressed : if the subject of the second clause is the same as that of the first no comma is necessary :—

(a) My squire laughed heartily at the conceit, and he made the landlord sit down with us.

(b) I attended the lecture and was delighted with the speaker's lucid explanations.

(6) after an absolute construction :—

(a) The ford having been captured, the army made good progress.

(b) The clergyman having concluded his sermon, the organist played the closing hymn.

(7) after a verb indicating that words have been spoken in direct speech :—

(a) He enquired, " Are you going to the match ? "

(b) " Don't be annoyed," he remarked, " for I have no intention of carrying through my plan."

The Colon (:). In modern punctuation the colon has two specialised uses :—

(1) to divide clauses where the second or following sentences illustrates or illustrate the meaning of the first. No capital letter should

be used after a colon unless the following word already demands a capital, *e.g.* a proper noun :—

(*a*) Mars is a great deal smaller than the Earth : its diameter is not much more than half of the Earth's, and its weight only about one-tenth of the Earth's.

(*b*) No man is perfect : to err is human.

(2) to introduce a quotation, or an enumeration, when it is usually followed by a dash :—

(*a*) After a pause, he made the following statement : "I am quite convinced of his guilt."

(*b*) You might please send me :—a writing pad and fountain pen, a box of paints and drawing pad, some brushes and a pen-knife.

The Semicolon (;) marks a pause more pronounced than that indicated by the comma. It may be used :—

(1) between co-ordinate clauses with different subjects when these clauses are not joined by conjunctions :—
It was high time to make the Wassail now ; therefore I had up the materials and made a glorious jorum.

(2) between clauses connected by Alternative or Illative conjunctions (*e.g.* else, therefore, then) :—

(*a*) "Accept the umpire's decision ; *otherwise* you'll be ordered off the field."

(*b*) That the penalty was unjust he could not maintain ; *for* he had previously awarded more severe penalties himself.

Note carefully that the parts of the above sentences separated by semi-colons are themselves complete sentences containing principal clauses.

The **Exclamation Mark** (!) is used after :—

(1) interjections and exclamations such as :—
Oh! Great Scott! Away with these!

(2) Apostrophe :—
You little devil! O Luxury!

(3) expressions of emotion :—
How horrible! What a disappointment!

The **Hyphen** (-), which is not so long as the **Dash** (—), is used to compound two or more words into one thought-unit :—ne'er-do-weel ; double-barrelled ; out-of-the-way ; oft-repeated.

N.B.—Many words are frequently hyphened that should be written entire, *e.g.* bluejackets ; redcoats ; archbishop.

The **Dash** (—) is used :—

(1) to mark an abrupt break in a sentence :—
To be, or not to be—that is the question.

(2) to indicate that a name has been omitted or intentionally suppressed :—
Mr. — voted against the amendment.

(3) after a multiple subject :—
Reputation, wealth, health and happiness —all were sacrificed by his stupid act.

(4) to indicate a parenthesis—one dash before and one after the inserted part—and used instead of **Brackets** ( ) :—

> Let but the commons hear this testament—
> Which pardon me, I do not mean to read—

The **Question or Interrogation Mark** (?) must be used after direct questions, and is included within the quotation marks.

" Who were present ? "

" Shall no man else be touch'd but only Caesar ? "

N.B.—Be careful not to use a question mark after an indirect question, *e.g.* :—

> He asked me why I did not comply with his wishes.

How often have we been misinformed ?— may also be an exclamation.

Diaeresis (··) (" taking asunder ") consists of two dots placed over a second vowel, when two vowels come together, to indicate that the vowels are to be pronounced separately, and not as a single vowel or diphthong :—

> aërial, naïve.

The **Apostrophe** (') in punctuation is used to show that a letter or letters has or have been omitted :—

> I'm for I am ; I'll for I shall or will ; e'er for ever ; touch'd for touched.

The **Asterisk** (Star) (*) is used as a reference to a note on a word or phrase usually found at the foot of the page. A group of asterisks is sometimes used to denote that letters or words have been purposely omitted.

Italics are types used by printers *which slope to the right* used for the purpose of emphasis or distinction. They are frequently used for foreign words or titles of books, as :—*coup d'état* ; *Ivanhoe.*

Note.—Roman type is perpendicular, thus :—ROMAN.

A **Caret** (∧) is a mark to show where something has been omitted, *e.g.* I ∧ seen that, etc.
have

The **Ampersand** (&) is the sign for *and* and is used frequently in names of firms *when printed,* as :—

Robert Gibson & Sons (Glasgow), Ltd.

Do not use this contracted form of *and* in composition unless when quoting names of firms or in a business letter.

(*Note.*—The word is a corruption of :—*and per se and*—*i.e.* & standing by itself means *and.*)

Inverted Commas or Quotation Marks, either double (" ") or single (' ') are used :—

(1) to mark the beginning and end of a quotation, *i.e.* the actual words used by a speaker or writer :—

(*a*) " I have no use for artificial flowers," he said.

(*b*) " I have no use," he said, " for artificial flowers."

(2) to denote the title of a book or play, a ship or a house, when the title is written, *e.g.* Shakespeare's " Hamlet." (If Shakespeare's Hamlet were written, readers would understand by it the character Hamlet and not the play " Hamlet.") The new battleship

"King George V."   She lives at "The Laurels."

When these names appear in print, italics are usually employed, thus :—*Hamlet*, *The Laurels*.

(3) to mark a quotation within a quotation. If double quotation marks have been used for the complete words spoken, then use single marks for the quotation within, or *vice versa* (the terms being exchanged). Thus :—

"In the wood," he said, " I discovered a notice which read, ' Trespassers will be prosecuted.'"   Or, 'In the wood,' he said, ' I discovered a notice which read, " Trespassers will be prosecuted." '

CAPITAL letters are used at the beginning of: —

(1) First words in sentences, as :—
    The dog killed the rabbit.

(2) Proper names and proper adjectives, as :—
    London ; French ; Spenserian.

(3) The names of days, months and festivals, as:—
    Tuesday ; August ; Hallowe'en.

(4) Quotations (unless only part quotations) as:—
    Pope wrote, " A little learning is a dang'rous thing."

(5) Each line of poetry, as :—
    Beside yon straggling fence that skirts the way,
    With blossom'd furze unprofitably gay.

(6) The name of the Deity, and nouns and pronouns representing it, as :—

O God! Thou hast, etc.

(7) Capital letters are also used for :—

(*a*) Titles of honour or office, as :—
Lord Palmerston ; George the Fifth ; The Lord Mayor.

(*b*) Initials in names, as :—
R. L. Stevenson.

(*c*) Titles of books, plays, etc., but when the title is made up of several words, then for the most important words only, as :—
The Master of Ballantrae ; The Merchant of Venice.

EXERCISES IN PUNCTUATION

1. **Punctuate the following :—**

a. As it was mexico provided no courts no police no regular postal facilities and no schools.

b. He believed that speculators bankers and money lenders there were growing rich at the expense of western farmers.

c. Douglas a squat dwarfish man with a huge head and lincoln an awkward lanky giant whose homely countenance was surmounted by a shock of rough black hair presented an extraordinary contrast.

d. the prospect of being beset in so slightly built a craft was to say the least unpleasant it looked very much as if fresh packs were driving down upon us from the very direction in which we were trying to push out yet it had become a matter of doubt which course it would be best to steer to remain stationary was out of the question the pace at which the fields drift is sometimes very rapid and the first nip would settle the poor little schooners business for ever.

e. as soon as the anchor was let go in hammerfest harbour we went ashore and having first ascertained that the existence of a port does not necessarily imply letters we turned away a little disappointed to examine the metropolis of finmark a nearer inspection did not improve the impression its first appearance had made upon us and the odour of rancid cod liver oil which seemed indiscriminately to proceed from every building in the town including the church has irretrievably confirmed us in our prejudice.

lord dufferins letters from high latitudes.

f. the failure of sir stafford cripps mission to india comes as a great disappointment but not following recent indications of the indian congress attitude as a surprise no blame attaches to sir stafford whose patience dexterity and sincerity have not been questioned throughout nor does any lie at the door of the british war cabinet for how could it in face of the external enemy have conceded more than it did regarding defence.

sunday times leader.

g. to a long life said i.
he hesitated to a long life said he with a sudden bark of laughter and with eyes fixed on one another we tilted the little glasses his eyes looked straight into mine and as i drained the stuff off felt a curiously intense situation the first touch of it set my brain in a furious tumult i seemed to feel an actual physical stirring in my skull and a seething humming filled my ears.

wellss story of the late mr elvesham.

h. stifling another yawn i did my best to imitate his demeanour the bookies were bawling two to one bar one cockbird stimulated by publicity now began to give himself the airs of a real restive racehorse chucking his head about flattening his ears and capering sideways in a manner which caused the onlookers to skip hastily out of range of his heels i say thats a classy looking quad exclaimed a youth who appeared to have purchased the paddock he consulted his card and i overheard his companion as they turned away saying something about his jockey looking a bit green weed better back nigels they say hell win for a cert.

sasoons the ringwell heavy weight race.

i. and there for a week the stricken partner lay unconscious of aught but the visions wrought by disease and fear on the eighth day at sunrise he rallied and opening his eyes looked upon york and pressed his hand then he spoke.

and its you i thought it was only whisky.

york replied by taking both his hands boyishly working them backward and forward as his elbow rested on the bed with a pleasant smile.

and youve been abroad how did you like paris so so how did you like sacramento

bully

and that was all they would think to say presently scott opened his eyes again.

im mighty weak.

youll get better soon.

not much.

francis bret hartes the iliad of sandy bar.

j. i have seen you several times lately said the broken gentleman who looked shabbier than before in the broad daylight but I didnt like to speak i live not far from here.

why so do i and i added without much thinking
what i said do you live alone.

alone oh no with my wife.

gissings christopherson.

2. **Which of the following (*a*) are wrongly printed
(*b*) should be hyphened (*c*) should not be hyphened ?**

all together	hand-barrow	hill-top
news paper	in to	alright
hankypanky	hang-man	upside down
onto	handy-man	up on
hand-and-glove	high-tea	speaking tube
singing book	rocking horse	roadroller
robin redbreast	roadstead	ran-sack
pic-nic	over-and-above	overseas
to-morrow	today	yester-day

3. **Give the usual abbreviations for :—**

indicative, adverb, adjective, able-bodied seaman,
in the year of our Lord, miles per hour, Authorised
Version, British Broadcasting Corporation, Bachelor
of Science, Pounds, shillings, pence.

4. **What do the following abbreviations stand for ?**

J.P., B.C., c.o.d., C.I.D., D.V., O.T.C., D.S.O., F.M.,
f.o.b., H.M.I.S., I.O.M., LL.D., M.D., Secy., N.N.E.,
Y.M.C.A., W.E.A., U.S.S.R., V.C., q.v., G.P.O.,
M.R.C.S., M.R.C.V.S., A.N.Z.A.C., *cf.*

CHAPTER VII

SYNTHESIS

In the early stages of writing English, you are warned that short sentences help you to express your ideas clearly and simply. The advice, so far as it goes, is admirable, but very soon you feel that a series of short sentences sounds jerky and dull and that ideas are not so isolated in your mind as they appear in short sentences. The attempt to write longer sentences, however, sometimes ends in confusion or in a wearisome repetition of *and, then, also, again, and so*. To avoid this, all that is required of you is to learn the simple rules of **Synthesis**, that is, *the combination of a number of short sentences into a larger sentence*. This, you will observe, is the opposite of Analysis.

The new sentence may take the form of the following kinds of sentence :—

I.—Longer Simple

Example :

{ Two large shaggy dogs stood at the door.
{ They were ready to rush upon the traveller.

Two large shaggy dogs stood at the door ready to rush upon the traveller.

II.—Compound

Example :

> The survivors were lean and sunburnt by long exposure to a tropical sun.
> They were as strong and bold as ever.

The survivors were lean and sunburnt by long exposure to a tropical sun but they were as strong and bold as ever.

III.—Complex

Example :

> The player at last saw the ball ahead and overhead.
> He went forward at full speed.

When the player at last saw the ball ahead and overhead, he went forward at full speed.

IV.—Compound-Complex

Example :

> At last he saw the brushwood pile.
> He hurried along the ridge.
> Close behind him were the swift moving tribesmen.
> He wished to escape from them.

At last he saw the brushwood pile and he hurried along the ridge, since close behind him were the swift moving tribesmen from whom he wished to escape.

Methods and Examples of Synthesis

Note.—First select a sentence or sentences to be the Principal Clause or Clauses in the new sentence.

I.—Longer Simple Sentence

1. Use of words in Apposition, Phrases qualifying the Subject or Object, Phrases modifying the Predicate.

Examples :

(*a*) {
The captain mostly would not speak when spoken to.
He was a very silent man by custom.

A very silent man by custom, the captain mostly would not speak when spoken to.

(*b*) {
Dick looked through the range-finder at the iceberg.
It was now moving towards us very slowly.

Dick looked through the range-finder at the iceberg *now moving towards us very slowly*.

(*c*) {
He lay down on the deck.
He was beneath a mound of damp, dirty coats.

He lay down on the deck *beneath a mound of damp, dirty coats*.

2. Use of a Present Infinitive, Gerund (with Preposition), Participle.

(*a*) {
The gentleman's interest was now aroused.
He asked the reason for this strange behaviour.

The gentleman's interest was now aroused *to ask* the reason for this strange behaviour.

(b) { He was overwhelmed by the number of his foes.
{ He continued to struggle for some time.

Overwhelmed by the number of his foes, he continued to struggle for some time.

(c) { He always agreed with the chief speaker.
{ He gained a reputation for wisdom.

By always agreeing with the chief speaker, he gained a reputation for wisdom.

II.—Compound Sentence

Use of Co-ordinating Conjunctions (and, but, yet, for, etc.).

(a) { We paid no further attention to the ship.
{ Fortunately, the sea remained calm during the night.

We paid no further attention to the ship *but* fortunately, the sea remained calm during the night.

(b) { The sun shone on the children.
{ They enjoyed the unaccustomed brightness.

The sun shone on the children *and* they enjoyed the unaccustomed brightness.

III.—Complex Sentence

1. Use of Relative Pronouns introducing Adjective Clauses (who, which, that, as, but, etc.).

(a) { There is an old pensioner in the village.
{ He has seen much service in the wars.

There is an old pensioner in the village *who* has seen much service in the wars.

9

(*b*) { We walked up a long avenue of aged elms.
       { Many rooks and crows were nesting.

We walked up a long avenue of aged elms in *which* many rooks and crows were nesting.

2. Use of Subordinate Conjunctions introducing Adverbial Clauses (when, where, if, as, although, since, etc.).

(*a*) { The cock was exhausted by his efforts.
       { He lay down on the ground, croaking his indignation.

When the cock was exhausted by his efforts, he lay down on the ground, croaking his indignation.

(*b*) { The regiment had suffered severely in the last battle.
       { The men were eager to meet the enemy.

Although the regiment had suffered severely in the last battle, the men were eager to meet the enemy.

Note.—Where there is only one Subordinate Clause, the Principal Clause will normally come last, if more than one, the Principal Clause will come between them.

3. By a combination of methods under 1, 2.

{ He was asked to sing at a concert.
{ He consented to sing a popular song.
{ He did not know the words perfectly.

When he was to sing at a concert, he consented to sing a song the words *of which* he did not know perfectly.

IV.—Compound-Complex Sentence

By a combination of two or more of the methods under I, II, III.

> We had a sound sleep.
> We attacked the engine again.
> It gave us some trouble for a time.
> At last we discovered the flaw.

After a sound sleep, we attacked the engine again *and although* it gave us some trouble for a time, at last we discovered the flaw.

EXERCISE I

a. **Combine the sentences in the following groups by using either present participles, or past participles. The first is done for you :—**

1. The children crowded round him. They eyed him from head to foot with great curiosity.

   The children crowded round him, *eyeing* him from head to foot with great curiosity, *or* The children, *crowding* round him, eyed him from head to foot with great curiosity.

2. Tito was obliged to make his way through chance openings in the crowd. He found himself at one moment close to the trotting procession.

3. Tito went straight to Bardo's chair. He paid his homage to Romola as he advanced.

4. The tea was cold by the time it arrived at the men's quarters. The feeding ground was in many cases a great distance from the fire.

5. Here they used to sit in the shade through a long lazy summer's day. They would talk listlessly over village gossip. They would tell endless sleepy stories about nothing.

b. Combine the sentences in the following groups by means of participles and adjective clauses. The first is done for you :—

1. The Mexicans made no further resistance. They were intimidated by the presence of their detested foe. This foe had forced his way into their city.

   The Mexicans, *intimidated* by the presence of their detested foe, *who had forced his way into their city*, made no further resistance.

2. A lighted lantern threw out a yellow glimmer. The glimmer barely illuminated the room. The lantern was hung over the stove.

3. A few priests were to be seen lingering on the terraces. These terraces wound round the sides of the pyramids. The priests were clad in their usual wild vestments.

4. News of this quarrel was soon communicated to Cortes. He sent at once to the fiery chiefs. He implored them to lay aside their differences. These differences would soon bring the expedition to ruin.

5. The aqueduct was raised on a strong though narrow dike. The aqueduct was constructed partly of brickwork and partly of stone. The dike transported the aqueduct across an arm of the lake.

EXERCISE II

Combine each of the following groups of sentences into a single sentence of the kind named. The verb of the new Principal Clause is in italics :—

Note.—Groups I-X contain hints for the necessary changes.

1. **Compound.**—We *will talk* afterwards about the shipwreck. We *must* now *defend* ourselves against the savages.

2. **Complex.**—The night *was* fast *closing* in. She returned homeward, laden with flowers (Adv. Cl. of Time).

3. **Simple.**—The Templar *was* a dangerous foe. He had been for many years a warrior in distant lands (Phrase).

4. **Simple.**—The colonel *summoned* Pedro and me into his presence. He wished to make more enquiries about us (Infin.).

5. **Simple.**—The branch *burned* brightly in my hand. It was of a resinous nature (Phrase).

6. **Complex.**—The paper had been sealed in several places (Adj. Cl.). The doctor carefully *unfolded* the paper.

7. **Complex.**—Isaac heard the terrible news (Gerund). He *raised* a piercing yell. It made the very vault resound (Adj. Cl.).

8. **Compound-Complex.**—The forges *were lit* again. Once more the work of repair *went on*. The men were worn out by their previous labours (Adv. Cl. of Concession).

9. **Compound-Complex.**—The town *was* brimful of excitement. He had quite forgotten his duties (Adv. Cl. of Consequence). A sight of the church clock *reminded* him of his task. It was very important for the safety of his friends (Adj. Cl.).

10. **Compound.**—My friend and I *repeated* our visit to the club. We *were* not *made* welcome on this occasion.

11. **Simple.**—The squire *dropped* down beside him on his knees. He was crying like a child.

12. **Simple.**—I *fixed* my umbrella in a step at the stern. It was like a mast standing over my head. It was intended to keep the sun off me.

13. **Complex.**—I *have heard* of a gentleman. He was under close confinement in the Bastille for seven years. During this time he tried many ways of distracting himself.

14. **Complex.**—The breeze *was* already at an end. It was a wind from the south. The jolly boat shoved off from the schooner. Several men remained on board the ship.

15. **Simple.**—I was on my way to the station. He *passed* me with great strides. His head was high among the low flying bats.

16. **Compound-Complex.**—I *peeped* out a second later. The coast was entirely clear. I *was* able to get away without any trouble.

17. **Complex.**—The sound of sea-booted footsteps died away forward. There was no longer any sound of life. Suddenly I *seemed* to be alone on the ship. It was rocking upon the midnight ocean.

18. **Complex.**—There *is* a cold tang in the air in the early morning. It will later give place to heat. The sun gathers strength later.

19. **Compound-Complex.**—One of the strangers *stepped* forward. He *made* a suggestion. Efforts should be made to barricade the house. It was their only means of protection. The Indians were possibly intending to attack.

20. **Compound-Complex.**—The negro *has* many hardships in life. He *gets* more satisfaction out of life than the white man. He makes fewer demands on life. He has a happy and contented nature.

EXERCISE III

Construct sentences in the following models :—
1. Adj. Cl.—Prin. Cl.
2. Prin. Cl.—Adv. Cl. of Place.

3. Noun Cl.—Prin. Cl.
4. Prin. Cl.—Adj. Cl.
5. Adv. Cl. of Reason—Prin. Cl.
6. Prin. Cl.—Adv. Cl. of Condition.
7. Prin. Cl.—Noun Cl.—Adv. Cl. of Time.
8. Adv. Cl. of Concession—Prin. Cl.—Adj. Cl.
9. Adj. Cl.—Noun Cl.—Prin. Cl.
10. Prin. Cl.—Adj. Cl.—Prin. Cl.

CHAPTER VIII

DIRECT AND INDIRECT SPEECH

(Sometimes termed Direct and Indirect Narration.)

DIRECT SPEECH

IN a composition a writer may require to introduce the actual words of a speaker. This task often presents difficulties to the young and inexperienced writer and he frequently goes wrong in putting in the correct punctuation marks.

The actual words spoken by a person are written without any alteration ; but in order to indicate that these words are the words actually spoken (or in some instances written, *e.g.* when quoting from a poet or writer),

1. **Quotation marks** are inserted at the beginning and end of the words. These marks consist of one pair of inverted commas at the beginning and one pair of apostrophes at the end. (Sometimes only one single inverted comma and one single apostrophe are used), *e.g.*

" Give me leave to depart," he said.

or

' Give me leave to depart,' he said.

2. **A comma** is put after the verb which indicates that the words are spoken : or, if the saying or

reporting comes after the spoken words, or after some of the spoken words, the comma comes after the words first quoted. *e.g.* He said, " I am tired." or, " I am tired," he said.

Notes.—

1. It would be monotonous always to use the one method of putting the reporting verb at the beginning. Especially when the quotation is long, it is more artistic to begin the quotation and then to insert the reporting verb and continue the quotation, putting in a comma after it and after the part quoted. *e.g.*

   " On the night of 3rd November," he began, " at about 5 p.m., I was standing at the corner of Barr St. and Main St. when I noticed a policeman approaching and trying all the doors of the shops as he came along."

2. If the first section of the spoken or quoted words forms a sentence, a period must be put in after the reporting verb and not a comma as above, where the reporting verb is inserted after a phrase. The continued quotation must begin with a capital letter. *e.g.*

   " I know my own mind," the witness replied. " The cross-examiner cannot induce me to change my evidence."

3. Remember that the punctuation required for the original words must be retained, including interrogation and exclamation marks. *e.g.*

   " Why do you persist in worrying me ? " he asked in a surly manner.
   " Get out ! If I see you again, I'll have you arrested."

INDIRECT OR REPORTED SPEECH

A speech is seldom recorded in the actual words of the speaker or in full in our newspapers. If a speech is reported in direct speech it is usually one made by a most important person (*e.g.* His Majesty the King) and the speech is not usually a long one.

Most speeches are *reported* and, in writing what the newspaper has to print, the reporter has two tasks to perform, namely :—

1. To change the direct into indirect or reported speech.

2. To summarise the contents (*i.e.* to make a précis) of the speech.

In converting a speech from the direct to the indirect form, certain changes are necessary, namely :—

1. Insert the conjunction **that** before the reported words.

2. Pay attention to the **tense** of the reporting verb (*e.g.* said, remarks, etc.). In writing, we should use one tense throughout our composition unless there are special reasons for departing from the tense used. (See Ch. II, p. 56, where this matter is fully dealt with.) It is a common fault with inexperienced writers to confuse past and present tenses. The keeping to one tense throughout a composition is called the observation of the sequence of tenses. The following rules will enable you to observe the necessary sequence in reporting direct speech :—

   (*a*) If the reporting verb (said, remarked) is in the past tense, the verbs that follow must also be in the past tense.

(*b*) If the reporting verb (says, will say) is in the present or future tense, the verbs that follow may be in any tense.

Direct.	He said, " I am tired."
Indirect.	He said that he was tired.

Direct.	He says, " I am tired."
Indirect.	He says that he is tired.

Direct.	He says, " I shall be tired."
Indirect.	He says that he will be tired.

Direct.	He will say, " I am tired."
Indirect.	He will say that he is tired.

Note.—If the words spoken state a universal truth (*i.e.* something we believe is true now, was true in the past and will be true in the future) then the present tense is used even after a reporting verb in the past tense.

Example :

Direct.	He said, " The world is a sphere."
Indirect.	He said that the world is a sphere.

When we observe the rules governing sequence of tense, we find the following changes must be made, when converting direct to indirect speech, when the reporting verb is in the past tense.

is becomes *was*		*shall* becomes *should*	
are becomes *were*		*will* ,, *would*	
has, have become *had*		*may* ,, *might*	
		can ,, *could*	

3. Pronouns, adjectives that refer to *position* (*e.g.* demonstrative, this, that), and adverbs of *time* and *place* must be altered as follows :—

Pronouns.

I, *me*, become *he* (*she*), *him* (*her*).
We, *us*, become *they*, *them*.
You becomes *him*, *her*, *they*, *them*.

Adjectives.

this becomes *that*.
these becomes *those*.

Adverbs.

now	becomes	*then*.
hither	,,	*thither*.
hence	,,	*thence*.
to-day	,,	*that day*.
to-morrow	,,	*the next day*.
yesterday	,,	*the previous day*, *the day before*.
ago	,,	*before*.
so	,,	*thus*.

(You will notice that words denoting *nearness* in time or place in direct speech become words denoting *distance* in indirect speech.)

4. When reporting questions, use a verb that indicates that a question has been asked, *e.g.* :—

Direct. " May I have a drink ? "
Indirect. He asked if he might have a drink.

In dealing with such sentences as follow, indicate by means of the verb you use the emotion or feeling expressed, *e.g.* approval, distrust, disapproval, disappointment ; commands and exclamations also must be indicated, so that the indirect form gives a clue to the original meaning.

Direct. " I am shocked by your conduct ! " his uncle said.

Indirect. His uncle exclaimed that he was shocked by his (nephew's) conduct.

Direct. " You are very punctual ! " James said to George, as he looked at his watch, having waited over an hour for him.

Indirect. James, having waited over an hour for George, after looking his watch, expressed his annoyance at George's lack of punctuality.

Direct. " Goal ! " the excited spectators howled, as the clever centre-forward scored.

Indirect. The excited spectators shouted their appreciation of the clever play of the centre-forward when he scored.

Direct. " Show me your exercise at once," shouted the angry master.

Indirect. The angry master ordered the pupil to show him his exercise at once.

N.B.—Vary your reporting verb to avoid monotony ; instead of always using said, use replied, answered, stated, affirmed, explained, told, etc. When turning direct into indirect speech, be careful to avoid any confusion in your use of pronouns, *e.g.*

Direct. He announced, " He is coming now."

Indirect. He (the speaker) announced that he (the person expected) was coming then.

If the names of the speaker and the person expected are known, insert them.

EXERCISE I

Convert the following passages into indirect speech :—

1. "I am going off to-morrow," he replied with annoyance.

2. "Are you feeling all right, now ? " he inquired.

3. "Shut that door at once, James ; there is a frightful draught," said his mother.

4. "What a mess you're in ! " she exclaimed.

5. "I shall take this article if you can send it to me by to-morrow," the lady says as she leaves the sorely-tried shop assistant.

6. "Take the surveyor's chain and measure this field," he ordered his assistant. "Don't make so many mistakes this time, remember," he added rather spitefully.

7. "You'll not deny that two and two make four ? " he shouted in a frenzy to the boy. "Your arithmetic is shocking ; and this mistake is inexcusable," he added.

8. Markheim could not refrain from smiling with a kind of bitter triumph. "No," said he, "I will take nothing at your hands ; if I were dying of thirst, and it was your hand that put the pitcher to my lips, I should find the courage to refuse. It may be credulous, but I will do nothing to commit myself to evil."

9. "Let us get away from here," said Elvira with a shiver. "All these people looking—it is so rude and so brutal." And then giving way once more to passion—"Brutes ! " she cried aloud to the candle-lit spectators—"brutes ! brutes ! brutes ! "

10. "I detest this practice," he said ; and after a pause he asked, "Have you never heard the old adage, ' A stitch in time saves nine '—and have you never thought of acting on it ? "

11. MRS. CANDOUR : What do you think of Miss
    Simper ?

    SIR BENJAMIN BACKBITE : Why, she has very
    pretty teeth.

    LADY TEAZLE : Yes, and on that account, when
    she is neither speaking nor laughing (which
    very seldom happens), she never absolutely
    shuts her mouth, but leaves it always on a jar,
    as it were—thus—(*shows her teeth*).

    MRS. CANDOUR : How can you be so ill natured ?

    LADY TEAZLE : Nay, I allow even that's better
    than the pains Mrs. Prim takes to conceal her
    losses in front. She draws her mouth till it
    positively resembles the aperture of a poor's-
    box, and all her words appear to slide out
    edgewise as it were thus : How do you do,
    madam ? Yes, madam (*mimics*).

    LADY SNEERWELL : Very well, Lady Teazle , I
    see you can be a little severe.

    LADY TEAZLE : In defence of a friend, it is but
    justice. But here comes Sir Peter to spoil
    our pleasantry.

EXERCISE II

Convert the following indirect statements into direct
speech :—

1. Rip remarked that he was a poor quiet man, a
   native of the place, and a loyal subject of the king
   whom he called upon God to bless.

2. He admitted that his results in the previous examination had been lamentable and promised that
   they would improve in the next.

3. He states that he admires George's courage on
   that occasion and asks to be judged sincere in the
   expression of that opinion.

4. The "Journal" reports that a group of generals, believing that now that the Nazi party has fulfilled its mission of strengthening Germany it should be replaced by a saner type of government, is behind the increased activity of the Monarchists, who are being regarded in Germany as "the party of to-morrow."

5. He now, therefore, assumed a look of importance, and in an angry tone began to examine the sailor, demanding in what engagement he was thus disabled and rendered unfit for service. The sailor replied in a tone as angrily as he, that he had been an officer on board a private ship of war, and that he had lost his leg aboard, in defence of those who did nothing at home.

6. The missionary states in his letter that following the occupation of the city of Shanghai people were compelled to register and declare ownership of wireless sets. They were allowed to retain their radios on the understanding that they would not disseminate any information obtained through them. Petrol was so scarce that private cars had completely disappeared from the thoroughfares and only street cars remained.

7. The entire German nation was, he said, in favour of Hitler's great and risky game. All Hitler's steps of systematic blackmail were universally and enthusiastically regarded by Germans as strokes of genius. Hitler did not create modern Germany. A Hitlerite Germany created Hitler.

8. Bailie K—— moved that the sub-committee's recommendation should be adopted by the Corporation. There was no question, he said, of exploitation of child labour. The position was that larger potato crops were being raised in order to augment the food supply and save shipping for war purposes.

CHAPTER IX

COMPOSITION

No doubt, like many another, you find Composition or essay writing difficult. Very often, in spite of all your pains, the result is so disappointing that you decide that writing an essay is a gift and that no amount of hard work will make you a good essayist. Yet there is no reason why you should not write clear, simple English, free from grammatical errors. It is possible to give you some guidance beyond the rather vague advice :—

> Have something to say,
> Think what you are to say,
> Say it,
> Say it well.

Remember that an essay should be, if possible, the expression of personal experience, whether gained by direct observation or from suitable works of reference, since only then can it be sincere and convincing. Generally, except when under examination, you are at liberty to select your subject from a number of topics. You are at liberty to treat the subject as you please, and very often you are given two or three days to turn it over in your mind.

You are better to begin cautiously, working from words to sentences, from sentences to paragraphs, and so to the full-sized essay. Here is some preliminary practice.

10

EXERCISE I

(a) Write down FIVE adjectives useful in describing each of the following :—

a cycle, an orange, a sheep dog, boiling cocoa, a submarine.

(b) Write down FIVE nouns useful in describing each of the following :—

a telephone, a farmyard, an elephant, a telegram, a class room.

(c) Write down FIVE verbs useful in describing each of the following :—

speech, anger, movement, surprise, shame.

(d) Write down FIVE adverbs useful in describing each of the following :—

dancing, sawing wood, skating, eating an orange, a class singing.

(e) Write down nouns to describe the sounds made by—

a cow, a motor car, a violin, a raven, bees.

(f) Write down adjectives to describe the smell of—

pepper, an onion, tobacco smoke, musty hay, a chemist's shop.

You have now considered the value of words. In a sentence you are required to express an idea clearly and concisely. The following exercise will help you to do so.

EXERCISE II

(a) Write down a sentence to contain each of the following group of words :—

a budgerigar............to speak ; a barometer......... pressure ; a glazier............window ; a cat.............. purring ; a storm at sea............wreck.

(*b*) **Write a definition, if possible in one sentence, of the following :—**

a clock, an orange, a needle, a corkscrew, a flute.

(*c*) **Write down THREE of the rules, in three sentences, for playing the following games :—**

cricket, net ball, dominoes, football, ludo.

As an essay is composed of one or more paragraphs, you will see the importance of practice in writing paragraphs. Each paragraph you write should contain a theme or topic made up of a series of ideas contained in the sentences that compose the paragraph. Try to make sure that one sentence leads naturally to another and avoid any gap in the meaning. Try to make your paragraphs fairly short, at least until you have had a good deal of practice, and take care not to introduce a fresh topic into the last paragraph.

EXERCISE III

Re-arrange the following sentences to form a good paragraph :—

1. And some fell among thorns : and the thorns sprang up, and choked them. And when he sowed, some seed fell by the wayside, and the fowls came and devoured them up. And when the sun was up, they were scorched ; and because they had no root, they withered away. But others fell in good ground, and brought forth fruit, some an hundredfold, some sixtyfold, some thirtyfold. Behold a sower went forth to sow. Some fell upon stony places, where they had not much earth ; and forthwith they sprung up, because they had no deepness of earth.

2. " There isn't any," said the March Hare. " I didn't know it was your table," said Alice ; " it's

laid for a great many more than three." " Have some wine," the March Hare said in an encouraging tone. " It wasn't very civil of you to sit down without being invited," said the March Hare. Alice looked all round the table, but there was nothing on it but tea. "Then it wasn't very civil of you to offer it," said Alice angrily. " I don't see any wine," she said.

3. The letters are then inked over and sheets of paper are pressed down tight upon them. So far as Europe is concerned, type was first used in Holland in the middle of the fifteenth century and was introduced into England by Caxton. Printing is a device for multiplying what is written by making copies of it. The inked letters leave their marks upon the paper, and these marks are the printed words. Little metal letters, called type, are arranged in such a way as to form the words that you want to print. As many copies can be made of what is printed as there are sheets of paper.

You will find the practice of using outlines very helpful in composition. The outline given, contains the main facts and your task is to fill in the appropriate detail. At times you may find it convenient or even essential to re-arrange the facts of the outline in order to secure the best order. Your final work will, of course, show no trace of notes.

EXERCISE IV

Expand the following outlines into paragraphs and furnish titles for each. (The number after each outline gives the number of sentences in the paragraph.)

1. Drake and his friends playing bowls—small armed vessel brings news that Spanish fleet is near—captains hurry to their ships—Drake insists on finishing game—players board their ships. **(4)**

2. Queer looking boy—snub-nosed, flat-browed, dirty
looking—short rather bow-legged—little sharp ugly
eyes—hat at back of head almost falling off—
hands in pockets of corduroy trousers—roystering,
swaggering young gentleman—about four feet six
in his bluchers. (5)

3. Breakfast in cockpit of the Goblin—proper breakfast—cocoa, Dutch bread, English butter, scrambled
eggs—Susan avoided easy way of boiling eggs—
melted butter in big frying pan—broke six eggs—
stirred with fork—only one slopped over—hiss and
splutter on stove—Daddy's surprise, pleasure and
thanks. (5)

EXERCISE V

(a) **Make the following descriptions clearer by adding
further detail in some three or four sentences :—**

1. The station was packed with holiday crowds.
2. She was as clean as soap and water could make
her.
3. It was a truly gigantic meal.
4. From the kitchen came savoury smells which he
had no difficulty in identifying.
5. The victim had suffered severe head injuries.

(b) **Write paragraphs, using the sentences in each group
as the first and last sentences of your paragraphs.**
(Add 4-5 sentences.)

1. I hate spring cleaning.
When will all this noise and confusion come to
an end ?
2. How hot it was !
The youngest sailor began to whistle for a wind.
3. It was the most exciting moment in the game.
And that is how we won the match.
4. Why should boys not do some housework ?
Much may be said on both sides.

5. Even the very children were scared by his looks. Yet he was really a very kind-hearted man.

EXERCISE VI

(a) **Complete the following outlines by adding suitable details and then give titles :—**

1. Great fire in crowded part of London—warehouses and dwelling houses affected—work of fire brigade.
2. Old shepherd—tall wiry figure—keen eyes—rough homespun—dog—knowledge of hills.
3. Value of microscope—reveal things invisible to the naked eye—microbes—blood—tissues—food.
4. Start of race—runners—strong wind—signal start —winner's method of running.
5. Modern dress—ugly not comfortable—lack of variety—personal taste not encouraged—tight-fitting clothes a mistake.

(b) **Prepare outlines for the following :—**

a cycling tour ; the street you live in ; a lifeboat-man ; a telescope ; making a slide ; a vacuum cleaner ; if I had a thousand pounds ; a motor car on fire ; the crowd at a football match ; my stamp album.

EXERCISE VII

(a) **Write a paragraph (5-6 sentences) on each of the following :—**

Buying a railway ticket.
My old football boots.
A petrol pump.
The uses of a pin.
How to make toast.
My favourite film.
A seaside boat hirer.
How to inflate a bicycle tyre.

Some Spring wild flowers.

My uniform (Boys' Brigade, Guides, etc.).

(b) **Write a paragraph as for the school magazine on the following :—**

The Staff *versus* Pupils Match.

Our school prefects.

Classroom gossip.

Things not done.

The school bell.

The best period of the week.

Late comers.

The school excursion.

Children's Hour on the Radio.

Distinguished visitors.

You may now be ready to tackle a complete essay. The first step is to make sure you know exactly what the title means, especially if it is in the form of a figure of speech or a proverb. If the essay requires definite information you must force yourself to recall all you know of the subject whether in the form of personal experiences or stories you have heard. You may at times draw on your imagination to add to your ideas, and, indeed, in writing on such a subject as a lion hunt, you must rely on what you have read or heard or seen at the cinema and what your imagination can add. How then are these ideas to be recalled ? Here are two methods you may try.

1. Write down the names of any things that the subject suggests, just as they come into your mind. You will find that one will suggest another once you start to write. Do not trouble about order at present until your list is more or less complete. Then select similar ideas and supply a suitable

descriptive heading for each. Next arrange your topics in a suitable order. Compose a suitable sentence to begin your composition and, using the material in your outline, write out the essay. Round off with a good sentence.

2. The second method is more orderly and may suit you better. Write down the words **Who ? When ? Where ? Why ? How ? What ?** in a column and apply each to your subject. Write down any ideas the questions suggest in short phrases or even words. The ideas under each heading will generally supply a paragraph which you may arrange as you think fit. Now begin your essay, paying particular attention to the first and last sentence.

If the subject is a wide one, concentrate on one aspect of it. A general subject like *Summer* is most successfully treated by dealing with say, *The Pleasures of Summer*. As far as possible, draw on your own experiences and always make clear in the first paragraph what aspect of the title you are dealing with.

Study the following methods of tackling an Essay.

A Farm

Make a list of (a) sights, (b) sounds, and (c) scents you associate with a farm.

(a) **Sights**—House, outbuildings, fields, woods, trees, moors, animals, machines, etc.

Now write down details you associate with each item, *e.g.* House—grey stone or whitewash, red tiles or blue slates, sheltered or exposed, homely or graceful, etc.

(*b*) **Sounds**.—Clatter of milk-pails, lowing of cattle, barking of dogs, rattle of carts, etc.

Now write down details you associate with each item, *e.g.* lowing of cattle—deep, pleasant, heard at certain times, etc.

(*c*) **Scents**.—Peat or wood smoke, hay, kitchen, flowers, cattle, etc.

Now write down details you associate with each item, *e.g.* sweet smell of hay, etc.

Here you have ample material for your essay. Now consider the wording of it, and try to select suitable nouns, verbs, adjectives, *e.g. lowing* of cattle, *swishing* tails, the house *nestled* in a hollow, *green* meadows, *blue* smoke.

The Royal Navy.

Use such interrogative words as are useful.

When ?—Long history—Alfred's navy—gradual development.

Why ? (of interest).—Famous tradition—Drake and the Spaniards; Blake and the Dutch; Nelson and the French; Jellicoe and the Germans.

What ? (is typical).—Spirit of the navy—Grenville and the *Revenge* ; Captain Fegen of the *Jervis Bay*—desperate odds.

How ? (does it work).—Duties of modern navy—destroyers and convoy work—corvettes and U-boats—minesweepers—aircraft carriers—seaplanes, the eyes of the fleet.

Where ? (is it essential).—Navy and control of the seas—essential to our safety.

From this emerges the following plan:--

   (1) Foundation of the navy.

   (2) Great traditions of the navy.

   (3) Spirit of the navy is the same.

   (4) Varied duties of the navy to-day.

   (5) Importance of the navy.

Friendship

When you are given an abstract noun as title, take simple experiences from your own life and then arrange the lessons and ideas which they suggest.

(1) Think of your friends and ask yourself why you like them. Such points as the following will arise: (1) same age; fond of same games; like to talk of same things ; admire same people, books, etc.; same quality you admire —kindness, courage, loyalty.

(2) Now ask yourself what kind of friend you would like to have—a famous boy footballer; an actor ; some one very brave, strong, clever, kind, witty, rich ?

From the answers to these questions you can arrange your ideas under the following headings:—

1. How is friendship formed ?

2. What do we find in friendship ?

3. What do we consider the most desirable friendship ?

4. How does friendship express our own nature ?

5. How does friendship develop and improve us ?

6. Final statement of the need for and value of friendship.

You may now consider the essay in detail. It consists of a **Beginning**, a **Middle** or **Body**, and an **End**.

The **Beginning** will be found in the first paragraph and should plunge into the subject without delay. You should generally avoid tracing past history unless the subject requires it. Give the reader some idea of what your subject is to be. If you are describing something, don't begin your first sentence with 'It' or "This," but repeat the noun.

In the **Body** of the essay you will give the main facts already arranged in your outline. Avoid such common errors as the use of " I," " I like," unless you require to state your private views. If you must use a pronoun, say "we," but avoid dull personal phrases such as " Let us consider." You should avoid long paragraphs.

The **End** should come naturally and be brief and concise. Make sure that you do not introduce a new and contradictory idea in the last paragraph.

EXERCISE VIII

Expand the following outlines by suitable details and dialogue into anecdotes. Supply titles :—

1. Three brothers in possession of one treasure, a pear tree—guarded it in turn at night—angel disguised as beggar asked for help from guard—promised his own share from tree when ripe—visit repeated to others on successive nights—similar promises given—when ripe, angel came to claim pears—brothers surprised, but prepared to keep promise—angel cast off rags—each brother given his heart's desire.

2. Two men in restaurant—waiter brought two steaks —one rather burnt—each wished other to serve— one at last persuaded—gave burnt steak to friend —other protested—if he served—would have kept burnt steak to himself—other replied that was what he had done—other should be grateful for that was what he had got.

Compositions are classified as :—

> Narration
> Description
> Exposition
> Argument
> Reflection.

(1) **Narrative** is used of any story, whether imaginary or based on fact. It may include the anecdote, incident or short story, and may be drawn from the writer's own or imaginary experience, from history or from biography. You must try to tell your story in an easy natural fashion and work towards a definite point or climax in the last paragraph. You will find that dialogue adds life to your story.

EXERCISE IX

(a) **Use the following sentences as opening sentences for anecdotes :—**

1. " Another trick like that and you'll suffer, my lad."
2. Just at midnight, he heard tapping at his window
3. It was another example of the importance of the old school tie.
4. Unobserved, he watched his taxi driver running along the platform and looking into each compartment.
5. Have you ever heard anything like this ?

(*b*) **Invent or find** suitable anecdotes with the following as last sentences :—

1. Well now, who still thinks Scotsmen are mean ?
2. So I never caught my big fish after all !
3. That's how the window was broken.
4. He had certainly earned his sixpence.

EXERCISE X

(*a*) **Write an anecdote to illustrate the following titles :—**

1. The elephant never forgets.
2. A cry in the night.
3. The wise mouse.
4. Too many cooks.
5. The lost shilling.

(*b*) **Tell an anecdote to illustrate the following :—**

1. Irish humour.
2. Scottish caution.
3. English love of cricket.
4. French politeness.
5. Negro fun or good nature.

The **Short Story** is generally longer than the anecdote and not only tells the story of an incident or a series of incidents, but adds a certain amount of description. You will find also that you are expected to make the people in the story life-like by bringing out their different natures. In Chapter XVI, you are told something of the structure of the short story which you should try to adopt to your own use.

EXERCISE XI

(*a*) **Write short stories with the following opening sentences.** (The number after each denotes the number of characters you should introduce, if possible.)

1. I was tired of his continual insults, but, when I received a blow, it was more than I could bear. (2).
2. It was a night of stars as the two horsemen approached the castle. (4).
3. I saw at a glance that the sailor was very much excited. (3).
4. To escape was not easy as we were closely watched. (3).
5. It all began as a joke. (3).

(b) **Write short stories with the following last sentences :—**

1. In the boat they found the stowaway, the only man left alive.
2. If it hadn't been for the signal . . . . . .
3. And there are the boots on my feet to prove it.
4. Well, I never thought that any girl could have done it.
5. The secret of the cave was never discovered.

(c) **Write short stories with the following titles :—**

1. The stolen cattle.
2. The secret of the heather ale.
3. The false alarm.
4. The amateur burglar.
5. An adventure in the forest.

You are sometimes asked to write a narrative essay which does not usually require such a definite plot as the short story, but the structure is very much the same. The subject may be part of a longer narrative, from history or from the life of some well-known person. Be careful here, as in the short story, of the beginning, and keep the important part until almost the last few words.

EXERCISE XII

(a) **Write a narrative essay on the following :—**

1. Spending sixpence at Woolworth's.
2. When I played Santa Claus.
3. My favourite story from the Bible.
4. A king burns the cakes.
5. An adventure with a cobra.

(b) **Write a narrative drawn from your own experience, your reading of fiction or history, or your imagination on the following :—**

1. Courage.
2. Treachery.
3. Obedience.
4. Fidelity.
5. Unselfishness.

(c) **Write an essay on the following topics :—**

1. A Roman legionary tells of his adventures in Britain.
2. A crusader tells how he came to Jerusalem.
3. An English archer returns from Agincourt.
4. How we fought the Armada, by one of Drake's sea dogs.
5. With Nelson at Trafalgar, by a powder-monkey.

(d) **Write an essay on the following topics :—**

1. A day on the prairie.
2. With my young brother at the dentist's.
3. A thrilling night ride.
4. An adventure in our street.
5. A schoolroom mishap.

The **Descriptive** essay comes naturally after Narrative. Of course, as you know, description enters into most forms of writing, but you may study it as a separate form. You will find that description varies from the simple description of a common object to the complex and difficult description of a great building, a landscape, a city scene, and so on. When you describe, tell exactly what you see or remember. Do not give a mere catalogue of facts, but adopt a definite attitude towards your subject and describe it from that point of view. Select what seem to you the most important facts and show how they affect you. Try to bring out such things as colour, sound, smell, movement, and try if you can to introduce suitable similes and metaphors. One method you may safely use, is to give a bird's eye view of the subject as a whole and then proceed in successive paragraphs to fill in important details.

EXERCISE XIII

(a) **Describe briefly and without naming the object :—**

1. Your school desk.
2. A fishing-rod.
3. A kitten.
4. A lumber-jacket.
5. A thermometer.

(b) **Describe fully what you dislike in the following :—**

1. The dullest book you know.
2. A dentist's rooms.
3. An unpopular uncle or aunt.
4. Some voices on the Radio.
5. Household tasks.

(c) **Describe fully the uniform of the following :—**

1. An airman.
2. A cowboy.

3. A waitress.
4. A clown.
5. A postman.

(d) **Describe from memory the following :—**

1. A holiday poster.
2. A film you liked.
3. A famous painting.
4. An interesting shop window.
5. A family photograph.

(e) **Give a word picture, as vividly as you can, of :—**

1. A busy street crossing.
2. A holiday crowd at a station.
3. An air-raid shelter.
4. A church tower.
5. A mountain stream.

(f) **Write a description of the following :—**

1. Prize-giving day.
2. A cinema queue.
3. The school garden.
4. A seaside pier.
5. In the barber's chair.

(g) **Compare and contrast the following :—**

1. The chimes of Big Ben and your alarm clock.
2. Before and after a bath.
3. Football and hockey.
4. A duck and an ostrich.
5. Your teacher in the classroom and on the sports field.

The **Character Sketch** is a special kind of descriptive essay, as you know, and may be conveniently studied separately. When you meet a person, you notice his appearance and dress and form your

11

opinion of him by what he says and does, and to a lesser degree, by what others say of him. Try to follow this method in your description. Give details to show such things as height, build, age, features, colour of hair, eyes, watching always for any mannerism or peculiarity that marks him off from others. Don't lay too much stress on dress, though it may reveal character. Deal next with what you know of him, whether generous or mean, brave or cowardly, kind or cruel, and try to show the reasons for your statements. Remember such matters as his wisdom or foolishness, his keenness or dullness. Try to sketch in the background of surroundings, people, everyday life and occupation, with which you associate him. If you are dealing with a character in a book, tell briefly the part he plays in the story. In conclusion, give your final opinion of him whether you approve, admire, despise, like or hate him. This, of course, should follow naturally from your preceding paragraphs.

EXERCISE XIV

(a) **Describe the following well-known film figures :—**
> Donald Duck, Snow White, Pluto, Mickey Mouse, One of the Seven Dwarfs.

(b) **Describe the following :—**
> A village cobbler ; a well-known footballer ; a school prefect ; your school janitor ; a policeman.

(c) **Describe in such a way as to make their identity clear without naming them :—**
> A classmate ; a famous statesman ; an inmate of the Zoo ; a well-known film star ; your favourite in fiction.

The **Expository Essay**, you will find, increases your respect for definite facts. Other types of essay encourage you to exercise your imagination, but here you have to record rather than invent. You are required to explain something to a reader who knows little or nothing about the subject. Sometimes you may find it necessary to say the same thing in different ways or to use several illustrations to make a point clear. When the explanation is a long one, it is worth while making a summary of your conclusions at various stages in the course of the essay. You should try to use simple words and short sentences in this type of essay and to keep out any ideas which have nothing to do with the subject. Here, especially, you will be tempted to say ' I ' or ' you,' to repeat ' and,' and to write notes instead of sentences. Avoid these carefully. The simplest form of Exposition is the definition in which you have already had some practice.

EXERCISE XV

Use the following outlines as material for essays :—

1. *Raisin Cake.*—1 lb. self-rising flour, $\frac{1}{4}$ teaspoonful salt, 6 oz. butter, $\frac{1}{2}$ lb. stoned raisins, $\frac{1}{2}$ teaspoonful mixed spice, $\frac{1}{2}$ lb. sugar, $\frac{1}{2}$ pint milk. Sift flour and salt into basin—rub in butter, add dry ingredients—mix to dough with milk—put in greased tin—bake for $1\frac{1}{2}$ hours in moderate oven.
2. *Building a Fuselage.*—Three parts—nose and cabin, tail, centre section—centre section divided down middle—sections built separately—accessories fitted before joining sections—work on side fuselage—fitting at same time—sections of centre part joined by L-shaped strips riveted at each edge of the two halves—upright edges of strips touch when

halves are put together—joined by U-shaped strip fitting over two upright edges.

Note.—Use sentences throughout.

EXERCISE XVI

(a) **Describe as clearly and briefly as you can the following :—**

How to make a rabbit hutch ; how to play cricket or hockey ; how to use a telephone ; how to take a photograph ; how to repair a puncture.

(b) **Describe the structure and method of using the following :—**

A petrol pump ; an automatic lighter ; an electric bell ; a sewing machine ; an electric iron.

(c) **Explain carefully the difference between the following:—**

A hammer and a mallet ; a toadstool and a mushroom ; a nail and a screw nail ; a knife and a pair of scissors ; a piano and an organ.

The **Argumentative Essay** gives you a chance of airing, and what is more important, justifying your views on a subject. You must try to convince your reader by your arguments and not merely assume what you think is right. Do not ignore the views of those who disagree with you or, what is worse, invent foolish beliefs which can be easily ridiculed. Make a start by stating clearly what you intend to prove and show how it differs from the other possible point of view. State your argument point by point, and then deal with possible objections in a fair and reasonable fashion. In the last paragraph, re-state what you set out to prove and let your last sentence give the conclusion you have reached. It is useful practice to write up class debates in the form of an essay.

EXERCISE XVII

Use the material in the following outline for an essay on :—" Are we too fond of games during school hours ? "

State your point of view, let us say the negative —games and their value—bring out best qualities in pupils—popular with all—need for amusement and diversion to prevent overstrain—sign of healthy children. On the other side deal with and refute objections—loss of time—neglect of studies—upsetting effect on pupils—leisure for games outside school—conclusion.

EXERCISE XVIII

Write essays on the following :—

1. Who dress most sensibly in summer, boys or girls ?
2. That a hiking holiday is better than a cycling holiday.
3. That every scholar should have workshop and garden training.
4. That the kilt is the best dress for boys.
5. That one should start with the breast stroke rather than the crawl stroke in learning to swim.
6. That August is the best holiday month.
7. That Rugby is a better game than Soccer.
8. That modern children are spoiled by their parents.
9. That all boys and girls should join some association, *e.g.* Boy Scouts, Girl Guides.
10. That there should be no home work.

The Reflective Essay you will find the most difficult. The subject very often seems vague and general. You are given an abstract noun like **Kindness** or **Courage** and told to write an essay. Yet it can be done. Start off by giving the title a particular application and connect the theme with your own experience, either actual or imaginary. When you have done this, you will find that you have something definite to deal with. Make sure that you start from the very beginning to deal with actual facts. If you find yourself writing down vague colourless statements, start over again.

EXERCISE XIX

Write essays on the following subjects :—

1. Toys of long ago.
2. A cyclist's view of motorists or *vice versa*.
3. The joys and trials of a teacher's life (by a pupil).
4. The truth about football (by a cricketer).
5. If I had a five pound note.
6. What I really dislike.
7. Love of one's country.
8. When I am twenty-one.
9. " Nothing but front stalls left."
10. Speeches I have listened to.

Letter Writing

You are generally not very old when you write your first letter and soon learn that careful spelling and well constructed sentences are expected of you, as well as good writing. Your early letters may take the form of a reply to an invitation to a party, a letter of thanks for a birthday gift, or a letter to your parents or school friends when on holiday. Later you may have to write what is called a formal letter in application for a situation or on some other business matter. Perhaps more than most school work, a letter seems to be of practical importance, and you will find no doubt a certain pleasure in letter writing.

Try to write naturally, that is, as you would speak to the person concerned, but be careful to give the proper form of the letter. In the first paragraph, state the purpose of the letter ; in those following, give any necessary information. Use the last paragraph as a conclusion, and let it be short. Don't write postscripts, even if you are a girl.

The **letter** may be classified as:—

1. Familiar or friendly—as, the letter to a school friend.
2. Social and semi-formal—as, the invitation to a party.
3. Formal or business—as, the formal invitation or letter of application.

The letter consists of:—

a. **Heading**, which includes the address and date (not day of week only), and is written in the right-hand top corner.
b. The **Salutation**, or method of naming the person or persons written to, which is written on the left-hand side a little below the date.

c. The **Body**, which contains the ideas of the letter and begins just below the salutation.

d. The **Subscription** or ending, which is on the right-hand side just below the last sentence of the body of the letter.

Note.—In formal and business letters, it is customary to write the name and address of the person written to, immediately above the Salutation.

Examples:

1. Social and Semi-Formal: AN INVITATION.

> 12 ROWAN ROAD,
> PERTH.
> *1st August,* 1942.

DEAR MRS. SMITH,

It will give us great pleasure if you will dine with us on Wednesday next, August 5th, at 7 o'clock.

> Yours sincerely,
> MARY BROWN.

2. Social and Formal: AN INVITATION.

Mr. and Mrs. William Thomson present their compliments to the Misses Brown and request the pleasure of their company at a party on Tuesday, October 11, at 7.15 p.m., to celebrate the coming of age of their son, John.

THE PRIORY,
CEDAR AVENUE,
BRISTOL.
25th September, 1941.

3. Formal business letter: AN APPLICATION.

97 MAIN STREET,
KILMARNOCK.
9th May, 1942.

Messrs. WILSON BROS.,
73 CHURCH STREET,
KILMARNOCK.

DEAR SIRS,

In reply to your advertisement in the *Evening Standard* of 7th May, for a junior clerk, I beg to offer myself as a candidate for the situation.

I am fifteen years of age and have completed a three years' Secondary Course in Victoria Higher Grade School, and have been awarded the School Intermediate Certificate with special distinction in French and German. I am at present taking a day course of commercial training which I shall continue in the evening, if necessary.

I enclose a copy of two recent testimonials, and have permission to refer any further enquiries regarding my attainments and character to Mr. Williams, my former headmaster.

If you should see fit to grant me an interview, I shall be glad to supply any further information you may require.

Yours faithfully,

ROBERT CRAIG.

1. Familiar or Friendly.

a. First paragraph should contain friendly references to the recipient and his affairs.

b. Select a few interesting topics and introduce personal references.

c. Don't write careless, inadequate letters and then you are spared apologetic phrases such as,

"I really have nothing to say," or "I must catch the post."

2. Formal Letter.

a. Retain use of third person for pronouns, possessive adjectives, tenses and auxiliaries of verbs.

b. Begin with the name of the writer; put the address and date at the end. There is no signature.

3. Business Letter.

a. In addition to parts of the ordinary letter, include the name or official description of the person or persons addressed, inserting this before the salutation.

b. Give the full date. It may be necessary for reference.

c. In the body of the letter avoid " *to-day* " or "*yesterday*," giving the exact day of the week and month, thus, Monday, 9th June.

d. If the letter is in reply to another, first acknowledge receipt and then answer the *matters* referred to in it.

e. In letters of application, give such information as may show your suitability.

f. Always sign your name in full.

EXERCISE XX

(*a*) **To what persons would the following forms of saluta-tion be suitable ?—**

My dear John ; Dear Sir ; Gentlemen ; Rev. and Dear Sir ; Dear Mr. Brown.

(*b*) **How would you address the following ?—**

A business firm ; a stranger ; your headmaster ; a school friend ; a member of parliament.

(*c*) **To what kind of letter would the following subscrip-tions be given ? Write out suitable salutations for each.**

Yours faithfully, I beg to remain, Your obedient servant, Very sincerely yours, Your loving son.

EXERCISE XXI

(*a*) **Write a letter suitable for the following:—**

1. To a shop-keeper, ordering household supplies.
2. To your headmaster, asking for a testimonial.
3. To a well-known person, asking for his autograph.
4. To a bookseller, asking about suitable prizes for boys.
5. To a nursery gardener, ordering seed for your allotment.

(*b*) **Write a letter in the third person suitable for the following:—**

1. An invitation to a party.
2. A complaint to a railway company regarding goods delivered in a damaged condition.
3. A complaint regarding your neighbour's dog.
4. A letter declining an invitation (give reasons).
5. A letter to a stranger, who has accused you of some offence and threatened to take legal pro-ceedings against you.

(c) **Write a letter suitable for the following:—**

1. To the manager of a seaside hotel, asking for holiday terms.

2. To a farmer, asking permission to camp on his land.

3. To a Lost Property Office, giving details of articles left in a bus.

4. To the editor of a local paper, protesting against home lessons.

5. To a sports outfitter, ordering equipment for the school cricket or hockey eleven.

(d) **Write a letter suitable for the following:—**

1. To a former school friend, giving school gossip.

2. To an American cousin, who has just arrived in this country.

3. A letter of thanks to an uncle, for a birthday present of ten shillings.

4. A challenge to the secretary of a rival sports club.

5. A complaint of a cat regarding injustice at the recent cat show.

EXERCISE XXII

(a) **Write an answer to the following advertisements:—**

1. Young lady wanted as companion and children's nurse ; highest references ; apply Brown, 12 Moor Road, Dundee.

2. Office boy for contractor's office wanted ; please state age and salary expected ; good opening for hard working lad ; apply Messrs. Raymond & Tully, 76 Queen Street, Liverpool.

3. Wanted, cottage, buy or let, unfurnished ; with garage or garage space ; nearness to city desirable ; Box 9872, *Morning Herald*.

4. Lost on 14th November, genuine gold signet ring with monogram ; handsome reward—1734, *Times Office*.

5. For sale or exchange, cycle in good condition, three speed gear, too small for present owner ; would suit boy ; 14-15 years ; what offers ?— Brown, 3 Tully St., Glasgow.

(*b*) **Write a series of letters on the following subjects:—**

1. An application for a post as apprentice or office boy or shorthand-typist.

2. A letter from the employer in (1) to the headmaster making enquiries about the applicant.

3. A reply from the headmaster to the employer.

4. A letter from the employer asking the applicant to call.

5. A letter from the successful applicant to the headmaster after the interview.

Postcards

The **Postcard** may be regarded as an abbreviated letter. Since space is limited, the arrangement or lay-out of the heading, salutation, etc. is much less formal, but should be neat and tidy. Rule off your jotter or exercise book in postcard sizes ($5\frac{1}{2} \times 3\frac{1}{2}$ inches), and then write and address the following notes or short letters.

EXERCISE XXIII

Write a postcard:—

1. To your cousin, inviting him for a week-end to your home.

2. To your parents, from a holiday camp.

3. To the secretary of your sports club, explaining why you cannot play on Saturday.
4. To the butcher, ordering Sunday's dinner.
5. As secretary of the school debating society, calling a committee meeting.

A **Telegram** is only used when speedy communication is essential and the normal charge is based on twelve words, including name and address of recipient, and signature of the sender. You will find that the wording of a telegram gives you excellent practice in cutting out all unnecessary words.

EXERCISE XXIV

Write a series of telegrams (not exceeding twelve words) **to convey the following information:—**

1. To your uncle whom you are visiting, telling him when and where your train arrives.
2. To a friend, postponing his visit to your home and giving a reason.
3. To your mother on holiday, informing her of illness at home. (Do not alarm her !)
4. To a live stock dealer, ordering some rabbits to be kept as pets.
5. To a friend, congratulating him on winning a scholarship, or other prize.

Dialogue, as you have seen, can do much to enliven every type of composition, but it can also be considered as a type in itself. You have, of course, noticed how the action of a play is carried on by dialogue, and how it reveals the characters of the speakers. When you write dialogue you must

try to make your dialogue do as much. Here are some hints which will help you to make your dialogue clear, simple and natural.

1. Begin a new line with each speaker.

2. Use shorter sentences than in normal composition and vary the form. Avoid mere " Yes " or " No " or " What ? " etc.

3. Make the speeches brief and to the point. Use common words and, at times, colloquialisms or even slang, when suitable for the speakers.

4. You may insert the name of the speaker in the margin as in a play, or inside the dialogue, as in a novel. Use speech-words and vary them according to the mood of the speaker, as—said, roared, growled, whimpered, threatened, interrupted. Modify speech words as—whispered timidly, screamed angrily. Vary position of speech word and name of speaker as—*William said* " This is a very interesting book." " This," *said William*, " is a very interesting book." " This is a very interesting book," *said William*.

Notes.—

When the names of speakers are introduced in the margin as in a play, omit quotation marks; when inserted in the dialogue as in a novel, use quotation marks.

When direct speech is broken by speech word, check punctuation by reading the direct speech only.

EXERCISE XXV

Write dialogues between the following:—

1. An airman and a sailor.
2. A cricket ball and a football.

3. A group of girls discussing the school dance, the morning after.

4. A night watchman and a stranger.

5. An employer and a candidate for a vacancy as office boy, typist, apprentice, etc.

6. A shepherd's dog and an old sheep.

7. A scrubber and a bar of soap.

8. An American and a schoolboy, at Stratford-on-Avon or at Burns's cottage.

9. A dentist and a nervous patient.

10. A group of four boys at the beginning of a new session.

Oral Composition

How often has your father or some other grown-up complained that they, that is, your teachers, may teach you to write sensibly but that they certainly don't teach you how to express yourself in ordinary speech. Whatever the truth of the complaint, there is no doubt that speech training and practice in speaking on a given subject are very important. Very few people even speak clearly and distinctly after a sentence or two without practice, and most of you are tongue-tied when first asked to speak before a class for more than a few seconds. After the first attempt, however, you generally gather confidence. The first plunge is the worst.

Oral Composition may be in the form of a **lecturette** on some topic in which you are interested, or may develop into a **debate** with two or four speakers taking the opposite sides. A chairman, usually the teacher, especially in the early stages of debating, introduces the speaker or speakers and, after the speech or speeches are over, asks for questions or comments.

Note.—

It is advisable to make each pupil responsible for at least one contribution to the discussion, and to take a note of what interests him during the speech.

When you are asked to give a talk on any subject, collect your material and write out a connected statement, which should be more or less memorised. From this, prepare a brief summary with the chief ideas underlined for reference. In the actual delivery you may read the speech (which is not advisable), speak without notes of any kind (which is difficult without practice), or use the summary for reference. If you can draw at all well on the blackboard, use diagrams to illustrate your explanations.

EXERCISE XXVI

Prepare a talk (of 10-20 minutes' duration) **on the** following:—

1. Model aeroplanes.
2. A collection of birds' eggs.
3. A camping experience.
4. How to recognize aircraft.
5. Games and tricks for a party.
6. How to make a toboggan.
7. The care of pets.
8. How to build a camp fire or to cook a camp meal.
9. The joys of cycling.
10. Evenings at the Scouts, Girl Guides, etc.

12

Class Debates tend to promote class activity and, **if** carefully managed, teach self-control. The " I'm right, you're wrong " attitude, and mere personal abuse, are gradually replaced by quiet speaking, good-humoured tolerance and careful argument. The speakers should always address the chairman, who will, of course, always say who is to speak during the discussion.

EXERCISE XXVII

Prepare a speech for the affirmative or the negative on the following subjects:—

1. Modern children have too much pocket money.
2. That cyclists should be taxed.
3. That every boy should have workshop experience in school.
4. That professionalism tends to destroy sport.
5. That schools should make more use of wireless lessons.
6. That girls should have pockets.
7. That it is better to excel at sport than at studies.
8. That a mixed class of boys and girls is less efficient and happy than one consisting of boys or girls only.
9. That there is little place for large dogs in city life.
10. That reading " penny dreadfuls " does more good than harm.

CHAPTER X

ERRORS IN COMPOSITION

ERRORS in composition occur chiefly through (1) neglect or ignorance of the Rules of Grammar, (2) neglect or ignorance of the Laws of Style, and (3) through faulty arrangement of words and phrases.

I. RULES OF GRAMMAR

A. Rules of Agreement

1. A **Verb** agrees with its subject in number and person, as, I *am*, thou *art*, he *is*.

2. A **Composite Subject**, *i.e.* one consisting of two or more nouns or pronouns in the singular number, joined by the conjunction *and*, takes a plural verb :—as, John, James and I *were* invited to the party.

Notes.—

1. Where two subjects express a single idea a verb may be in the singular number :—as, His power and control *was* strictly limited. All beer and skittles certainly *is* not life. Bread and butter *satisfies* a hungry man.

2. Some nouns, apparently plural in form, take a singular verb ; as,

The news of the war *is* disappointing.
The wages of sin *is* death.

3. A **Subject**, consisting of two or more nouns or pronouns in the singular number, joined by either—or, or neither—nor, takes a singular verb, as :

Either John or James *has* the correct answer.
Neither David nor I *am* content.

4. When a **Subject** consists of two or more nouns or pronouns in different numbers and of different persons, joined by *and*, the verb is in the plural number, and agrees with the first person rather than the second, and with the second rather than the third, as:

Her sister and I *were* chosen to represent the school.

5. When a **Subject** consists of two or more nouns or pronouns in different numbers and of different persons, joined by either—or, neither—nor, the verb agrees with the last noun or pronoun:—**as,**

Either Ella or you *were* present.
Neither Thomas nor I *was* present.

6. When a **Subject** consists of two singular nouns, joined by *along with*, *as well as*, the verb is in the singular number:—as,

Dr. Johnson, as well as his biographer, James Boswell, *was* a member of the club.

7. When the **Subject is a Collective Noun** or a Distributive Pronoun, or none, or many a, the verb is in the singular:—as,

The orchestra *was* late owing to the accident.
Each *was* given an apple.
None but the brave *deserves* the fair.
Many a man *has* made the same mistake.

Notes.—

1. If the person using the Collective Noun is thinking of the individual members that compose the group, he uses a plural verb; if he thinks of the group as acting as a group, he uses a singular verb :—as,

> The jury *were* sworn in at 10 a.m.
> The jury *was* not long in returning its verdict.
> A certain number of them *was* chosen.
> A number of people *are* handicapped in life.

N.B.—Be careful not to use a Collective Noun in the same sentence, treating it (1) as a unity and (2) as composed of individual members :—as,

> The team *was* delighted with its victory and they *were* entertained to tea after the match.

2. Since none may mean not any as well as no one, a plural verb may be used :—as,

> When the survivors *were* counted none *were* missing.

8. **Pronouns** agree in gender, number and person with the nouns for which they stand. The Case of Pronouns depends on their relation to the other words in their own clauses :—as,

> Sheila had to stay at home because she had to help her mother.
> He, who was always willing to help his friends, became destitute because they would not help him.

Notes.—

1. When a Relative Pronoun has two Nouns or Pronouns of different persons, either of which might be the antecedent, it agrees with the Noun or Pronoun on which the greater emphasis is placed :—as,

I am a man of few words who *act(s)* on **the** spur of the moment.

I is 1st person, man is 3rd person. Act or acts is possible, but since man is closer than I, most people would prefer acts.

2. The Relative Pronoun should be placed as close as possible to its antecedent to prevent ambiguity :— as,

> The man entered the room who was on holiday from the city.

This is wrong, because the antecedent of who is man, not room.

3. *And who, and which* should never be used unless preceded by *who* or *which* :—as,

> During her term in hospital she unfortunately contracted an unusual disease and which proved most difficult to cure.

If the writer had written " a disease which was unusual and which " etc., the sentence would have been correct.

9. **This** and **that** agree in Number with the nouns which they qualify.

Note.—

This (pl. these) refers to something nearer the speaker than what is referred to by that (pl. those) :—as,

> This window is cleaner than that.
> These books are dearer than those.

10. Two negatives make an affirmative:—as,

> I don't want nothing—*i.e.* I want something, whereas the speaker most probably meant " I don't want anything."

EXERCISE I

Re-write the following faulty sentences in correct English :—

1. Robert, you and I is going to the concert.
2. His temper and passion makes him livid.
3. Neither you or I are able to do it.
4. The news of the war are very depressing.
5. Either you nor he cannot be allowed to depart.
6. The doctor as well as the undertaker were present.
7. The visitor along with a porter arrive at the front door.
8. Many a man hope for a stroke of good fortune.
9. Each of the children were given an apple.
10. Everyone present expect a present.
11. The crew is undoubtedly deserving punishment, but they ought not to lose their pay.
12. The crowd was very unruly, but they dispersed quietly when the police was summoned.
13. The boy jumped into the boat who had misbehaved himself.
14. The ship who sailed that afternoon left her moorings.
15. The woman which she met was obviously ill.
16. Let you and I settle this matter.
17. This is between you and I and the gatepost.
18. For me, it was unfortunate ; for he, it was a tragedy.
19. Myself am responsible.
20. Who did you speak to ?
21. Those who you formerly selected will attend.
22. The men who you refer to have arrived.
23. Those whom you know were formerly present failed to put in an appearance.
24. I and the others mentioned gained prizes.

25. We and our neighbours joined to form a fire party.
26. The snake was regarded as sacred and sacrifices were made to them in foreign lands.
27. This room whose floor was anything but level was my quarters for a year.
28. The sick man and who was a foreign sailor was taken away in the ambulance.
29. These sort are to be avoided.
30. He boarded the ship which was a daring thing to do.
31. He jumped over the high wall which showed his recklessness.
32. Somebody saw it. I forget whom.
33. This is one of the greatest swindles which has been perpetrated on the public.
34. Here is the purse which I used and is empty now.
35. He doesn't know nothing.

B. The Noun and Pronoun—Case, etc. Use of Correct possessive.

1. A **Noun** in the possessive singular is marked by an apostrophe s ('s) ; in the possessive plural it is marked by s apostrophe (s') : as; lady's, ladies'.

Notes.—

1. Nouns not monosyllabic, the last syllable of which begins and ends with " s," classical names, certain idiomatic phrases mark the possessive by an apostrophe only :—as,

    Moses' nose, Cassius' treason, for conscience' sake.

2. Nouns which mark the plural by internal change of vowel have an apostrophe s ('s) for both possessive singular and possessive plural :—as,

    Woman's, women's.

3. The apostrophe should *not* be added to nouns denoting inanimate objects :—as, the table's leg, the window's cord. The exceptions to this rule are such idiomatic expressions as :—Out of harm's way, a day's journey, the world's end.

2. When **two or more Nouns** in the possessive case are in apposition, the sign of the possessive is placed after the last one only:—as, Messrs. Mair, Hunter and Young's client: for " Our Lord, Jesus Christ's sake."

Note.—

If two nouns are in the possessive case, joined by *and*, and if separate possession is intended, both nouns should have the apostrophe s : as,

> Mr. Jones's and Mr. Brown's supporters both entered the square at the same time.

3. **Possessive Pronouns** (or Adjectives) take no apostrophe:—as,

> The dog bit *its* tail. What's *yours* is mine.

4. **Nouns or Pronouns with a following Gerund** are in the possessive case:—as,

> You'll excuse my intruding.
> You cannot prevent my finding out your secret.

5. **Each other** is used of two persons, **one another** of more than two:—as,

> John and Mary told each other the news.
> The four of them related their adventures to one another.

6. **Each** may be used of two, or more than two persons ; **one another** is only used of more than two:—as,

> Each of the two soldiers had a bomb.
> Each of the soldiers in the platoon had a bomb.

All the soldiers in the company were loyal to one another.

7. **One** should be followed by one's, not his, her, their, etc.

One ought not to do such things for the sake of one's reputation.

Notes.—

One in the above sentence is an indefinite demonstrative pronoun and demands a pronoun or pronouns of the same kind after it. Inexperienced writers are tempted to follow this pronoun with a definite personal pronoun or with definite pronouns of both genders :—as,

One should not boast of his (or her or their) exploits in company.

A similar confusion is also likely to occur when the pronouns that are compounds of—one and—body are used as subjects (*e.g.* anyone, everyone ; anybody ; nobody ; somebody). To write :—

" If anyone arrives during my absence, tell him or her to await my return " is correct but awkward.

To write :—

If anyone arrives during my absence tell *them* to await my return—is wrong, because them is plural, anyone is singular.

You are advised to be very sparing of the use of *one*. Frequent use of the indefinite pronoun *one* makes your composition very artificial. Other pronouns, such as *everyone*, *everybody*, etc., make traps for the unwary. You may avoid the use of the " one " construction by

a. Using all, or people :—as,

People should not boast of their exploits in public. Let all look after themselves (instead of " Let each look after himself or herself).

b. Using the passive instead of the active voice :—as,

Such things should not be done in public (instead of : One should not do such things in public)

EXERCISE II

Re-write the following faulty sentences in correct English :—

1. The window's cord was broken.
2. One of Cassius's friends was Brutus.
3. Moses's power came from God.
4. The telephone's receiver was damaged.
5. James's, John's and David's bicycles were found under the hedge.
6. The taper's light was feeble.
7. I had a collision with the car and damaged it's radiator.
8. You cannot prevent us entering here.
9. You must stop him shouting.
10. He sang for his' supper.
11. The dog caught it's tail in a trap.
12. The hat is her's.
13. Each gave a present to the other so all four were pleased.
14. Since David and Jonathan loved one another so much, they have been considered as model friends.
15. When " Auld Lang Syne " was sung, each gave his hand to the other and then the vast hall emptied.
16. The members of the climbing party proved loyal supporters of each other.
17. If one had to enter a house in the old days, he would find the place filled with beautifully carved furniture, and it's maker would tell you all about it and how long it took him to make each article.

18. If one talks to himself he runs the risk of being arrested.

19. You ought to go to church for we are taught to do so.

20. They escorted we home.

C. The Verb—Tenses, etc.

1. **Transitive Verbs** govern the objective case:—as,

> He carried *her* over the stream.
> He kicked the *ball* into the goal.

Note.—

Pronouns have a different form in the objective case from that of the nominative. Our nouns are not inflected, *i.e.* do not change their form for the different cases. When in doubt about the case of a noun, make an analysis of the clause.

2. The **Verbs** *to be*, *seem*, *appear*, *become*, *remain*, *grow*, *etc.*, along with passive verbs of making, naming, appointing, electing, crowning, calling, creating, etc., take the same case after them as before them:—as,

> He was elected *Emperor*. He became *president*.
> He remained *manager* for the rest of his life.

Note.—

In such instances as these, the verb might be called a verb of statement—no real action is implied : the subject and the noun after such verbs are equivalents.

3. *Bid*, *can*, *dare*, *feel*, *hear*, *let*, *make*, *see*, *may*, *must*, *need*, *shall*, *will*, are followed by the infinitive mood without to:—as,

> He let me *advance*.   I shall *come*.   He may *go*.

Notes.—

1. All verbs govern following verbs in the infinitive mood, but, generally, the " to " sign of the infinitive is written :—as,

    I told him to go.
    He permitted me to enter.

    The verbs under 3 are exceptional in this respect.

2. The past of ought and must is expressed by a following perfect infinitive :—as,

    He must surrender.   He must *have surrendered.*
    He ought to apply himself.   He ought *to have applied* himself.

3. Verbs of expecting, hoping, intending, etc., are followed by the Present Infinitive, *not* by the Perfect Infinitive :—as,

    He intended to come—*not* to have come.

4. The **Past Participle** and not the Past Tense is used after the auxiliary verb have:—as,

    I have come, *not* I have came.

Note.—

Be careful to distinguish between the past participle and past tense of the following verbs :—Swim, bear, cleave, eat, fall, sink, lie (to recline), ring, saw, see, swing, strew, fly.

5. **Sequence of Tenses.**—*a.* A past tense should follow a past tense:—as,

    He was annoyed when he *failed* to find the treasure.
    He studied hard that he *might* be dux.
    He pacified the mob when it *threatened* him.
    He would not surrender because he *dreaded* what they would do to him.

Note.—

After a verb in the past tense statements of permanent and universal acceptance follow in the present tense :—as,

> Columbus believed that the world *is* round.
> He was then convinced that all men *are* mortal.

b. A present or a future tense in the principal clause may be followed by any tense in the dependent clause:—as,

> I feel I *am* not welcome.
> I shall feel I *am* not welcome.
> I feel I *have* not *been* welcome.
> I shall feel I *have* not *been* welcome.
> I feel I *shall be* welcome.
> I feel I *was* not welcome.
> I shall feel I *was* not welcome.
> I am beginning to feel I *am* not welcome.

6. **Shall, Will.**—*a.* When simple future tense is intended, the following are the correct auxiliaries to use:—

	Sing.	*Plural.*
1st person,	I shall.	We shall.
2nd person,	Thou wilt (you will).	You will.
3rd person,	He will.	They will.

b. When a promise, a threat or a command is intended, the following should be used:—

	Sing.	*Plural.*
1st person,	I will.	We will.
2nd person,	Thou shalt (you shall).	You shall.
3rd person,	He shall.	They shall.

Examples of some of the above uses:—

I shall speak at the meeting = merely future tense.

I will „ „ „ „ = determination to speak.

You will then proceed to headquarters = merely future tense.

You shall then proceed to headquarters = an order.

They will be free = merely future tense.

They shall be free = determination on the part of the speaker to secure their freedom.

c. **Should and Would.**

1. In principal clauses should is used to imply the meaning of *ought to* for all three persons:—as,

> I (you, he, we) should be pleased to assist as I (you, he, we) have benefited from the funds.

2. In principal clauses would is used to imply some condition or intention or determination:—as,

> I (you, he, we) would not promise aid as the cause was unworthy.
>
> The child would insist on weeping.
>
> We would be pleased if you could see your way to comply with these instructions.

7. **The omission (ellipsis) of the Principal Verb** in contracted clauses or in answers, after the auxiliaries *may, can, shall, will, have, be,* is permissible only when the form understood is the same as the form expressed:—as,

> I never have and never will support such a cause.

The verbs of the two clauses ought to be:—have supported and will support. The perfect tense of the verb of the first clause demands the past participle *supported*, which does not appear in the sentence; it must therefore be supplied. The correct version is:—

> I never have supported and never will support such a cause.

On the other hand, study this sentence:—

> I cannot and do not support such a cause.

The principal verb of the first clause and the auxiliary verb *do* of the second both demand the present infinitive form which is found in the sentence (one verb governing a following verb in the infinitive mood): accordingly, the sentence as it stands is correct.

8. A **Participle** should qualify the subject of the nearest finite verb ; otherwise it becomes misrelated or unrelated:—as,

> Cycling down hill, he suddenly observed a block in the road.

In this sentence the present participle *cycling* does the work of an adjective and qualifies he, the subject of the finite verb.

> Thinking that everything was ready, the signal for the start was given.

In this sentence, *thinking* is not related to any subject stated in the sentence. Some change is required:—as,

> He (perhaps the judge or starter) thinking that everything was ready, gave the signal for the start.

Notes.—

1. The participle may be used impersonally in such examples as :—

> Barring accidents, we should arrive at four p.m.
> Generally speaking, he was well behaved.

2. Frequent errors occur in letter endings such as :—

> Hoping to see you soon,
>
> Your loving friend,
>
> JIM.

First of all, there is no predicate here, so it cannot be a sentence. If " I am " is added after soon, then it becomes a sentence and the *hoping* qualifies " I."

9. A **Gerund** must be qualified unless it has the same subject as the finite verb:—as,

> Through mistaking his identity, the police arrested the wrong man.

But: Through their mistaking his identity, the prisoner was allowed to escape.

EXERCISE III

Re-write the following faulty sentences in correct English :—

1. Let us to do it.
2. I shall to visit you soon.
3. Bid him to dance.
4. He hoped to have attended the meeting.
5. He intended to have been present.
6. He expected to have gone before them.
7. I had rang the bell before entering.
8. I seen it myself.
9. The Channel has been swam several times.
10. The river overfled its banks.

11. The distance was flew in three hours.

12. In early times it was not believed the world was round.

13. I ask him to send them and he replied that he could not.

14. He did not even know that two and two were four.

15. The child should insist on weeping.

16. He would be pleased to help as so much has been done for him.

17. We will arrive at 2.30 p.m.

18. We will expect you about noon.

19. We shall proceed no further with this business because it is wrong.

20. I must insist on it—you will go to sea.

21. I assure you I have not and never could sing.

22. He hoped to but never managed.

23. No reward has or can be offered.

24. He wanted to and walked the rest of the way.

25. I never have and never will support any lottery.

26. Cantering up the avenue, the view was magnificent.

27. Swinging through the air, we watched the monkeys with delight.

28. For sale—car by commercial damaged by air raid.

29. Hoping for an early reply,

Yours faithfully,

J. NIVEN.

30. Walking along by the side of the lake, the hill was visible.

31. Considering the condition of trade these days, the accounts are highly satisfactory.

32. Mantelpiece offered for sale by proprietor carved by famous sculptor.

33. On account of being absent, the goods were given to others.

34. On account of fouling the points, the accident occurred.

35. Through avoiding contact, the spread of the disease was confined to a small area.

36. He was annoyed at the jockey mounting the wrong horse.

37. He failed to appreciate the lawyer pleading with such emotion for such a poor specimen of humanity.

D. The Adjective—Comparison, etc.

1. The **Comparative Degree** of the adjective is used when two things, or two sets of things, are compared:—as,

Willie is *taller* than John.

This selection is *wider* than that.

Notes.—

1. Comparatives are generally followed by than. Exceptions :—superior, inferior, exterior, interior. The Comparatives of these Latin forms are followed by to.

2. The thing compared must be always excluded from the class with which it is compared when we use the Comparative Degree :—as,

She is taller than any girl in the room, ought to be She is taller than any *other* girl in the room.

3. Adjectives denoting shape, direction, nationality, and adjectives of material require great care when being compared.

(Yet we do use the comparative in such expressions as :—Tom's limbs are rounder than John's. But if some one is British, can he be more British ?)

4. Many adjectives on account of their meaning ought not to be compared, *e.g.* infinite, unique. impossible, everlasting.

2. The **Superlative Degree** of the adjective is used when more than two things are compared:—as,

She is the *tallest* girl in the class.

Note.—

When we use the Superlative Degree the thing compared must be included in the class with which the comparison is made :—as,

She is the prettiest of the other girls, ought to be She is the prettiest of all the girls.

3. The use of the **Definite and Indefinite Articles.**—The faults with the use of the articles are either omitting them when they ought to be inserted or inserting them when they ought to be omitted.

He made outstanding success of his task (*an* must be inserted before outstanding).

James, youngest of the sons, succeeded (*the* should be inserted before youngest).

The poet and painter may mean one person : if two separate persons are intended, then write:—

The poet and the painter.

4. *Like* is an **adjective**, not a **conjunction**:—as,

They all said he was *like* me.

Don't be a naughty boy *like* James was. This is wrong: put as (a conjunction) or such as instead of like.

EXERCISE IV

Re-write the following faulty sentences in correct English :—

1. He was superior than him.
2. John had one brother and he was the tallest.
3. He was braver than all the others.
4. James was cleverer than anybody in his class.
5. Mary is the heaviest of all the other girls.
6. Choose the easiest of the two alternatives.
7. He was one most unique example of extravagance.
8. To do it that way would be more impossible even than to do it the other way.
9. The black and white dogs met in the park.
10. A yellow and black flag is the national standard.
11. He is taking active interest in the movement.
12. James, youngest of the family, succeeded to the estate.
13. The poet and prose writer are not so privileged.
14. Do not sing like he does.
15. Do it like we used to do.

E. The Preposition.

1. A preposition governs the objective case:—as,

   I gave the book to *her*.

2. *Without, except* are prepositions and not conjunctions:—as,

   He completed the task *without* my aid.
   All the members of the team, *except* the goal-keeper, were capped.

3. *Between* refers to two persons or things; *among* refers to more than two:—as,

> Divide it *between* the two of you.
> He distributed the gifts *among* his many friends.

F. The Conjunction.

1. *Whether or not* is used rather than whether or no.

2. *Neither* must be followed by *nor*, *either* by *or*, *not only* by *but also*:—

> *Neither* you *nor* I can afford to neglect our work.
> You'll *either* go to school *or* (go) to bed.
> They found *not only* gold *but also* precious stones.

Note.—

The first correlative must be placed before the same part of speech as the second.

EXERCISE V

Re-write the following faulty sentences in correct English :—

1. Divide the apple among the two of you.
2. The crowd divided the spoil between themselves.
3. Neither he or his brother had stolen it.
4. Either expecting success nor hoping to evade disaster, they took the decision.
5. Not only was he lazy but also dishonest.
6. He gave she an apple.
7. I cannot get out without I do my lessons.

II. LAWS OF STYLE.

Errors in composition may occur through
  A. Wrong selection of words.
  B. Using wrong forms of words.
  C. Faulty arrangement of words.

A. Selection of Words.

Make sure that the words you select for your composition are sanctioned by a dictionary and that you use them as reputable modern writers would use them.

If we comply with these general directions, we find that there are certain classes of words which we are not permitted to use in composition unless we have a particular reason for doing so. For example, certain words are used only in Scotland and they might not be understood by readers other than Scottish.

You should avoid using:—

1. Words that are no longer in use (*i.e.* obsolete words or **archaisms**) such as:—*wight, yclept.*

2. Words that are used only in conversation and that are not regarded as sufficiently dignified when written (unless in dialogue). This class of words is called **Colloquialisms**, Slang or Vulgar terms.

Examples:

pal, rotter, digs (lodgings), *tough guy, can't, don't.*

3. Words that are used only by specialists— **Scientific**, **Legal** and **Technical terms**.

Examples:

heterodyne, transhumance.

4. Words and phrases from **foreign languages**, unless they have been fully adopted by our language.

Examples:

bête noire, quo vadis ? *réchauffé.*

5. Words that have been invented, termed **Neologisms**, or Coinages, such as:—*elevenish, squanderise, to third degree* (someone).

6. Words that are used only in certain districts called **Dialect terms**, such as :—*anent, loup, ingle.*

B. Be certain that you use words in their **proper sense**. For example, never use the verb to aggravate to convey the meaning of to annoy: to aggravate means to make worse (*e.g.* to aggravate the pain). Individual and person do not mean the same. If people cannot get your meaning accurately, there must be something faulty in your attempt to express it. As we write or speak primarily to convey meaning, a writer or speaker ought to do his utmost to express accurately the meaning he desires to convey.

Avoid having your meaning indistinct (**ambiguity**). This fault in writing frequently occurs through:—

a. Using a word capable of being interpreted in different ways, as:—

His smart appearance delighted us—may mean—

(1) The neatness of his dress or (2) his arrival up to time.

Please *observe* the rules—may mean—

(1) Read and note the rules, or
(2) Obey the rules.

b. Confusion in the use of pronouns causes
ambiguity: this fault is very common with careless
and inexperienced writers.

> The Captain told the orderly that *he* would
> arrive in good time and that *he* would be
> present when the attack took place.

The pronoun *he* may refer to the Captain or to
the orderly.

c. The leaving out of necessary words also causes
ambiguity:—as,

> The teacher scolded the boys more than the
> parents.

This might mean (1) The teacher scolded the
boys more than he scolded the parents, or (2) The
teacher scolded the boys more than the parents
scolded the boys.

C. Faulty arrangement of words and phrases.

Consider these sentences:—

a. Erected to the glory of God and to the memory
of John Faithful, killed accidentally by his
brother David.

> In the above sentence the arrangement of
> the words is at fault: it should be:—
> Erected by his brother David to the glory
> of God and to the memory of John Faithful,
> killed accidentally.

b. Those who oppose our policy in India are
many.

> Here we are in doubt whether this means
> (1) Those in India who oppose our policy
> are many, or (2) Those who oppose our

Indian policy (*i.e.* our policy relating to India) are many.

c. He did not play the piano yesterday as he wished.

This might mean (1) He did not play the piano yesterday at all, though he wished to do so, or (2) He did not play the piano yesterday in the manner in which he wished to play it—*i.e.* he played badly.

A few General Rules to guide you in keeping to the normal order of words:—

1. The usual order of a sentence is:—Subject, predicate and object:—as,

The dog killed the rat.

Notes.—

1. A complement follows the object if the verb is transitive :—as, They elected him emperor.

2. The indirect object when used without a preposition precedes the direct object :—as, She gave him a sixpence. But :—She gave a sixpence to him.

2. When you are composing, keep as close together as you can things that should be thought of together. This means that qualifying or modifying words, phrases and clauses should be placed as close as possible to the words they qualify or modify.

Accordingly, relative pronouns will require to be placed close to their antecedents.

He shot the dog that had run away from home with a pistol.

If we put the phrase " with a pistol " after dog, we are still breaking Rule 2.

With a pistol he shot the dog that had run away from home. This correction complies with Rule 2 and improves the sentence.

> Mr. Jones was much annoyed with the doctor because he did not call, having summoned him twice.

Applying Rule 2, we get:—

Mr. Jones, having summoned the doctor twice, was very much annoyed with him because he did not call.

> The man met with an accident and died in hospital whom I called on yesterday.

Here we find the antecedent *man* and the relative pronoun *whom* too far apart.

By keeping them close together the sentence is greatly improved, thus:—The man, on whom I called yesterday, met with an accident and died in hospital.

> He felled his opponent with his heavy club swinging it round his head.

Swinging is a present participle and refers to he: accordingly, we must put it close to he.

Swinging his heavy club round his head, he felled his opponent.

3. Do not use unnecessary words or repeat your meaning unnecessarily (**Redundancy**).

He wrote his *own* autobiography. This statement is at fault, because autobiography means a life story of someone written by that person. One man may write the biography, but he cannot write the autobiography, of another man.

EXERCISE VI

Re-write the following faulty sentences in correct or good English:—

1. The prisoner effected a speedy getaway.
2. He said it was a lot of baloney.
3. He was a tough guy and no mistake.
4. At 10.30 p.m. he kicked the bucket.
5. I can assure you I was fair fed up.
6. Don't be angry at me.
7. He corresponded to him regularly.
8. He asked me whither he should accept or no.
9. When he spotted the prisoner, he was astonished.
10. She did nothing but aggravate him.
11. The modern transport of to-day is superior than that of any other age.
12. His own autobiography was a best-seller.
13. He was granted the sole salt monopoly for the country.
14. It is obvious and patent that he suffers from a deterioration of his kidneys.
15. The vehicle was an automobile, that went by itself.
16. He is the same individual as called yesterday.
17. WANTED—Chauffeur-gardener to look after chickens over military age. (*Advertisement.*)
18. Don't kill your wife with washing. Let us do it for you. (*Laundry advertisement.*)

ERRORS DUE TO FAULTY IDIOM.

There are certain generally accepted and re-garded as fixed ways of expression peculiar to languages or peculiar to the language spoken in a district (*i.e.* a dialect).

Sometimes this idiom conforms to the rules of grammar, but sometimes it does not. For example, " It's me! " is not strictly grammatical, as the verb *to be* takes the same case after it as before it. Yet " It's me! " is accepted as good English—idiomatic English.

We are not using idiomatic English if we say:—

I don't love him like you do.

Like is not a conjunction: the conjunction *as* is required instead of like.

Your special attention is directed to the use of the phrases *there is* and *there are*. In such phrases we use what may be called a Provisional or anticipatory subject as the real subject follows.

For example, Once upon a time there were three bears. Three bears is the real subject. We could express the same sentence thus:—" Once upon a time three bears were—but this would not be good idiomatic English. Note that what follows the expressions there is (was) there are (were) *conditions the number of the verb in the phrase*. Far too many young writers make the mistake of following the expression *there is* (was) with a plural subject :—as,

There was many people present: or, there are (were) by a singular subject:—as,

There were a large crop of potatoes this autumn.

Idiomatic usage demands the use of the correct preposition after verbs if the intended meaning is to be conveyed. Thus, we congratulate a person *on* his success not for his success. We dissuade someone *from* doing something not against.

EXERCISE VII

Correct the following expressions which are unidiomatic :—

1. The new member of the House made his *first* speech.
2. He *fixed* his colours to the mast.
3. He *raised* the sponge.
4. To temper the wind for the *sheared* lamb.
5. To show the *cleft* foot.
6. She was *addicted* to charitable acts.
7. Amazed *with* his luck.
8. Covered *by* glory.
9. He dabbled *with* stocks.
10. He *rummaged* the drawer.
11. He ransacked through the house.
12. The biter was *bitten*.
13. She went down on her *bent* knees to plead her cause.

EXERCISE VIII

Supply suitable prepositions to go with the following verbs and use verbs and preposition correctly in phrases or sentences :—

boast—	composed—	infested—
conform—	dispense—	antagonistic—
confide—	comment—	advised—
consequent—	distrustful—	agree—
result—	responsible—	treat—
triumph—	acquiesce—	different—

EXERCISE IX

There is something wrong with the following sentences ; correct the idiom or the expression of it :—

1. He was at his wit's ends in the matter.
2. He had it at his finger's end.

3. Unfortunately she enjoys poor health.
4. Their friendship was close knitted.
5. The jumper was close knit.
6. As he was our best runner, he was the hope to the House.
7. That was a mean trick—under the belt in fact.
8. He was an adherent to the Labour Party.
9. He was a chip off the old block.
10. Get a move on—don't rest with your oars.
11. A stitch in time saves several.
12. There's many a slip 'twixt the cup and the mouth.
13. He was penny wise and shilling foolish.
14. There's no use trying to make bricks without clay.

EXERCISE X

Correct the mistakes in or improve the expression of the following, which were intended as sentences. They have been selected from pupils' compositions. Put your knowledge of analysis to a practical use :—

1. Through the summer cricket and tennis occupies the attention of enthusiasts.
2. Unless one has spent this season in the country one has no conception of the anxiety and bustle that takes place on the farm.
3. At school even there is a sign of autumn as boys bring chestnuts to play at different games with.
4. The corn and wheat has been late in ripening.
5. The fading of the flowers and falling of the leaves in the parks and gardens are a sign of autumn.
6. The birds mostly migrate to other warmer lands.
7. With the battle of the Atlantic still raging the difficulties of the Royal Navy become more and more heavier by the fact that an Enemy Raider

may easily slip into the Atlantic and attack a convoy, then make of into the Autumn fog leaving the desolate seamen to their fate.

8. Carver, like a mad dog, punched John with his bloody fist foaming at the mouth.

9. Theatres are only frequented infrequently as the seats are dearer than the picture house.

10. The further one is away from the screen in a picture house the better it is, which is the very opposite from the theatre.

11. In modern houses of to-day the walls are thin.

12. The old form of transport which was by means of a coach which was pulled by a pair of horses, or sometimes four.

13. His reactions are like most people in retirement.

14. There are a great variety of books.

15. Thus it is safer to spend your time cleaning the bicycle rather than repairing same.

16. I can't give them soup too often.

17. The people of Britain have grown more vegetables this year than ever before which, if Britain had not been a lazy country, would have taken place years ago.

18. Scenery in the films is much more varied to that of the theatre.

19. When the Nazi airmen wrought destruction on many homes.

20. This year men who glean the fields are scarce and so while taking a walk in the country many parties of boys are giving a hand.

21. All the flowers and plant growth is wakening up from their long winter sleep.

22. A play in a theatre lasts a good deal longer than any films and therefore more material is required.

23. If this does not happen the show is not a success which does not help the producer.

24. The old music is very nice to listen to and one does not usually get fed up no matter how long he listens for.

25. Where green is gradually giving way to brown and the wind whistling through the trees blowing dead crisp leaves off the already quite sapless branches and fungi round the bottom of the trunk.

26. Nearing the island, Goatfell stood boldly out from the other mountains.

27. Under the ground there run wires, which when a vehicle passes over them, the lights change.

28. The child lay awake some time watching the fire-light, when at last he fell asleep.

29. We heard a strange sound, but we soon realised it was only an owl.

30. Portia's father stated in his will that no one might marry her unless they chose the right casket.

31. Among them was the Prince of Morocco and the Prince of Arragon.

32. We looked at the windows coming up the road to see if they were properly blacked-out.

33. I thought of a good idea.

34. I shall try and find the book for to-morrow.

35. With my pocket money I would buy a useful book such as a dictionary, which will help you all through your life.

36. Talking of the Great War, the Highland regiments have shown conspicuous gallantry.

37. You then count the money your left.

38. Nearly every highlander has a clan of some sort which in the olden days were robbers and murders.

14

39. A postman has a tiring job as you have to go up and down stairs of tenement buildings.

40. I watched the queue diminish until it was about two or three people before me.

41. The Germans lashed me and on returning to my cell I was full of cuts and full of blood.

42. They knew what would of happened.

43. That was how the boys wanted more food.

44. Seeing that he had no sword he wrestled with his foe.

45. After I had finished my tea I got dressed.

46. Nearly every shop you passed there was always a queue.

47. The queues are because of the war as the ships are needed to bring war materials.

48. When I explained he thought differt.

49. The gas is harmless only that it makes the victim groggy.

50. It never said anything about blood in the bond.

51. It was an old man that owned the shop because I knew him.

52. The document only said a pound of flesh.

53. The war in Poland was getting worse.

54. We managed to get a board.

55. I have to go a long way to get to the place.

56. The next thing I minded was lying on my back on a sofa.

57. The Australians have shown their metal in this war.

CHAPTER XI

ARE YOU MENTALLY ALERT ?

THERE are so many things that we forget, so many things that we fail to notice, so many things that we misunderstand that it is necessary to train ourselves to exercise our memories, to sharpen our powers of observation, to pay close attention to what we hear or read and, perhaps most important of all, to know where to find the information we require. This chapter contains a number of exercises of different kinds which may help you towards these ends.

EXERCISE I

Complete the following :—

1. Boy scout is to cub, as girl guide is to............
2. Dog is to pup, as cat is to............
3. Goose is to gander, as buck is to............
4. Teacher is to pupil, as professor is to............
5. Twilight is to night, as dawn is to............
6. Pen is to sword, as writer is to............
7. Beef is to ox, as venison is to............
8. Navy is to W.R.N.S., as Air Force is to............
9. Master is to man, as mistress is to............
10. Man is to woman, as monastery is to............

EXERCISE II

In each of the following series of words, all the words but one belong to a definite class. Name the class and the exception in each group :—

1. Apple, plum, cherry, onion, strawberry.
2. Iron, ebony, brass, zinc, lead.

3. Shoe, sandal, clay, gaiter, mocassin.
4. Duck, hen, goose, turkey, lark.
5. Pea, barley, filbert, lentil, bean.
6. Lion, tiger, deer, cougar, puma.
7. Blenheim, Skua, Fulmar, Junker, Wellington.
8. Malay, Afghan, Moor, Hindu, Persian.
9. Paris, Morocco, Calcutta, Cape Town, New York.
10. Sun dial, compass, watch, chronometer, metronome.

EXERCISE III

Arrange the words in the following groups in order of their significance, importance, or value, or force :—

1. Mob, army, congregation, crowd, gang.
2. Speak, whisper, scream, shout, bellow.
3. Gleam, glitter, glisten, glint, glimmer.
4. Pain, anguish, feeling, suffering, agony.
5. Stench, odour, smell, perfume, aroma.
6. Tolerate, suffer, approve, endure, permit.
7. Vanity, presumption, pride, conceit, arrogance.
8. Hut, mansion, hovel, bungalow, palace.
9. Hold, clench, grasp, clutch, grip.
10. Tarpon, salmon, sprat, whale, herring.

EXERCISE IV

Arrange in pairs the proverbs that seem to contradict each other :—

1. Out of sight, out of mind.
2. Fine feathers make fine birds.
3. Many hands make light work.
4. What's done cannot be undone.
5. Too many cooks spoil the broth.
6. Absence makes the heart grow fonder.
7. A rolling stone gathers no moss.

8. All is not gold that glitters.
9. Home-keeping youths have ever homely wits.
10. It is never too late to mend.

EXERCISE V

What is wrong with the following definitions?

(Remember that a full definition should give the class to which the thing belongs and the points of difference between it and all other members of the class.)

1. A banana is a yellow fruit.
2. Tea is what you drink instead of coffee.
3. An egg is a breakfast fruit.
4. A policeman is a man who hates criminals.
5. Man is a two-legged animal without feathers.
6. Oats are food for men in Scotland and for horses in England.
7. A kangaroo is like a rabbit but larger.
8. Medicine is something out of a bottle and has a nasty taste.
9. A trust is a body of people who control a certain commodity—*e.g.* Brains Trust.
10. An ambassador is an honest man sent to lie abroad for the good of his country.

EXERCISE VI

The following sentences contain parts of different proverbs. Rearrange them to restore the original proverbs :—

1. A burnt child gathers no moss.
2. Make hay before you leap.
3. Little strokes wait for no man.
4. A stitch in time is worth two in the bush.
5. A rolling stone is better than no bread.
6. Pride goes while the sun shines.
7. A bird in the hand dreads the fire.

8. Half a loaf saves nine.
9. Look before a fall.
10. Time and tide fell great oaks.

EXERCISE VII

Give the questions to which the following are the answers :—

1. A great naval victory at which Nelson died.
2. The name of the inn which belonged to the parents of Jim Hawkins in *Treasure Island*.
3. Taxes levied on goods coming into the country.
4. The Jew in *The Merchant of Venice*.
5. The boy who remained on the deck of a burning ship.
6. The Bible of the Mohammedans.
7. The name given to a German submarine.
8. The colour of this light is red and it is on the left-hand side of the ship.
9. It is the biggest bell of St. Stephen's Tower at the Houses of Parliament.
10. The name of this printer's character is ampersand.

EXERCISE VIII

Which of the following statements suggest that our future is decided by (*a*) our own efforts, (*b*) God, or Fate, or Luck ?

1. If your name is on the bullet, it won't miss you.
2. Trust in God and keep your powder dry.
3. If chance will have me king, why chance may crown me without my stir.
4. The best man always wins.
5. Heaven helps those who help themselves.
6. Waves and winds are on the side of the skilled navigator.
7. Put a stout heart to a stey brae.

8. God is on the side of the biggest battalions.
9. Man is man and master of his fate.
10. There's a divinity that shapes our ends.
    Rough-hew them how we will.

EXERCISE IX

From what reference book, person, or association would you seek information on the following problems ?

1. The health of your dog.
2. Keeping bees.
3. Making a will.
4. A continental tour.
5. Income Tax.
6. Notifying a birth, death, etc.
7. Eye-strain.
8. Daily proceedings in Parliament.
9. Producing a school play.
10. Buying a house.

EXERCISE X

What industry, activity, association or persons do you associate with the following ?

Fleet Street, Hollywood, Covent Garden, Paternoster Row, Scotland Yard, Threadneedle Street, Downing Street, Wall Street, Monte Carlo, The Rand.

EXERCISE XI

Explain briefly the following :—

1. How to tell the place of registration of a motor car.
2. When and why a policeman wears a white coat.
3. How to tell a cigarette smoker.
4. Why fish are darker on the upper part of the body.
5. Why the men at the rear of a procession marching to the music of a band at the head of the procession are unable to keep in step with the men at the front.

6. Why you prefer having a pound (weight) of half-crowns to a half-pound of crowns.

7. Why some birds pretend to be injured when you come near their nests.

8. Why a football crowd is more excitable than a cricket crowd.

9. Why railway embankments are planted with grass.

10. How many stars and how many stripes are there in the American Flag and the reason.

EXERCISE XII

Pick out the proverbs which correspond in meaning with the statements that follow :—

1. *When the cat's away, the mice will play.*
2. *A shoemaker should stick to his last.*
3. *New brooms sweep clean.*
4. *It's of no use crying over spilt milk.*
5. *One swallow does not make a summer.*
6. People should express opinions only on what they understand.
7. Servants and schoolboys take advantage of the absence of their masters.
8. What's done cannot be undone.
9. Because a thing happens once, it does not mean that it will happen always.
10. People are generally enthusiastic when they take up a new job.

Recast the meaning of the following sentences as well-known proverbs :—

1. An inferior generally copies his master.
2. Appearances are often deceptive.
3. Those who have faults should not criticise others.

4. Don't do anything decisive until you have carefully considered the possible results.

5. We learn caution from our mishaps.

EXERCISE XIII

What is absurd about the following?

1. I will be drowned and nobody shall save me.

2. Is that your own hare or a wig ? (said to a man carrying a hare).

3. Red hair is a sign of bad temper.

4. As the red light was showing, we started to cross the street.

5. The statement of the Irishman who said, that if he knew where he was to die, he would never go near the place.

6. The musical tourist who was anxious to hear the Sound of Jura.

7. Britain has always muddled through so why should we worry about making mistakes ?

8. For half-a-crown, I shall send you instructions how to make a fortune.

9. A man is at liberty to marry his widow's niece.

10. Surely you believe this ; everybody knows it is true.

EXERCISE XIV

What are the occupations of the persons described in the following quotations ?   Give reasons.

1. He was the mildest mannered man
   That ever scuttled a ship, or cut a throat.

2. His shrapnel helmet set a-tilt,
   His bombing waistcoat sagging low,
   His rifle slung across his back.

3. My tears must stop, for every drop
   Hinders needle and thread.

4. When Barney Buntline slewed his quid
   And said to Billy Bowline.

5. A matron old, whom we——name
   Who boasts unruly brats with birch to tame.

6. When any sick to me apply
   I physics, bleeds and sweats 'em,
   If after that they choose to die
   Why Verily !   I. LETTSOM.

7. Crouched in the dripping dark
   With steaming shoulders stark,
   The men who hew the coal to feed my fire.

8.   Some watcher of the skies
   When a new planet swims into his ken.

9. When he with fruitless pain skimm'd the brook
   And the coy fish rejects the skipping hook.

10. And because he prospered with sickle and scythe,
    With cattle afield and labouring ewe,
    Antony was uncommonly blythe.

EXERCISE XV

Give reasons for the following facts:—

1. Arctic explorers often grow beards.

2. Street hawkers are generally hoarse.

3. Outside pipes are generally wrapped up.

4. A marble is often put in an iron kettle.

5. Men of the Air Force are usually young and alert.

6. Students are said to have a stoop.

7. Metal teapots often have wooden handles.

8. Sailors walk with a rolling gait.

9. Many American words and phrases are entering the language.

10. A boy feels tired when asked to do an errand for his mother, but hurries off to play football.

CHAPTER XII

INTERPRETATION

THERE is no longer the intensive study of poetry and prose which used to be common in schools. As a result, you read a great deal more during your school course, but it is probably true that your study of literature is not so exact or critical. It is for this reason that you will find Interpretation specially useful, for, in it you are required to make a close study of selected passages, to understand them fully and to express the meaning in your own words. You will see how the great writers handle grammar, figures of speech, and other devices of style, and you will find that your ability to handle the English language is steadily improving in consequence. Here are some of the rules you must observe in this kind of work.

Some Hints on Interpretation

1. Read the whole passage carefully until you have given yourself the chance to understand it thoroughly.

2. Read over the questions set and make sure you understand what is required.

3. Mark the section of the passage containing the answer to each question.

4. Always answer in sentences and, unless otherwise directed, in your own words. You may use single words or short phrases from the

passage, if they are simple and in common use. Never use words or phrases from the passage which require explanation.

5. Number each new exercise and begin it with a new paragraph.

6. Do not add information which is not contained in the passage unless the question, and this is unlikely, requires it.

7. If you quote from the passage, *e.g.* a phrase or a figure of speech, use quotation marks.

8. Write down words and phrases you are asked to explain and give the meaning as used in the passage.

Note.— Abstract words, e.g. *philanthropy, can best be explained by thinking of definite examples.*

9. A summary should always be very much shorter than the original passage and contain only the essential facts.

Study the following examples :—

1. **Read this passage carefully and then answer the questions :**—

THE THRUSH'S NEST.

Within a thick and spreading hawthorn bush,
  That overhung a molehill large and round,
I heard from morn to morn a merry thrush
  Sing hymns to sunrise, and I drank the sound
With joy; and, often an *intruding guest*,
  I watched her *secret toils* from day to day—
How true she warped the moss, to form a nest,
  And modelled it within with wood and clay;

And by and by, like heathbells gilt with dew,
  There lay her shining eggs, as bright as flowers,
Ink-spotted over shells of greeny blue ;
  And there I witnessed, in the sunny hours,
A brood of *Nature's minstrels* chirp and fly,
Glad as that sunshine and the laughing sky.

(a) Describe in three short sentences what the poet saw in the hawthorn bush.

(b) Describe the eggs of the thrush.

(c) Give three words that express (1) happiness and (2) brightness.

(d) Give the meaning of the following phrases as used in the passage :—
  intruding guest, secret toils, nature's minstrels.

(e) Point out one example of metaphor, simile, personification.

(f) Make a particular analysis of the sentence :—
  Often . . . day to day.

(a) The poet saw the bird make her nest by twisting moss, and shaping it from the inside with wood and clay
  He saw that the eggs were laid in the nest.
  He saw the young birds as they sang and flew about.

(b) The eggs of the thrush were bright and greenish-blue in colour, and were spotted as with ink.

(c) The words are (1) merry, sing, joy ; (2) gilt, shining, bright.

(d) *Intruding guest* ; an uninvited, but not unwelcome, visitor.
  secret toils ; labours kept concealed.
  Nature's minstrels ; singers by instinct.

(e) Metaphor : I drank the sound.
  Simile : like heathbells gilt with dew.
  Personification : the laughing sky.

(g)   **Particular Analysis**

SUBJECT		PREDICATE			
Noun or Equivalent	Enlargement of Subject	Finite Verb	Object	Complement	Extension
I	an intruding guest	watched	her secret toils		often (degree) from day to day (time)

2. **Read the following passage carefully and then answer the questions which follow it :—**

PASSAGE FROM SOHRAB AND RUSTUM.

Go to ! if Iran's chiefs are old, then I
Am older : if the young are weak, the King
Errs strangely : for the King, for Kai Khosroo,
Himself is young, and honours younger men,
And lets the aged *moulder* to their graves.
Rustum he loves no more, but loves the young—
The young may rise at Sohrab's *vaunts*, not I.
For what care I, though all speak Sohrab's fame ?
For would that I myself had such a son,
And not that one slight helpless girl I have,
A son so fam'd, so brave, to send to war.
And I to *tarry* with the snow-hair'd Zal,
My father, whom the robber Afghans vex,
And clip his borders short, and drive his herds,
And he has none to guard his weak old age.
There would I go, and hang his armour up,
And with my great name *fence* that weak old man,
And spend the goodly treasure I have got,
And rest my age, and hear of Sohrab's fame.

(a) What is the name of the speaker ? From what line
    do you learn this ?

(*b*) Why is he angry with the King ? What is the name of the King ?

(*c*) What mark of age does his father show ?

(*d*) Explain how his father is troubled.

(*e*) How does the speaker wish to end his life ?

(*f*) What shows that he is not jealous of Sohrab ?

(*g*) Scan lines 1, 2. Name the metre.

(*h*) Explain : moulder, vaunts, tarry, fence.

(*a*) The name of the speaker is Rustum. See line 6.

(*b*) The King, being a young man, honours young men and does not care if old men live or die. The name of the King is Kai Khosroo.

(*c*) His hair is white.

(*d*) The Afghans trouble him, seize the lands on the frontier, and carry off his cattle.

(*e*) He would like to live with his father, give up warfare and protect his father by his fame. He would spend his great wealth, live quietly, and hear of the deeds of Sohrab.

(*f*) He wishes he had a son like Sohrab and would like to hear of his renown.

(*g*) Go to ! if Iran's chiefs are old, then I

Am older : if the young are weak, the King

The metre is Iambic Pentameter.

(*h*) *Moulder* : rot.

vaunts : boasts.

tarry : wait.

fence : enclose and protect.

3. Read the following passage carefully and then answer the questions which follow :—

As a train approaches a station, it comes to the distant signal, painted yellow and showing a yellow light at night. This signal gives the driver early warning of the position of the home signal, enabling him to check his speed to be ready to stop at the home signal if this has not been lowered in the meantime. That is, if the distant signal is set " all clear," the driver knows that the home signal is also at " all clear," but if the distant signal is at " danger " the home signal may be at " danger."

Although he may pass the distant signal when set at " caution," he must be prepared to pull up at the home signal. For this reason the distant signal is placed sufficiently far from the home signal to enable the train to be pulled up at the latter if necessary. The standard distance in Great Britain between distant and home signals varies from 600 yards on a rising gradient to 1,000 yards on a falling gradient.

(a) Why is the distant signal visible by day or by night ?

(b) Explain briefly the use of the distant signal to the driver.

(c) What information does the distant signal give regarding the home signal ?

(d) Which warning controls both signals ?

(e) Name the three settings of the signals.

(f) What is the importance of the distant signal ?

(g) Distinguish between a rising gradient and a falling gradient.

(h) Make a general analysis of the sentence : " Although he . . . signal."

(a) The distant signal is painted yellow and shows a yellow light at night.

(b) It prepares the driver for the home signal and thus enables him to check his speed.

(c) If it is at " all clear," so also is the home signal.

(d) The " all clear " controls both signals.

(e) The three settings are ' all clear,' ' danger ' and ' caution.'

(f) There is sufficient distance to allow the driver to pull up at the home signal.

(g) A rising gradient is one in which the slope of the ground is upwards and a falling gradient is one in which the slope is downwards.

(h) **General Analysis**

No.	CLAUSE	KIND	RELATION
A	He....................... signal	Prin.	Independent.
a₁	Although............... signal	Adv.	of Concession, mod. " must be prepared."
a₂	When (it is) set at caution **Complex Sentence**	Adv.	of Time, mod. " may pass."

4. Read the following poem and then answer the questions which follow it :—

To DAFFODILS.

Fair Daffodils, we weep to see
  You haste away so soon ;
And yet the early-rising Sun
  Has not *attained* his noon.
    Stay, stay
  Until the hasting day
    Has run
  But to the *even-song* ;
And *having prayed together*, we
Will go with you along.

We have short time to stay, as you,
  We have as short a Spring ;
As quick a growth to meet decay
  As you, or anything.
      We die,
As your hours do, and dry
      Away,
Like to the Summer's rain ;
Or, as the pearls of morning's dew,
Ne'er to be found again.

(a) What thought arouses the pity of the poet ?

(b) What request does he make ?

(c) What are the three stages common to mankind and the flowers ?

(d) Name two other things that pass away as quickly.

(e) Explain : attained, even-song, having pray'd together, pearls.

(f) Give an example of apostrophe, personification, simile.

(a) The poet regrets that the daffodils should fade so quickly.

(b) He asks the daffodils to wait until the end of the day, and states that we human beings will then accompany them.

(c) Both men and flowers have a period of early life, a period of growth, and one of decay.

(d) The two mentioned in the poem are (1) the summer's rain, (2) the morning's dew.

(e) *attained* : reached.
even-song : an evening service.
having pray'd together : as the daffodils fade, the flowers bend over just as the heads of human beings do in prayer.
pearls : round and bright drops.

(*f*) Apostrophe : " Fair daffodils."

Personification : the hasting day has run but to the close."

Simile : like to the summer's rain.

5. **Read the following passage and then answer the questions which follow it :—**

JOHN RIDD RIDES THE MARE.

First she reared upright in the air, and struck me full on the nose with her comb, till I bled worse than Robin Snell made me ; and then down with her fore-feet deep in the straw, and her hind-feet going to heaven. Finding me stick to her like wax, for my mettle was up as hers was, away she flew with me swifter than ever I went before, or since, I trow. She drove full-head at the cob-wall—" Oh, Jack, slip off," screamed Annie—then she turned like light ; when I thought to crush her, and ground my left knee against it. " Mux me," I cried, for my breeches were broken, and short words went the furthest—" if you kill me, you shall die with me." Then she took the court-yard gate at a leap, knocking my words between my teeth, and then right over a quick set hedge, as if the sky were a breath to her ; and away for the water-meadows, while I lay on her neck like a child at the breast and wished I had never been born. Straight away, all in front of the wind, and scattering clouds around her, all I knew of the speed we made was the frightful flash of her shoulders, and her mane like trees in a tempest. I felt the earth under us rushing away, and the air left far behind us, and my breath came and went, and I prayed to God, and was sorry to be so late of it.

(*a*) Explain briefly the THREE devices of the mare in her attempt to unseat the rider.

(*b*) Quote THREE references to illustrate Jack's state of alarm.

(c) How did he realise the speed of the mare's gallop to the water-meadows ?

(d) Give TWO examples of simile.

(e) Make a general analysis of the sentence : " Finding me . . . I trow."

(a) (1) The mare reared up on her forelegs and hind legs alternately.

(2) The mare galloped at full speed towards the wall and then, turning sideways, crushed his leg against it.

(3) Leaping over the courtyard gate and a hedge, the mare galloped at great speed towards the water- meadows.

(b) (1) " I wished I had never been born."

(2) " My breath came and went."

(3) " I prayed to God and was sorry to be so late of it."

(c) He saw the terrifying movement of her shoulders and her mane tossing about. The ground seemed to run past, and the air was left behind.

(d) Simile : " I stuck to her like wax."

" her mane like trees in a tempest."

(e) ### General Analysis

No.	CLAUSE	KIND	RELATION
A	Finding me stick to her like wax away she flew with me swifter . . .	Prin.	Independent.
a_1	than ever I went before .	Adv.	Degree mod. " swifter."
a_2	or ever [I went] since .	Adv.	Degree mod. " swifter."
B	For my mettle was up .	Prin.	Co-ord. with A.
b.	as hers was . . .	Adv.	Manner mod. " was."
	Compound-Complex		

6. Read the following passage and then **answer the** questions which   follow it:—

THE FIGHT IN THE ROUND-HOUSE.

By this, my pistols were ready, and there was nothing to do but listen and wait. While the brush lasted, I had not the time to think if I was frighted ; but now, when all was still again, my mind ran upon nothing else. The thought of the sharp swords and the cold steel was strong in me ; and presently, when I began to hear stealthy steps and a brushing of men's clothes against the round-house wall, and knew they were taking their places in the dark, I could have found it in my mind to cry out aloud.

All this was upon Alan's side ; and I had begun to think my share of the fight was at an end, when I heard some one drop softly on the roof above me.

Then there came a single call on the sea-pipe, and that was the signal. A knot of them made one rush of it, cutlass in hand, against the door ; and at the same moment, the glass of the skylight was dashed in a thousand pieces, and a man leaped through and landed on the floor. Before he got his feet, I had clapped a pistol to his back, and might have shot him, too ; only at the touch of him (and him alive) my whole flesh misgave me, and I could no more pull the trigger than I could have flown.

(*a*) State THREE reasons for the fears of the writer.

(*b*) What part of the round-house has (*a*) Alan, (*b*) David (the writer), to defend ?

(*c*) What was the signal for the attack ?

(*d*) Write down the words that suggest the speed and force of the attack.

(*c*) What references suggest that this attack took place at sea ?

(*f*) What prevented David from shooting his opponent ?

(g) Make a general analysis of the sentence :—" Before he got . . . shot him, too."

(a) (1) He had nothing to do but wait and think.
    (2) He thought of the deadly weapons of his enemies.
    (3) He heard the sounds made by the men preparing for the attack.

(b) Alan had to guard the wall and David the roof and the window in it.

(c) The signal was a single sound made on a sea-pipe.

(d) The words which suggest speed and force are, knot, rush, dashed in a thousand pieces, leaped.

(e) The references to the sea pipe, cutlass, round-house, suggest the sea.

(f) The touch of a living body made him reluctant to destroy a fellow being.

(i)   **General Analysis**

No.	CLAUSE	KIND	RELATION
A	I had clapped a pistol to his back . . .	Prin.	Independent.
a_1	Before he got to his feet	Adv.	Time, mod. " had clapped."
B	And [I] might have shot him, too . . .	Prin.	Co-ord. with A.

Compound-Complex

EXERCISES IN INTERPRETATION

Section I—Passages suitable for Forms I and II.

1. Read the following passage carefully and then answer the questions which follow it:—

    No summons calls them to the tower,
    To spend the *hospitable* hour.

To Scotland's camp the Lord was gone,
His *cautious* dame, in bower alone,
Dreaded her castle to unclose,
So late, to unknown friends or foes.
On through the *hamlet* as they paced,
Before a porch whose front was graced
With bush and flagon trimly placed,
Lord Marmion drew his rein :
The village inn seemed large, though *rude* ;
Its cheerful fire and hearty food
Might well relieve his *train*.

(a) Why did the lady keep the castle closed ?

(b) What time of day did this happen ?

(c) How did Marmion recognise the inn ?

(d) Explain the meaning of the following words as used
in the passage :—
    hospitable, cautious, hamlet, rude, train.

(e) Write out the first two lines and mark the accented
syllables.

2. **Read this passage very carefully and then answer
the following questions:**—

My hawk is tired of perch and *hood*,
My idle greyhound *loathes* his food,
My horse is weary of his *stall*,
And I am sick of captive *thrall*.
I wish I were, as I have been,
Hunting the hart in forest green,
With bended bow and bloodhound free.
For that the life is meet for me.
I hate to learn the ebb of time
From yon dull steeple's drowsy chime,
Or mark it as the sunbeams crawl,
Inch after inch, along the wall.
The lark was wont my *matins* ring,
The sable rook my *vespers* sing ;

> These towers, although a king's they be,
> Have not a hall of joy for me.
> No more at dawning morn I rise
> And sun myself in Ellen's eyes,
> Drive the *fleet* deer the forest through,
> And homeward *wend* with evening dew ;
> A blithesome welcome blithly meet,
> And lay my *trophies* at her feet,
> While fled the eve on wing of glee,—
> That life is lost to love and me !

(a) What is the occupation in life of the speaker in the passage ? What has happened to him, and where is he living ?

(b) Show, from the passage, where you get your answers to (a).

(c) Describe a day in the former life of the speaker.

(d) How does he spend his days now ?

(e) Explain :—hood, loathes, stall, thrall, matins, vespers, fleet, wend, trophies.

(f) Make a general analysis of lines 5, 6, and 7.

(g) Point out and explain one figure of speech.

3. **Read the following passage carefully and then answer the questions which follow it:—**

> The *livelong* day Lord Marmion rode :
> The mountain path the Palmer showed,
> By glen and streamlet winded still,
> Where *stunted* birches hid the rill.
> They might not choose the lowland road,
> For the Merse *forayers* were *abroad*,
> Who, fired with hate and thirst of prey,
> Had scarcely failed to bar their way.
> Oft on the trampling band, from crown
> Of some tall cliff, the deer looked down ;
> On wing of jet, from his repose
> In the deep heath, the blackcock rose ;

Sprung from the gorse the timid roe,
Nor waited for the bending bow ;
And when the stony path began,
By which the *naked* peak they wan,
Up flew the snowy ptarmigan.

(a) Who guided the party of Marmion ?

(b) Why did they not take the lowland path ?

(c) What animals are mentioned ?

(d) Explain the meaning of the following words as used in the passage :—livelong ; stunted ; forayers ; abroad ; naked.

(e) What letter is not pronounced in ptarmigan ?

(f) Write out the first two lines and mark the accented syllables with an X.

4. **Read carefully the following poem and then answer the questions which follow it :—**

THE ROMAN ROAD.

The Roman Road runs straight and bare
As the pale parting line in hair
Across the heath. And thoughtful men
Contrast its days of Now and Then,
And delve, and measure, and compare ;
Visioning on the vacant air
Helmed legionaries, who proudly rear
The Eagle, as they pace again
          The Roman Road.

But no tall brass-helmed legionnaire
Haunts it for me. Uprises there
A mother's form upon my ken,
Guiding my infant steps, as when
We walked that ancient thoroughfare,
          The Roman Road.

                                        T. HARDY.

N.B.—**Give your answers in sentences.**

(a) Name a Roman Road.

(b) When thoughtful men see this road, what does it make them picture to themselves?

(c) Why do thoughtful men " delve, measure and compare " ?

(d) Give *one* noun that conveys the meaning contained in the words " thoughtful men that measure and compare."

(e) Of what does the Roman Road remind the poet ?

(f) Write down a simile used in the poem.

(g) Mark the syllables that are stressed or accented in the first line.

5. Read the following **poem** carefully **and answer the** questions which follow it :—

THE SCARECROW.

All winter through I bow my head
    Beneath the driving rain ;
The North Wind powders me with snow
    And blows me black again ;
At midnight neath a maze of stars
    I flame with glittering *rime*,
And stand, above the stubble, stiff
    As mail at morning-prime.
But when that child called Spring, and all
    His host of children, come,
Scattering their buds and dew upon
    These acres of my home,
Some *rapture* in my rags awakes ;
    I lift void eyes and scan
The skies for crows, those *ravening* foes
    Of my strange master, Man.
I watch him striding lank behind
    His clashing team, and know

Soon will the wheat swish body high
    Where once lay *sterile* snow ;
Soon shall I gaze across a sea
    Of *sun-begotten* grain,
Which my unflinching watch hath sealed
    For harvest once again.

(*a*) Describe what the scarecrow sees in winter.

(*b*) Describe what happens in spring.

(*c*) Describe the scene in summer.

(*d*) Give the meaning of the following words :—rime ;
    rapture ; ravening ; sterile ; sun-begotten.

(*e*) Make a general analysis of the last four lines.

6. **Read the following passage carefully and then
answer the questions which follow it:**—

Sweet was the sound, when oft at evening's close
Up yonder hill the village murmur rose ;
There, as I passed with careless steps and slow,
The mingled notes came soften'd from below ;
The swain responsive as the milkmaid sung,
The sober herd that low'd to meet their young :
The noisy geese that gabbled o'er the pool,
The playful children just let loose from school ;
The watchdog's voice that bay'd the whisp'ring
    wind,
And the loud laugh that spoke the *vacant mind* :
These all in sweet confusion sought the shade,
And fill'd each pause the nightingale had made,
But now the sounds of population fail,
No cheerful murmurs fluctuate in the gale,
No busy steps the grass-grown foot-way tread,
For all the bloomy flush of life is fled.
All but yon widow'd, solitary thing
That feebly bends beside the plashy spring ;
She, wretched matron, forc'd, in age, for bread,
To strip the brook with mantling cresses spread,

To pick her wintry faggot from the thorn,
To seek her nightly shed, and weep till morn ;
She only left of all the harmless train,
The *sad historian* of the pensive plain.

(*a*) Where was the poet when he heard the sounds ?

(*b*) What sounds were made by (1) birds, (2) animals, (3) human beings ?

(*c*) What proof is there of the present absence of any traffic ?

(*d*) What does the one survivor do for food, fire, and shelter ?

(*e*) Explain the phrases as used in the passage :—vacant mind ; sad historian.

(*f*) Give *three* examples of onomatopoeia.

(*g*) Write out the last two lines, scan them, and name the metre.

7. **Read the following passage carefully and then answer the questions which follow it :—**

The Water Rat was restless, and he did not exactly know why.   To all appearances the *summer's pomp* was still at fullest height, and although in the tilled acres green had given way to gold, though rowans were red-dening, and the woods were dashed here and there with a tawny fierceness, yet light and warmth and colour were still present, without any chilly fore-warnings of the passing year.   But the constant chorus of the orchards and hedges had shrunk to a *casual evensong* from a few yet unwearied performers ; the robin was beginning to assert himself once more ; and there was a feeling in the air of change and departure.   The cuckoo had long been silent ; but many another *feathered friend*, for months a part of the familiar landscape and its small society, was missing too, and it seemed that the ranks thinned steadily day by day.   Rat, ever observant of all winged movement, saw that it was taking daily a *southing tendency* ; and even as he lay in bed at night he thought he could make out, passing in the darkness overhead, the beat and quiver of *impatient pinions*, obedient to Nature's call.

(a) What signs of autumn were to be noticed in the vegetation ?

(b) How did the coming of autumn affect the birds ?

(c) What do we call this yearly movement of the birds ?

(d) What sound did Rat hear at night ?

(e) Explain : summer's pomp ; casual evensong ; feathered friend ; southing tendency ; impatient pinions.

(f) Make a particular analysis of the sentence :
But the constant . . . performers."

8. **Read the following passage and then answer the questions which follow it :—**

Meanwhile Pizarro and his followers were experiencing all the miseries which might have been expected from the character of the *barren* spot on which they were all imprisoned. They were, indeed, relieved from all *apprehensions* of the natives, since they had quitted the island on its occupation by the white men ; but they had to endure the pains of hunger even in a greater degree than they had formerly experienced in the wild woods of the neighbouring continent. Their principal food was crabs and such shell-fish as they could *scantily* pick up along the shores. *Incessant* storms of thunder and lightning, for it was the rainy season, swept over the devoted island, and half-drenched them with a perpetual flood. Thus, half-naked, and pining with famine, there were few in that little company who did not feel the spirit of enterprise quenched within them or who looked for any happier *termination* of their difficulties than that afforded by a return to Panama. The appearance of Tafur, therefore, with his two vessels, well stored with provisions, was greeted with all the rapture that a crew of a sinking wreck might feel on the arrival of some unexpected *succour* ; and the only thought, after satisfying the immediate *cravings* of hunger, was to embark and leave the detested isle for ever. —*The Conquest of Mexico.*

(*a*) Where had Pizarro and his followers come from, and where were they now situated ?

(*b*) " Imprisoned " does not here mean " in a prison building." What does it mean ?

(*c*) What sufferings had they to endure ?

(*d*) From what danger were they saved ? Why ?

(*e*) What do you think Pizarro was doing in this region ? In what sentence does the writer say that they had no wish to continue the work ? How did the adventure end ?

(*f*) Explain :—barren ; apprehensions ; scantily ; incessant ; termination ; succour ; cravings.

(*g*) Make a general analysis of the first sentence and a particular analysis of : " Incessant storms of thunder and lightning swept over the devoted island."

9. Read the following passage very carefully a number of times and then answer the questions which follow :—

Over against a London house, a corner house not far from Cavendish Square, a man with a wooden leg had sat for some years, with his remaining foot in a basket in cold weather, *picking up a living* in this wise :— Every morning at eight o'clock, he stumped to the corner, carrying a chair, a *clothes-horse*, a pair of trestles, a board, a basket, and an umbrella, all strapped together. Separating these, the board and trestles became a counter, the basket supplied a few small lots of fruit and sweets that he offered for sale upon it and became a foot-warmer, the unfolded clothes-horse displayed a choice collection of halfpenny *ballads* and became a *screen*, and the stool planted within it became his post for the rest of the day. All weathers saw the man at the post. This is to be accepted in a double sense, for he *contrived* a back to his wooden stool by placing it against a lamp-post. When the weather was wet, he put up his umbrella over his *stock-in-trade*, not over himself ; when the weather was dry, he *furled* that faded article, tied it round with a piece of *yarn*, and laid it crosswise under the trestles ; where it looked like an *unwholesomely-forced* lettuce that had lost in colour and crispness what it had gained in size.

(a) Suggest a title for this passage.

(b) Point out three references to the fact that the man had lost a leg.

(c) How was he able to carry so many articles ?

(d) To what two uses did he put (1) the basket, (2) the clothes-horse ?

(e) Despite its sadness, the passage contains two comical items. What are they ?

(f) Explain the double sense in " at the post."

(g) Explain :—picking up a living, clothes-horse, ballads, screen, contrived, stock-in-trade, furled, yarn, un-wholesomely-forced.

(h) Parse :—London, house, had sat, for, remaining.

10. **Read the following passage carefully and answer the questions that follow :—**

Richard Mayne was a wealthy yeoman of the old school, sturdy, boisterous, bold and kind, always generous and generally good-natured, but cross-grained and obstinate by fits, and sometimes purse-proud—after the fashion of men who had made money by their own industry and shrewdness. He had married late in life and above him in station, and had now been for two or

three years a widower with one daughter, a girl of
nineteen, of whom he was almost as fond as of his greyhound Mayfly and for pretty much the same reasons—
that both were beautiful and gentle and his own, and
both admired and coveted by others—that Mayfly had
now three cups and that Lucy had refused four offers.

(a) Write down *three* words from the passage describing
the unpleasant side of Richard Mayne's character.

(b) Write *six* words from the passage describing the
pleasant side of Richard Mayne's character.

(c) Which did Mayne love more—Lucy or Mayfly ?

(d) What age was Lucy when her mother died ?

(e) Write down, from the passage, *two* words opposite
in meaning.

(f) Write and complete this sentence :—

Richard Mayne had made money because he
was.....................and...................... (Two
adjectives.)

Section II—Passages suitable for Forms II and III.

**1. Read the following carefully, then answer the
following questions :—**

" SHERWOOD TO-DAY."

Sherwood in the twilight, is Robin Hood awake ?
Grey and ghostly shadows are gliding through the
brake ;
Shadows of the *dappled* deer, dreaming of the morn,
Dreaming of *a shadowy man* that winds a shadowy horn.

Where the deer are gliding down the shadowy glen
All across the glades of fern, he calls his merry men—
Doublets of the *Lincoln green* glancing through the May
In Sherwood, in Sherwood, about the break of day—

Calls them and they answer : from *aisles* of oak and ash
Rings the " Follow, follow," and the boughs begin to
    crash,
The ferns begin to flutter and the flowers begin to fly
And through the crimson dawning, the *robber band* goes
    by.

(*a*) Explain briefly the meaning of the words and phrases
in italics.

(*b*) Each quatrain describes a picture. Describe each
of these pictures in your own words (about six lines
each).

(*c*) Scan lines 10 and 11. What change of metre has
taken place ?

(*d*) How does the poet suggest quick movement in line 11 ?

2. **Read the following passage carefully and then
answer the questions :—**

Perched on my city office-stool
I watched with envy, while a cool
And *lucky* carter handled ice—
And I was wandering in a trice,
Far from the gray and grimy heat,
Of that *intolerable* street,
O'er sapphire berg and emerald floe,
Beneath the still, cold, ruby glow
Of *everlasting* Polar night,
Bewildered by the queer half-light,
Until I stumbled, unawares,
Upon a creek where big white bears
Plunged headlong down with flourished heels,
And floundered after shining seals
Through shivering seas of blinding blue.
And as I watched them, ere I knew,
I'd stripped, and I was swimming, too,
Among the seal-pack, young and hale,
And thrusting on with *threshing tail*,

16

With twist and twirl and sudden leap
Through crackling ice and salty deep—
Diving and doubling with my kind,
Until, at last, we left behind
Those *big white, blundering bulks of death,*
And lay, at length, with panting breath
Upon a far untravelled floe,
Beneath a gentle drift of snow. . . .

—*W. W. Gibson.*

(a) What is the occupation of the person who is supposed to write the poem ?

(b) What proofs have you that what he saw was in a day dream ?

(c) What prompted his dream ?

(d) Why does the poet call the carter *lucky* and the street *intolerable* ?

(e) Why is Polar night called *everlasting* ? Is this word correctly used here ?

(f) What is meant by *threshing* tail ?

(g) What season of the year was it when the writer has his dream ? Give the proofs in the poem to support your answer.

(h) What is meant by " big, white, blundering bulks of death " ?

(i) Write the first three lines and mark the accented syllables in them.

3. **Read the following poem carefully and then answer the questions below :—**

In dim green depths rot *ingot-laden* ships,
While gold dubloons that from the drowned hand fell
Lie nestled in the ocean-flower's bell
With Love's gemmed rings once kissed by now dead lips.

And round some wrought-gold cup the sea-grass whips
And hides lost pearls, near pearls still in their shell,
Where seaweed forests fill each ocean-dell,
And seek dim sunlight with their countless tips.

So lie the wasted gifts, the long-lost hopes,
Beneath the new hushed surface of myself ;
In lonelier depths than where the diver gropes
They lie deep, deep ; but I at times behold
In doubtful glimpses, on some reefy shelf,
The gleam of irrecoverable gold.

—Eugene Lee-Hamilton.

(a) Describe, *in your own words,* using *all* the information
   supplied by the poet, the scene depicted by him
   in the first eight lines.

(b) In the last six lines, the poet draws a comparison
   between his wasted gifts and the sunken treasure.
   described in the first eight lines. Using your own
   words, avoiding figurative or metaphorical language,
   make this comparison as clear as you can.

(c) Explain clearly what you understand by :—
   (1) Ingot-laden.
   (2) Where seaweed forests fill each ocean-dell,
       And seek dim sunlight with their countless tips.
   (3) In lonelier depths then where the diver gropes.
   (4) The gleam of irrecoverable gold.

**4. Read the following poem carefully and then answer
the questions below :—**

COURAGE.

Courage is but a word, and yet, of words
The only sentinel of permanence ;
The ruddy watch-fire of cold winter days,
We steal its comfort, lift our weary swords,
And on. For faith—without it—has no sense ;
6 And love to wind of doubt and tremor sways ;
7 And life for ever quaking marsh must tread.

Laws give it not ; before it prayer will blush ;
Hope has it not ; nor pride of being true ;
'Tis the mysterious soul which never yields,
But hales us on and on to *breast* the rush
Of all the *fortunes* we shall happen *through* ;
And when Death calls across his shadowy fields—
Dying, it answers ; " Here ! I am not dead ! "

                                    —*John Galsworthy*.

(a) State in your own words what the poet has to say
about courage.

(b) Write down completely the first two metaphors
which the poet uses to describe courage and explain
them.

(c) You will notice that both these metaphors are such
as a soldier might use—they are military. Why are
they   particularly   appropriate   in   this   poem ?
Write down any other phrases which show that the
poet thinks of life as a battle.

(d) Write down a line which includes an example of
inversion.

(e) Write lines 6 and 7 in prose order.

(f) Give a general analysis of the poem from " Hope
has it not " to the end.
Parse fully : breast ; fortunes ; through.

5. **Read the following poem and then answer the
questions below :—**

ENGLAND.

Arise up, England, from the smoky cloud
That covers thee, the din of whirling wheels ;
Not the pale spinner, *prematurely* bowed
By his hot toil, alone the influence feels
Of all this deep necessity for gain :
Gain still ; but *deem* not only by the strain
Of engines on the sea and on the shore,

Glory, that was thy *birthright*, to retain.
Oh thou that knewest not a conqueror,
Unchecked desires have multiplied in thee,
Till with their *bat-wings* they shut out the sun ;
So in the dust thou goest moodily,
With a bent head, as one who gropes for *ore*,
Heedless of living streams that round him run.
—*Lord Hanmer.*

(a) Give the meaning of the sonnet in your own words,
ensuring that you bring out clearly what the poet
is warning the people against.

(b) Give the meaning of the following words (*in italics*)
as they are used in the passage ; " prematurely " ;
" deem " ; " birthright " ; " bat-wings " ; " ore."

(c) Write down words from the poem containing (1) a
simile, (2) an example of metonymy.

(c) Give a general analysis of the poem from line 6—
but deem, to the end—run.
Parse fully ; deem ; glory ; birthright ; till ; so.

6. **Read the following poem carefully and answer the
questions below :—**

SEA FEVER.

I must down to the seas again, to the lonely sea and
the sky,
And all I ask is a tall ship and a star to steer her by,
And *the wheel's kick* and the wind's song and the
white sail's shaking,
And a grey mist on the sea's face and a grey dawn
breaking.

I must down to the seas again, for the call of the
running tide
Is a wild call and a clear call that may not be denied ;
And all I ask is a windy day with the white clouds flying,
And the flung spray and the *blown spume*, and the
sea-gulls crying.

I must down to the seas again, to the *vagrant gipsy life*,
To the gull's way and the whale's way where the wind's
    like a whetted knife ;
And all I ask is a merry yarn from a laughing fellow-
    rover,
And quiet sleep and a sweet dream when *the long
    trick's* over.

(a) What does Masefield mean by " Sea Fever " ?

(b) Give three words or phrases which make you feel
that the poet was a real sailor.

(c) What kind of ship is described ? How do you know ?

(d) Give two examples of personification and one of
simile.

(e) Give the meaning of the following phrases :—
the wheel's kick; blown spume; vagrant gipsy
life; the long trick.

(f) Make a general analysis of the first two lines of the
second stanza.

7. Read the following passage and then answer the
questions which follow it:—

The wild hunter can still further check or altogether
prevent observation by moving on hands and knees,
when his weight is *widely distributed*. In the particular instance of a fish he endeavours to come to the
margin of the water at the rear of the fish, whose eyes
are so placed that it can see best in front. When he
has arrived at the margin, and has to rear himself up,
if from hands and knees, or, if already upright, when
he commences his work, he tries to conceal his arms,
or, rather, to *minimise their peculiar appearance* as
much as practicable by keeping them close to his sides.
All this time I am supposing that you are looking at
the poacher from the fish. To a fish or any wild animal
the arms of a man are suspicious. No other creatures

that they know possess these *singular appurtenances*, which move in almost any direction, and yet have nothing to do with locomotion. You may be sure that this great difference in the *anatomical construction* of a man is recognised by all wild animals once they are compelled, for their own safety, to observe him. Arms are so entirely opposite to all the variety of limb possessed by the varieties of living creatures.

(a) Why does the hunter move on hands and knees ?

(b) Why does the hunter approach the fish from the rear ?

(c) What precautions does he take regarding his arms ?

(d) Why are the arms of a man suspicious to the fish or wild animals ?

(e) Explain the meaning of the phrases as used in the passage :—widely distributed ; minimise their peculiar appearance ; singular appurtenances ; anatomical construction.

(f) Make a general analysis of the sentence :—You may be sure . . . to observe him.

8. **Read the following passage carefully and answer the questions that follow it:—**

The thud, thud of a horse's hoof does not alarm fish. Basking in the sun under the bank, a jack or pike lying close to the surface of the water will remain unmoved, however heavy the sound may be. The vibrations reach the fish in several ways. There is what we ourselves should call the noise as conveyed by the air, and which in the case of a jack actually at the surface may be supposed to reach him direct. Next there is the vibration passing through the water, which is usually pronounced to be a good medium. Lastly, there is the bodily movement of the substance of the water. When the bank is hard and dry the latter amounts only to a slight shaking but it frequently happens that the side of a brook or pond is soft and " gives " under a heavy weight. Some-times the edge is even pushed into the water, and the brook in a manner squeezed. You can see this when the cattle walk by the margin ; the grassy edge is pushed out, and in a minute way they may be said to contract the stream. It is in too small a degree to have the least apparent effect upon the water, but it is different with the sense of hearing which is so delicate that the bodily movement thus caused may be reasonably believed to be audible indeed to the jack.

(a) Enumerate the different ways in which the vibra-tions reach the fish. (Answer in your own words.)

(b) How do the different conditions of the bank affect the movement of the water ?

(c) What word in the first part of the last sentence tells you what " sense " is alluded to there ? Which sense is it ?

(d) Form adjectives from the following nouns :—
    vibration ; substance ; effect ; sense.

(e) Give the derivation of conveyed, contract, audible.

(f) Make a general analysis of the last sentence.

9. **Read the passage carefully and then answer the questions which follow:—**

The history of England in the seventeenth century differs from that of other European countries in one very important respect. While in France and in some of the states of Germany, the power and authority of the crown increased throughout the century, in England, the Crown was much less powerful under William III than it had been under Queen Elizabeth. There was no danger from without, and the island kingdom was free to develop its *internal* differences. The main features of interest in the period are two struggles—a conflict between king and Parliament for the *supreme* power in national affairs, and a conflict between two different types of Protestants, the Church of England and the Puritans, who had been increasing in numbers throughout the reign of Elizabeth. The two conflicts were closely connected, for the Church of England supported royal claims to *absolute* power, and the Puritans *advocated* the claims of Parliament to limit the royal authority.

(a) In what respect did English history in the seventeenth century differ from that of other European countries ?

(b) Why was Britain free to develop during that century ? Answer in a sentence.

(c) What were the two main conflicts of that period ?

(d) In what way were the two conflicts connected ?

(e) Give the meanings of *internal, supreme, absolute, advocated* as used in the passage.

(f) Invent a suitable title for the passage.

10. **Read this passage carefully, and answer the questions that follow it :—**

THE ATTACK ON THE ARMADA.

The Spanish fleet was anchored close to the edge of the *shoal* water, and to attack it where it lay was impossible. It was determined to drive them out into the Channel with fire-ships, of which they were known to be afraid. Sir Henry Palmer proposed to cross to Dover and fetch some worthless *hulks* ; but time would be lost, and there was not a day nor an hour to spare. Among the *volunteer* vessels which had attached themselves to the fleet there were many that would be useless in action, and as fit as the best for the service for which they were now needed. Eight were taken, and the *rigging smeared* rapidly with pitch, the hulls filled with any useless material which could be *extemporised* that would contribute to the blaze. The sky was cloudy.

The moon was in its last quarter, and did not rise till morning ; and the tide, towards midnight set directly down from the English position to where the ships of the Armada, seeking shelter from the bend in the coast, lay *huddled* dangerously close.   Long, low, sighing gusts from the westward promised the rising of a gale.

(*a*) What preparations did the English make to deal with the Spanish Armada ?
Why did they not make a direct attack ?

(*b*) How did natural circumstances aid the English ?

(*c*) Give the meaning of the following words :—

shoal ;   hulks ;   volunteer ;   rigging ;   smeared ; extemporised ;   huddled.

(*d*) Analyse the sentence beginning " Among the volun-teer vessels.   .   .   ."

CHAPTER XIII

HISTORY OF THE LANGUAGE

Roots and Derivatives

THE words in our language are derived from a great many sources.

The derivation of a word may be defined as the tracing of a word back to its original root. The principal sources of our language are :—

1. **Old English.**
2. **Celtic.**
3. **Latin.**
4. **Greek.**
5. **Romance Languages** (French, Italian, Spanish, etc.).
6. **Scandinavian.**
7. **Names of places and persons.**

but, in addition, we have borrowed words from practically all spoken languages at some time or other, through missionary, trade, exploration or war contacts.

When we seek the derivation of a word, we require to know the following terms :—

The Root (or stem) of a word is that part of it which cannot be further broken up, from which many words are usually derived, *e.g.* in the words reduce, adduce, produce, reducible, adducible, producible, *duc* (from the Latin verb *ducere*) is the root.

A **Prefix** (pre, from Latin *pre*, before ; fix, from Latin *figere*, to fix) is a letter, syllable or word put before another word to affect its meaning— *e.g.* ordinary, extra-ordinary.

A **Suffix** (suf for *sub*—Latin under) is a particle placed after the root of a word which influences the meaning, *e.g.* work, worker, -er is the suffix denoting the agent.

The word **Affix** (Latin *ad*—to) is used of either a prefix or a suffix, as the word denotes something added to the root of a word and that addition may be before or after.

Accordingly, if asked for the derivation of re-ducible, we should write :—

Prefix: *re*—from Latin, meaning back.
Root: *duc*, from Lat. *ducere*, to lead.
Suffix: *ible* is a Lat. adjectival suffix.

The Principal Elements in English

1. **Old English** supplies us with:—

(a) Demonstrative Adjectives; *e.g.* (this, that)

(b) Pronouns; *e.g.* (me, I, one, we).

(c) Numerals; *e.g.* (first, second, third).

(d) Prepositions; *e.g.* (from, to, on).

(e) Conjunctions; *e.g.* (and, but, lest).

(f) Strong, Auxiliary and Defective Verbs; *e.g.* (swim; have, be, shall, will, may, do; quoth).

(g) Adverbs of Time and Place; *e.g.* (then, here).

Note.—

Although there are more words of Latin than of English origin in the dictionary, the above list contains such words as we cannot avoid using when we write— we must use them very frequently.

2. **Celtic** place names are fairly common in our place names, *e.g.*—

> *Aber*: a river mouth: Aberdeen.
> *Ben*: a mountain: Benmore.
> *Dun*: a fort: Dumbarton.
> *Kil*: a church: Kilmarnock.
> *Strath*: a wide valley: Strathmore.

3. **Latin** has provided us with most of our words; in modern times, names for new inventions are frequently borrowed from Latin and Greek, *e.g.* television.

> *a.* Words of the **First Period**. The Jutes, Angles and Saxons found certain Latin words used by the Britons, a relic of the Roman occupation from A.D. 43 to 410.
>
> > *Castra*: a camp: Lancaster, Chester.
> > *Fossa*: a ditch: Fosbridge.
> > *Colonia*: a colony: Lincoln.
> > *Portus*: a harbour : Portsmouth.
> > *Strata*: paved (road) : Stratford.
>
> *b.* Words of the **Second Period**.
>
> The words then incorporated were (i) chiefly in connexion with Augustine's Conversion to Christianity of the English in 597 A.D.; and (ii) words connected with commerce.

    (i) Angel, bishop, monk, priest, psalter, disciple, creed, font.

    (ii) butter, lettuce, pepper.

c. Words of the **Third Period**.

These were introduced by the Norman-French after their Conquest in 1066. Such words chiefly relate to:—

    (i) Feudalism and War:—baron, squire, joust, homage, siege, lists, herald, duke.

    (ii) Government and Law:—Parliament, assize, judge, jury, justice, vassal.

    (iii) Church :—pilgrim, penance, friar, pity, chapel.

    (iv) Hunting and Cookery:—venison, quarry, chase, beef, rabbit, veal, mutton.

d. Words of the **Fourth Period**.

A great many words were introduced through the Renaissance, greatly helped by the Invention of Printing. Such words are in appearance very like their Latin originals: *e.g.* locate, dislocate, allocate, location, locally (Latin—*locus*, a place).

    vital, devitalise (Latin—*vita*, life).

    clamour, clamant, exclaim, declaim, proclaim (Latin—*clamo*, I shout).

    credible, credulous, incredible (Latin—*credo*, I believe).

4. **Greek**. Many Greek words have entered our language through Latin. A great many words

for technical and scientific inventions have been introduced directly from Greek.

telephone ; telescope ; photograph ; barometer.

5. **Romance Languages.**

a. French.
blonde; trait; camouflage; chauffeur; coup d'état,

b. Italian (chiefly connected with music and art).
canto; stanza; tenor; concert; palette; opera; sonnet.

c. Spanish.
armada; cork; cigar; castanet; grandee; negro.

6. **Scandinavian.**

By : a town : Whit*by*.
Tarn : a lake : *Tarn*syke.
Beck : a brook : Wans*beck*.
Thorpe : a village : Al*thorpe*.
Fiord : an inlet : Mil*ford*.

7. **Names from Places and Persons.**

bedlam (St. Mary of *Bethlehem*); magnet (magnesia in Thessaly); parchment (Pergamum); tawdry (St. Audrey's Fair); canary (Canary Islands) ; Bessemer ; cardigan ; macadamise; shrapnel (General Shrapnel); grog (the nick-name of Admiral Vernon, because he wore grogram breeches) ; filbert (Saint Philbert).

PREFIXES.

English (or Teutonic).

a-, a form of *on*, asleep,
    aweary.
after-, afternoon.
be-, behalf, behoof.
down-, downfall.
for-, { 1. *not*, forbid.
      { 2. *utterly*, forlorn.
fore-, *before*, foretell.
gain-, *against*, gainsay.
in-, im-, en-, em-, inborn, endear.
mis-, *wrongly*, mistake.
off-, *from*, offspring.

on-, onward.
out-, *from*, outset.
over-, oversee.
to-, *this*, to-morrow.
un-, { 1. *not*, unclean.
     { 2. *back*, undo.
under-, understand.
up-, upstart.
wan-, *without*, wanton.
with, { 1. *against*, withstand.
      { 2. *again*, withdraw.

Latin Prefixes.

ab-, a-, abs-, *from*, abuse.
ad-, *to*, adore.
ambi-, *around*, ambiguous.
ante-, *before*, antecedent.
bis-, *twice*, biscuit.
circum-, *around*, circumnavigate.
con-, *together*, conduct.
contra-, *against*, contradict.
de-, *down*, denote.
ex-, e-, *out of*, extract, eject.
in-, *into*, invade.
in-, *not*, innocent.
inter-, *between*, interfere.

ob-, *against*, * oppose.
pene-, *almost*, peninsula.
per-, *through*, perform.
post-, *after*, postpone.
prae-, pre-, *before*, prevent.
pro-, *before*, proceed.
re-, *back*, reflect.
se-, *apart*, seclude.
sine-, *without*, sinecure.
sub-, *under*, subdue.
super-, *over*, supernatural.
trans-, *across*, transgress.
vice-, *instead of*, viceroy.

* The final consonant of a prefix is frequently assimilated with the succeeding consonant to make the pronunciation easier, as :—*op*pose for *ob*pose.

Greek Prefixes.

a-, an-, *not*, anarchy.
amphi-, *on both sides*, amphibious.
ana-, *up*, analysis.
anti-, *against*, antipathy.
apo-, *from*, apostrophe.
cata-, *down*, catastrophe.
di-, *two*, dissyllable.
dia-, *through*, diameter.
en-, em-, *in*, emporium.

epi-, *upon*, epitaph.
hyper-, *over*, hyperbole.
hypo-, *under*, hypocrite.
meta-, *after*, metaphor.
para-, *beside*, paraphrase.
peri-, *round*, perimeter.
pro-, *before*, prophet.
pros-, *towards*, prosody.
syn-, *together*, syntax.

SUFFIXES.

English Suffixes.

1. Denoting agent:— *-er, -ar, -or, -en, -ster.*
   worker, beggar, spinster.

2. Denoting State, Action, or Condition:— *-dom, -hood, -ing, -ness, -red, -ship, -th.*
   kingdom, manhood, hatred, friendship, truth.

3. Denoting Diminution (Diminutives):— *-en, -ing, -ling, -kin, -ock.*
   chicken, duckling, lambkin, hillock.

4. Adjectival:— *-ed, -en, -ful, -like, -less, -some.*
   wicked, wooden, godless, winsome.

5. Adverbial:— *-ly, -wards, -wise, -way.*
   surly, upwards, likewise, straightway.

6. Frequentative:— *-k, -le, -l.*
   stalk, startle, kneel.

7. Causative:— *-en, -se, -er.*
   fatten, cleanse, falter.

Latin, Greek, and French Suffixes.

1. Denoting Agent:— *-ain, -an, -ee, -eer, -ier, -or, -trix, -ant, -ent.*
   tenant, captain, doctor, engineer.

2. Denoting State, Condition:— *-age, -ance, -ence, -ess, -tion, -sion, -lence, -our, -ery, -ry, -ty.*
   nonage, distance, honour, verity.

3. Diminutives:— *-aster, -et, -le, -icle, -cule, -ule, -et, -let, -ette, -ot.*

   poetaster, ballot, rivulet, particle.

4. Adjectival:— *-al, -an, -ain, -ane, -ant, -ate, -able, -ese, -esque, -ile, -ian, -ine, -ive, -ose, -ous.*

   loyal, ignorant, picturesque, grandiose.

5. Causative:— *-fy, -ish, -ise (ize).*

   magnify, flourish, minimise.

THE FORMATION OF NOUNS

1. Nouns are formed from Nouns:—
   - (*a*) By a change in the word itself:—as font, *fount*; stick, *stake*; rod, *rood*; head, *hood*.
   - (*b*) By a Prefix:—as *re*action, *in*gratitude, *mis*-statement.
   - (*c*) By a Suffix:—as king*dom*, maid*en*, boy*hood*.

2. Nouns are formed from Adjectives:—
   - (*a*) By a change in the word itself:—as hot, *heat*; proud, *pride*.
   - (*b*) By a Suffix:—as wise, wis*dom*; safe, safe*ty*; good, good*ness*.

3. Nouns are formed from Verbs:—
   - (*a*) By a change in the word:—as bear, *birth*; live, *life*; dig, *ditch*.
   - (*b*) By a Prefix:—as *off*spring, *down*fall.
   - (*c*) By a Suffix:—as marry, marri*age*; deny, deni*al*.

THE FORMATION OF ADJECTIVES.

1. Adjectives are formed from Nouns by a Suffix:—as wood, wood*en*; grace, grac*ious*; success, success*ful*.

2. Adjectives are formed from Adjectives:—
   (*a*) By a Prefix:—as noble, *ig*noble; regular, *ir*regular.
   (*b*) By a Suffix:—as white, whit*ish*; four, four*th*.

3. Adjectives are formed from Verbs by a Suffix:—as charm, charm*ing*; elude, elus*ive*.

THE FORMATION OF VERBS.

1. Verbs are formed from Nouns:—
   (*a*) By a change in the word:—as half, *halve*; proof, *prove*; sit, *seat*.
   (*b*) By a Prefix:—as *be*head, *un*mask.
   (*c*) By a Suffix:—as length*en*, typi*fy*.

2. Verbs are formed from Adjectives:—
   (*a*) By a change in the word:—as safe, *save*; hale, *heal*.
   (*b*) By a Prefix:—as *be*dim; *re*new.
   (*v*) By a Suffix:—as civil*ise*, bright*en*.

3. Verbs are formed from Verbs:—
   (*a*) By a change in the word:—rise, *raise*; lie, *lay*; fall, *fell*.
   (*b*) By a Prefix:—as *gain*say, *fore*see.
   (*c*) By a Suffix:—as tal*k* (tell), shov*el* (sho**ve**).

Latin Roots (Nouns and Pronouns).

ager	field	agriculture
alter	one of two	alternate
annus	year	annual
aqua	water	aqueduct
arma	arms	armament
astrum	star	disaster
canis	dog	canine
caput	head	capital
civis	citizen	civil
corpus	body	corporal
crux	cross	crucifix
culpa	fault	culpable
dens	tooth	indented
dies	day	journal
domus	house	domicile
eques	horseman	equestrian
fama	report	infamy
filius	son	filial
finis	end	infinite
fons	spring	fountain
frater	brother	friar
gens	nation	gentile
genus	kind (noun)	degenerate
gloria	glory	glorify
homo	man	human
hostis	enemy	hostile
ignis	fire	ignition
insula	island	insular
iter	journey	itinerant
janua	gate	janitor
lex .	law	legal
liber	book	library
locus	place	dislocate
luna	moon	lunacy
magister .	master	magistrate

mare	.	.	sea	maritime
mors	.	.	death	mortal
navis	.	.	ship	navigate
nomen	.	.	name	nominate
nox	.	.	night	nocturnal
oculus	.	.	eye	oculist
opus	.	.	work	co-operate
ovum	.	.	egg	oval
pater	.	.	father	paternal
pax	.	.	peace	pacify
pons	.	.	bridge	pontoon
puer	.	.	boy	puerile
radix	.	.	root	eradicate
rex .	.	.	king	regal
senex	.	.	old man	senility
stella	.	.	star	constellation
tempus	.	.	time	temporary
terra	.	.	earth	territorial
umbra	.	.	shadow	umbrella
unda	.	.	wave	undulate
urbs	.	.	city	urban
verbum	.	.	word	verbal
via .	.	.	way	deviate
vir .	.	.	man	virile
vita	.	.	life	vital
vox	.	.	voice	vocal

Latin Adjectives

aequus	.	.	equal	equation
altus	.	.	high	altitude
audax	.	.	bold	audacity
bonus	.	.	good	bounty
brevis	.	.	short	abbreviate
celer	.	.	swift	accelerate
dexter	.	.	right	ambidextrous

facilis	.	.	easy	facilitate
felix	.	.	happy	felicitate
fortis	.	.	strong	fortify
gravis	.	.	heavy	grief
liber	.	.	free	liberate
magnus	.	.	great	magnify
minor	.	.	less	diminish
novus	.	.	new	novice
omnis	.	.	all	omniscient
primus	.	.	first	primitive
proximus		.	next	approximate
sanctus	.	.	holy	sanctify
satis	.	.	enough	satisfy
similis	.	.	like	simile
verus	.	.	true	aver

Latin Verbs

ago	.	.	act	action
amo	.	.	love	amiable
augeo	.	.	increase	auction
cano	.	.	sing	chant
capio	.	.	take	captor
cedo	.	.	yield	succession
clamo	.	.	shout	clamant
credo	.	.	believe	credible
cresco	.	.	grow	crescent
curro	.	.	run	current
doceo	.	.	teach	docile
duco	.	.	lead	conduct
facio	.	.	make	factor
fido	.	.	trust	confidence
fluo	.	.	flow	fluent
frango	.	.	break	fracture
fugio	.	.	flee	fugitive
habito	.	.	dwell	inhabitant

impero	. .	command	empire
jacio	. .	throw	projectile
jungo	. .	join	conjunction
laudo	. .	praise	laudable
lego	. .	gather	collect
levo	. .	raise	lever
loquor	. .	speak	colloquial
ludo	. .	play	elusive
mitto	. .	send	emissary
moveo	. .	move	emotion
nascor	. .	am born	natal
noceo	. .	harm	innocent
oro	. .	pray	inexorable
patior	. .	suffer	patient
penetro	. .	enter	penetrate
peto	. .	seek	petition
placeo	. .	please	implacable
pono	. .	place	opposite
puto	. .	think	compute
rego	. .	rule	regulation
rogo	. .	ask	interrogate
scio	. .	know	science
scribo	. .	write	scripture
sedeo	. .	sit	session
sequor	. .	follow	consecutive
sto .	. .	stand	station
tango	. .	touch	tangible
teneo	. .	hold	retain
texo	. .	weave	textile
traho	. .	draw	traction
utor	. .	use	utility
venio	. .	come	convention
video	. .	see	vision
vinco	. .	conquer	convince
voco	. .	call	vocal
volo	. .	fly	volley

Greek Nouns

agon	. . contest	agony
anthropos	. man	anthropology
arctos	. . bear	arctic
astron	. . star	astronomy
atmos	. . vapour	atmosphere
baros	. . weight	barometer
biblion	. . book	Bible
bios	. . life	biology
chronos	. . time	chronometer
demos	. . people	democracy
helios	. . sun	heliograph
hippos	. . horse	hippodrome
kuklos	. . wheel	cycle
metron	. . measure	thermometer
pathos	. . feeling	pathetic
phos	. . light	phosphorus
polis	. . city	metropolis
theos	. . god	atheist
therme	. . heat	thermal

Greek Verbs

grapho	. . write	telegraph
phileo	. . love	philanthropy
skopeo	. . see	telescope

Greek Adverbs and Adjectives

eu .	. . well	euphony
monos	. . alone	monotony
poly	. . many	polygamy
tele	. . afar	telephone

EXERCISES

1. Form Nouns from the following:—

happy, rich, poor, high, broad, long, ridiculous, penal, sweet, common, unique, vulnerable, soluble, malevolent, pessimistic.

2. Form Adjectives from the following:—

oak, wool, noble, rot, swell, fail, produce, diminish, music, instrument, imagine, curl, sink, sale, notice, Dickens, Shakespeare, Burns.

3. Form Verbs from the following:—

short, like, quick, glory, signal, stupid, real, cant, cover, scandal, soft, local, slave, dim.

4. Point out the Prefixes and Suffixes in the following words, giving their meaning and stating from which language each is derived:—

overcome, underrate, conduct, analyse, synthetical, forego, mistakenly, exceed, intercommunicable, anteroom, ambidextrous, friendship, wisdom, contradictory, hillock, offshoot.

5. Give the derivation of:—

Argosy, calico, August, dunce, hollyhock, Jacobin, Jacobite, jersey, amok, camouflage, monsoon, Blighty, lynch, mackintosh, meander, muslin, sherry, tantalise, volt, ampere, savvy, malapropism, laconic, mesmerise, copper, fuchsia, grog.

CHAPTER XIV

POETRY—PROSODY

Poetry is usually written in metrical form and has been defined as the art of expressing in melodious words the thoughts that arise from feeling and imagination. Prose is usually primarily concerned with conveying meaning, giving information. You must remember, however, that the spirit of true poetry is to be found in prose form and that much that is written in metrical form fails to be true poetry because it has not been the product of feeling and imagination. Upon the treatment of the theme will depend the answer to the question, " Is this poetry or prose ? "

The poet will usually be more careful about the selection and arrangement of his words than the prose writer. The poet uses words that have a musical quality and, although both prose writer and poet may use figures of speech, the figures that the poet uses will appeal more to our sense of beauty and to our feelings than those of writers of prose.

Poetry is usually in metrical form, that is, the words form a fairly regular succession of groups of syllables, called **feet**, which are composed of accented (stressed) and unaccented (unstressed) syllables. For example, if we take the first line of Scott's *Lay of the Last Minstrel*, there are certain sounds in the line which we would naturally accent as we speak them, thus :—

The w̄ay| was l̄ong|, the w̄ind| was c̄old||

Prosody is the name given to the laws of metre. In order to study prosody, the following terms should be understood:—

A **Syllable** is a word or part of a word that is pronounced *as one sound*. Notice that a syllable will contain at least a vowel (including y) and may contain consonants, *e.g.* accommodate is pronounced ak-kom′-mo-dāt. We accent or stress the second syllable.

Metre is the regular recurrence of a group of syllables that are accented similarly, *e.g.*

The mĭn|strēl wăs| ĭnfīrm| ănd ōld||

Here we have a line of eight syllables and every alternate syllable is either unaccented or accented. We can divide the line into four groups of two syllables, the first unaccented, the second accented.

This succession of the same group gives us a regular **Rhythm,** or measured flow.

A **Foot** in prosody means a group of syllables accented in a certain way. Thus a foot is the unit of metre.

The commonest feet in English poetry are:—

Two Syllable Feet

NAME	ADJECTIVE	COMPOSED OF	DENOTED BY
Iambus (iamb.)	Iambic	unaccented + accented	⌣ — or *x a*
Trochee	Trochaic	accented + unaccented	— ⌣ or *a x*
Spondee	Spondaic	two accented syllables	— — or *a a*
Pyrrhic	Pyrrhic	two unaccented syllables	⌣ ⌣ or *x x*

Three Syllable Feet

NAME	ADJECTIVE	COMPOSED OF	DENOTED BY
Anapæst	Anapæstic	two unaccented + one accented	‿ ‿ — or $x\,x\,a$
Dactyl	Dactylic	one accented + two unaccented	— ‿ ‿ or $a\,x\,x$
Amphibrach	Amphibrachic	unaccented + accented + unaccented	‿ — ‿ or $x\,a\,x$

In addition to metre, most poetry also has **Rhyme**, which is a similarity of sound in the endings of two or more words, usually found at the ends of lines.

This similarity of ending sound should begin at the accented vowel and continue to the ends of the words, and the consonants preceding the rhyming sounds should be different in order to form a perfect rhyme, *e.g.*

"There's not a joy the world can give like that it takes a*way*,
When the glow of early thought declines in feelings dull de*cay*;"

" way " and " cay " form a perfect rhyme because
(1) ay is the accented vowel sound in each line ;
(2) w and c, the preceding consonants, differ.

Notice that in rhyme it is *sound*, not spelling, that matters ; *cough* does not rhyme with *though*.

Assonance occurs when there is a similarity of sound in vowels but not in succeeding consonants, *e.g.* feel, need.

Words usually rhyme in *one* syllable ; this is called masculine or single rhyme. When two syllables **rhyme,** we have feminine or double rhyme, *e.g.*

> "Whate'er the theme, the maiden sang
>   As if her song could have no *ending*;
> I saw her singing at her work,
>   And o'er the sickle *bending*."

The rhyming of three or more syllables (polysyllabic) is used chiefly for humorous effect as in Butler's *Hudibras* :—

> "Beside, he was a shrewd phil*osopher*,
> And had read ev'ry text and gl*oss over*; "

Middle Rhyme occurs when an accented sound in the middle of a line corresponds with the sound at the end of it, *e.g.*

> "Oh hark, O he*ar*! how thin and cl*ear*,
>   And thinner, clearer, farther going!
> O sweet and f*ar* from cliff and sc*ar*
>   The horns of Elfland faintly blowing! "

Two lines rhyming form a **couplet,** *e.g.*

> "Nae man can tether time or tide ;   *a*
> The hour approaches Tam maun ride ; "   *a*

When the lines are iambic pentameter the couplet is called the **Heroic Couplet,** *e.g.*

> "O blest retirement, friend to life's decline,   *a*
> Retreats from care, that never must be mine."   *a*

Rhyme occurring at the end of every second line is called *alternate, e.g.*

> "The hand of the reaper   *a*
>   Takes the ears that are hoary,   *b*
> But the voice of the weeper   *a*
>   Wails manhood in glory."   *b*

Blank Verse is the name given to lines of poetry that do not rhyme ; most lines in Shakespeare's plays, and in many long narrative poems, do not rhyme, *e.g.*

> " But the majestic river floated on,
>   Out of the mist and hum of that low land,
>   Into the frosty starlight, and there mov'd,
>   Rejoicing, through the hush'd Chorasmian waste."

Alliteration (sometimes called Head Rhyme) is the recurrence of the same initial letter or letters in words, *e.g.*

> " Nor cast one *l*onging *l*ingering *l*ook behind."

Try to become familiar with the *rhythm* of each metre.

EXAMPLES OF VARIOUS METRES

Iambic metre is the commonest in our speech and poetry ; if you remember that the normal line of a Shakespearean play is iambic, that should help.

> " This precious stone set in a silver sea,
>   Which serves it in the office of a wall,
>   Or as a moat defensive to a house,
>   Against the envy of less happier lands."

Trochaic metre :

> " While your hearts are growing colder,
>   While your world is growing older."

Anapæstic metre :

" And the eyes of the sleepers waxed deadly and chill,

And their hearts but once heaved, and for ever

grew still."

Dactylic metre :

" Take her up tenderly,

Lift her with care ;

Fashion'd so slenderly,

Young, and so fair !

You should notice that the use of each type of metric foot produces a *characteristic rhythm* and the poet uses the rhythm that best suits his purpose, just as a musician chooses the measure he desires for his music. Study Browning's *How They Brought the Good News from Ghent to Aix* and his *Cavalier Song* and you will see how suitable for these poems are the metres chosen.

SCANSION

To scan a line of poetry, we mark each syllable in accordance with whether it is accented or unaccented and then mark off the feet. We also name the metre used, and we designate the lines according to the number of feet in the line.

Monometer is a line of one foot (unusual).
Dimeter   ,,   ,,   two feet.
Trimeter   ,,   ,,   three feet.
Tetrameter   ,,   ,,   four feet.

Pentameter is a line of five feet.
Hexameter   „   „   six feet (Alexandrine).
Heptameter   „   „   seven feet (uncommon).

Before scanning a line, read the line and, if it has a definite rhythm, this should soon be apparent.

Remember to mark each word **as you pronounce it.** You must not make up your mind that because the first foot is an iambus that it necessarily follows that the other feet are also iambs. Do not be disappointed if you find lines of poetry irregular : too much regularity in metre would be monotonous Sometimes a line contains a syllable or syllables over and above the requirements of the metre used in the poem, or a syllable or syllables short of the requirements of the metre. In *The Ancient Mariner*, by Coleridge, for example, the usual stanza or verse is composed of four lines, lines one and three iambic tetrameter, lines two and four iambic trimeter :

" The Sun now rose upon the right :

Out of the sea came he,

Still hid in mist, and on the left

Went down into the sea."

The lines are regular as regards the number of syllables but not entirely regular in metre.

Let us examine the next stanza :

" And the good south wind still blew behind,

But no sweet bird did follow,

Nor any day for food or play

Came to the mariner's hullo ! "

There are nine syllables in the first line. Because it has an extra unaccented syllable we call this line **hypermetrical**.

Here is a third stanza :

> " Water, water, everywhere,
>
> And all the boards did shrink ;
>
> Water, water, everywhere,
>
> Nor any drop to drink."

Since the first line has only seven syllables, one short of the usual, it is called **catalectic**.

If you attempt to scan some modern poetry, you will find yourself in difficulties. Many modern poets use *Vers Libre* (free verse) in which there is no apparent regularity of metre.

Example :—

> " Yes, when the stars glisten'd,
>
> All night long, on the prong of a moss-scallop'd stake,
>
> Down, almost amid the slapping waves,
>
> Sat the lone singer, wonderful, causing tears.
>
> He call'd on his mate ;
>
> He pour'd forth the meanings which I, of all men, know."
>
> WALT WHITMAN'S " *Out of the Cradle Endlessly Rocking.*"

STANZAS

When we speak about a verse of poetry we usually mean a group of lines of a definite pattern, often called a **Stanza**. Remember that the word **verse** may also mean a single line of poetry.

The stanzas are usually regular, each being of the same number of lines, each corresponding line of the same length and metre. The term stanza may also be used of divisions, irregular in length, resembling paragraphs in prose, such as are found in *L'Allegro*.

Some of the common stanzas used in English poetry are :—

The Ballad Stanza : The commonest form is that in which the metrical Psalms are written, but the stanza varies in different ballads :

(a)	" The Lord's my shepherd, I'll not want,	a
	He makes me down to lie	b
	In pastures green ; He leadeth me	c
	The quiet waters by."	b
(b)	" As I was walking all alone	a
	Between a water and a wa',	b
	And there I spied a wee wee man,	c
	And he was the least that e'er I saw."	b

The Burns Stanza : As the name implies, this was used frequently by Burns :

" I'm truly sorry man's dominion	a
Has broken nature's social union,	a
And justifies that ill opinion	a
Which makes thee startle	b
At me, thy poor earth-born companion,	a
An' fellow mortal ! "	b

The Spenserian Stanza was first used by Spenser in his *Faerie Queene*. Notice particularly the ninth line, a hexameter, called an **Alexandrine.**

" From scenes like these old Scotia's grandeur
   springs,   *a*
  That makes her lov'd at home, rever'd abroad ;   *b*
  Princes and lords are but the breath of Kings ;   *a*
  ' An honest man's the noblest work of God ' :   *b*
  And certes, in fair virtue's heav'nly road,   *b*
  The cottage leaves the palace far behind ;   *c*
  What is a lordling's pomp ? A cumbrous load,   *b*
  Disguising oft the wretch of human kind,   *c*
  Studied in arts of hell, in wickedness refin'd ! "   *c*

The Sonnet is a poem of fourteen lines of iambic pentameter, having a definite rhyme scheme. The English type has two varieties—the Shakespearean and the Spenserian ; and there is the Classical or Italian type.

English Type		Classical or Italian Type
Shakespearean	**Spenserian**	
Quatrain { *a* *b* *a* *b*	{ *a* *b* *a* *b*	Octave — Quatrain { *a* *b* *b* *a*
Quatrain { *c* *d* *c* *d*	{ *b* *c* *b* *c*	Quatrain { *a* *b* *b* *a*
Quatrain { *e* *f* *e* *f*	{ *c* *d* *c* *d*	Volta or Turn
Final Couplet { *g* *g*	{ *e* *e*	Sextet { *c* *c* *d* *d* *e* *c* *c* *d* *d* *c* *e* *d*

Notes.—

(1) The Shakespearean type has 7 rhyming **sounds**, is made up of 3 quatrains and has a final couplet.

(2) The Spenserian type has 5 rhyming sounds, the last rhyming sound of the first quatrain linking with the second quatrain and the last rhyming sound of the second linking with the third and it also has a final rhyming couplet.

(3) The Classical or Italian type has a definite volta or turn after the octave and has no rhyming couplet.

The Elegiac Stanza: Because of the popularity of Gray's *Elegy Written in a Country Churchyard*, the stanza used in that poem is usually regarded as the elegiac stanza in English poetry; but elegies have been written in various stanzas (*e.g.* Milton's *Lycidas*, Shelley's *Adonais*, Cowper's *Toll for the Brave*).

> " The curfew tolls the knell of parting day,   *a*
>   The lowing herd winds slowly o'er the lea,   *b*
>   The ploughman homeward plods his weary way,   *a*
>   And leaves the world to darkness and to me."   *b*

WORD MELODY

There is a strong probability that many words owe their origin to the sounds which they represent. We may caution some one, " Don't *bang* the door ! " The fire burns with a merry *crackle*. Silk *rustles*, bees *buzz* and ducks *quack*. We realise that words have sound values as well as merely sense values. A poet aims at the most suitable expression and that usually is the most pleasing and effective. All good writers, whether of prose or poetry, take the sound values of words into account as well as the sense. As Pope writes.

" The sound must be an echo to the sense."

This device of using words the sounds of which suggest the sense of the words is called **Onomatopoeia** and this onomatopoetic (or onomatopoeic) effect is most frequently found in poetry.

By choosing suitable vowels and consonants, a poet can produce artistic effects in his work. When Yeats, in his poem *The Lake Isle of Innisfree*, wrote :

" I hear *l*ake water *l*apping with *l*ow *s*ounds by the *s*hore,"

he made no haphazard choice of vowels and consonants. His words are purposely chosen to imitate the sound of water lapping on the shore:

Study the following examples for sound effects :

" And ere three shrill notes the pipe uttered,
    You heard as if an army muttered ;
    And the muttering grew to a grumbling ;
    And the grumbling grew to a mighty rumbling."

" Bang, whang, whang goes the drum, tootle-te-tootle the fife,
    Oh, a day in the city square, there is no such pleasure in life ! "

        " Sweet and low, sweet and low,
            Wind of the western sea,
        Low, low, breathe and blow,
            Wind of the western sea ! "

Read Tennyson's poem *The Brook* and mark his selection of verbs to imitate the various sounds of the water at different parts of the course of the stream :

"I *chatter*, chatter as I flow."
"I *wind* about and in and out."
"I *steal* by lawns and grassy plots."
"I *slide* by hazel covers."
"I *murmur* under moon and stars."

Notice that onomatopoetic effect can be emphasised by *metrical arrangement, imitating the movement described*. In Browning's *The Cavalier's Escape*, for example, the metre imitates the movements of the horses :

"Trample ! trample ! went the roan,
    Trap ! trap ! went the gray ;
But pad ! pad ! pad ! like a thing that was mad,
    My chestnut broke away."

The suddenness of a tropical sunset is effectively emphasised in Coleridge's lines :—

"The sun's rim dips ; the stars rush out ;
At one stride comes the dark."

EXERCISE

In the following extracts one word used by the poet is omitted. In brackets after each are words which might be used, including the word the poet preferred. Try to select the poet's word, taking into consideration the sound and sense most suitable for the occasion:—

(*a*) And here the —— of eager nations ran
In murmur'd pity, or loud roar'd applause.
(talk, noise, buzz, sound.)

(*b*) And every soul, it passed me by,
Like the —— of my cross-bow !
(ping, twang, buzz, whizz.)

(c) While the Cock with lively din,
Scatters the rear of darkness thin,
And to the stack or the barn door,
Stoutly —— his dames before.
(walks, marches, struts, creeps.)

(d) A needless Alexandrine ends the song,
That, like a wounded snake —— its slow length along.
(hauls, drags, glides, slides.)

(e)   Yet still the sails made on
A pleasant noise till noon,
A noise like of a hidden brook
In the —— month of June.
(leafy, sunny, lovely, flow'ry.)

(f) And the owlet —— to the wolf below,
That eats the she-wolf's young.
(sings, calls, whoops, booms.)

EXERCISES IN PROSODY

I.

Scan the following extracts; describe the metre; point out examples of alliteration and onomatopoeia. Where the extract is a stanza, describe it and give its rhyme scheme:—

1. When Britain first at Heaven's command
   Arose from out the azure main.

2. Ruin seize thee, ruthless King !

3. Welcome, wild North-easter !
   Shame it is to see.

4. Not a word to each other ; we kept the great pace
   Neck by neck, stride by stride, never changing our place.

5. See you the dimpled track that runs,
   All hollow through the wheat ?
   O that was where they hauled the guns
   That smote King Philip's fleet.

6. Here comes the elephant
   Swaying along
   With his cargo of children
   All singing a song :
   To the tinkle of laughter
   He goes on his way,
   And his cargo of children
   Have crowned him with may.

7. One road leads to London,
   One road leads to Wales,
   My road leads me seawards
   To the white dipping sails.

8. " You are old," said the youth, " one would hardly
      suppose
      That your eye was as steady as ever ;
   Yet you balanced an eel at the end of your nose—
   What made you so awfully clever ?

9. When captains courageous whom death could not
      daunt,
   Did march to the siege of the city of Gaunt,
   They mustered their soldiers by two and by three,
   And the foremost in battle was Mary Ambree.

10. John Gilpin was a citizen
    Of credit and renown,
    A train-band captain eke was he
    Of famous London town.

11. O hark ! O hear ! how thin and clear,
       And thinner, clearer, farther going !
    O sweet and far from cliff and scar
       The horns of Elfland faintly blowing !
    Blow, let us hear the purple glens replying ;
    Blow, bugle ; answer, echoes, dying, dying, dying

12. What is this life if, full of care,
    We have no time to stand and stare.
    No time to stand beneath the boughs
    And stare as long as sheep and cows

13. There's not a joy the world can give like that it takes
    away,
    When the glow of early thought declines in feeling's
    dull decay.

14. What are garlands and crowns to the brow that is
    wrinkled ?
    'Tis but as a dead flower with May-dew besprinkled.
    Then away with all such from the head that is hoary !
    What care I for the wreaths that can only give glory !

15. Heard a carol, mournful, holy,
    Chanted loudly, chanted lowly,
    Till her blood was frozen slowly,
    And her eyes were darken'd wholly,
        Turn'd to Camelot ;
    For ere she reached upon the tide
    The first house by the water-side,
    Singing in her song she died,
        The Lady of Shalott.

16. And in a later time, ere yet the Boy
    Had put on boy's attire, did Michael love,
    Albeit of a stern unbending mind,
    To have the young one in his sight, when he
    Wrought in the field, or on his shepherd's stool
    Sate with a fettered sheep before him stretched
    Under the large old oak, that near his door
    Stood single.

17. The knight breathed free in the morning wind,
    And strove his hardihood to find :
    He was glad when he passed the tombstones gray,
    Which girdle round the fair Abbaye.

18. O for one hour of Wallace wight ;
    Or well skill'd Bruce, to rule the fight,
    And cry, " Saint Andrew and our right ! "
    Another sight had seen that morn,
    From Fate's dark book a leaf been torn,
    And Flodden had been Bannockbourne !

II

1. **Without altering the order of the following words, write them as lines of blank verse (iambic pentameter), suitably punctuated:—**

   (*a*) So saying from the pavement he half rose slowly with pain reclining on his arm and looking wistfully with wide blue eyes as in a picture him Sir Bedivere remorsefully regarded thro' his tears and would have spoken but he found not words.

   (*b*) I have been toiling more than seventy years and in the open sunshine of God's love have we all lived yet if these fields of ours should pass into a stranger's hand I think that I could not lie quiet in my grave.

2. **Without altering the order of the following words, write them, with suitable punctuation—**

   (*a*) *As a four-lined stanza rhyming a b a b :—*

   I murmur under moon and stars in brambly wildernesses I linger by my shingly bars I loiter round my cresses.

   (*b*) *As a five-lined stanza rhyming a b b a b :—*

   I look down over the farms in the fields of grain I see the harvest that is to be and I fling to the air my arms for I know it is all for me.

   (*c*) *As a four-lined stanza of iambic pentameter rhyming a b a b :—*

   One morn I miss'd him on the custom'd hill along the heath and near his favourite tree another came nor yet beside the rill nor up the lawn nor at the wood was he.

CHAPTER XV

FIGURES OF SPEECH AND LITERARY DEVICES

" As weak *as a kitten* " ; " as hard *as iron* " ; " March comes in *like a lion* and goes out *like a lamb* " ; " he ran *like a hare* " ; " he was *a regular brick* "—these expressions are fairly common in everyday speech yet many people who use them are unaware that they are using figures of speech. This should prove that figures of speech are not confined to poetry or even to carefully composed prose.

In a figure of speech we depart from the ordinary, literal use of a term. If we say or write that some one is a regular *pillar of the church*, we mean that that person is one of the chief supporters of the church, just as a pillar is an actual support for a roof or a balcony.

We use figurative language to make our meaning clearer than it would be without the use of the particular figure of speech used. We also use figures of speech to add force and beauty to our meaning and, in poetry, you will find this to be particularly true, because a poet aims at creating beauty of language, whereas a writer of prose often contents himself with being satisfied that his meaning has been illustrated more clearly.

Some figures of speech are based on a *resemblance between things compared.*

If you refer to your chum as " a regular brick," you mean he is reliable, dependable, he will not " let you down." The origin of this colloquial expression is probably the fact that a brick does not crumble or collapse easily. This is the quality common to your chum and a brick.

FIGURES BASED ON RESEMBLANCE

SIMILE.	PERSONIFICATION.
METAPHOR.	PARABLE, ALLEGORY, FABLE.

A **Simile** (Latin adj. meaning like or similar) is a figure of speech in which we state that one thing is *like* another **or** *as* another in one particular respect.

Examples :

1. He was as poor *as a church mouse*.
2. He was *like a bull in a china shop*.

The point of resemblance in (2) is awkwardness or clumsiness.

These examples are very simple and short ; they may illustrate the meaning well enough but they are neither beautiful nor original. In poetry we usually find the similes to be long, elaborate, beautiful and original.

Here are a few examples of simile from the poets :

" Like a glow-worm golden
   In a dell of dew,

Scattering unbeholden
Its aerial hue
Among the flowers and grass, which screen it from
the view."

" Their sails, as black as a starless night,
Came moving on— "

" As idle as a painted ship
Upon a painted ocean."

" Then like a pawing horse let go,
She made a sudden bound " (describing a ship).

" Like one that on a lonesome road
Doth walk in fear and dread,
And having once turned round, walks on,
And turns no more his head ;
Because he knows a frightful fiend
Doth close behind him tread."

A Metaphor is a figure of speech in which one thing is stated to be another ; one thing is put in place of another because there is one point of resemblance between the two things compared. For example, the camel has been called " the ship of the desert." The point of resemblance here is that just as a ship was found to be the best means of crossing the sea, so the camel was best adapted for crossing the desert.

Examples :

" Dew-drops are the gems of morning,
But the tears of mournful eve ! "

" And death is a low mist which cannot blot
The brightness it may veil."

" When I have fears that I may cease to be
Before my pen has glean'd my teeming brain."

Notes.—

1. In simile and metaphor there should be only **one** point of resemblance between the things compared and this resemblance should be clear.

2. You must not use **mixed metaphor,** *i.e.* you must not confuse the images.

   For example, to state that " the hand that rocks the cradle rules the world " would mean that women rule the world ; but to state that " the hand that rocks the cradle has kicked the bucket " would be nonsense. " To kick the bucket " is a slang expression meaning to die, by hanging. (Try to find the origin of the expression.) A hand being hanged is ridiculous.

3. Not every *like* or *as* introduces a simile. For example, " The duck is like the goose," " Wellington was like Napoleon "—these are true comparisons.

4. A simile can be made into a metaphor and a metaphor into a simile, *e.g.*

   " He curbed his passion " (metaphor).

   " He controlled his passion as if with a curb " (simile).

5. When a simile or metaphor is too far-fetched, too difficult to allow us to see the resemblance, it largely defeats its purpose. Such out-of-the-way similes or metaphors are called **Conceits.**

In **Personification** (sometimes called Personal Metaphor) we imagine something to be a person or having the qualities and feelings of a person.

> " April, April,
>   Laugh thy girlish laughter ;
> Then, the moment after,
> Weep thy girlish tears."

We can see from this example that the poet (Sir Wm. Watson) is treating the month of April as a girl and that he brings out the qualities of April, sun and shower, in laughter and tears.

The using of initial capital letters in abstract nouns is not regarded as good personification. This practice was common among the XVIIIth century poets, *e.g.*

> " With distant voice neglected Virtue calls,
>   Less heard and less, the faint remonstrance falls,
>   Tir'd with contempt, she quits the slippery reign,
>   And Pride and Prudence take her seat in vain."

Parable, Allegory, Fable are based on Resemblance.

A Parable takes the form of a simple story based on a series of similes but the writer or speaker intends to convey some spiritual meaning, using the simple narrative for this purpose. (An earthly story with a heavenly meaning.)

Christ used many parables as his audiences were simple folk. If you study the parable of the Sower, you will find that Christ, after telling the simple story, explains that the seed is the word of God and what happens to the seed is what really happens to the word of God among different people.

An **Allegory** is a story based on metaphor that is maintained throughout the story. Bunyan, in his " Pilgrim's Progress," tells of the adventures that befall a man whom he calls Christian. A child may think that the difficulties that confront Christian are real wordly, concrete obstacles, but an older reader at once realises that these difficulties are spiritual ones, the kind that all good Christians meet with in trying to live a good life (*e.g.* when Christian meets Giant Despair he has, for the time, lost hope).

A **Fable** is a story based on personification in which birds, beasts and fishes are made to talk like human beings and the object of the writer is to teach a moral, that is, a lesson to help us to live a good life.   (See Aesop's Fables.)

FIGURES BASED ON CONTRAST

ANTITHESIS.	EPIGRAM.
PARADOX.	PUN.

In **Antithesis** (*a placing opposite*) we contrast one thing with another (or with others), thus stressing the difference between them.

Examples :

Better to *reign* in *Hell* than *serve* in *Heaven.*

For *men* must *work* and *women* must *weep.*

And fools who came *to scoff* remained *to pray.*

Revenge triumphs over death ; *love slights* it ; *Honour aspireth* to it ; *grief flieth* to it.

Epigram and Paradox

An **Epigram** nowadays means a short, pithy and usually a clever saying.

Examples :

Brevity is the soul of wit.

Waste not, want not.

For the apparel oft proclaims the man.

A **Paradox** is that extreme form of the epigram in which a definite contradiction is made, but an underlying truth becomes apparent on thinking over the meaning of the statement.

Examples :

A *favourite* has no *friend*.

In the midst of *life* we are in *death*.

To spend too much time in studies is *sloth*.

A **Pun** consists in using the same word in different senses or in playing on two words which have the same sound but different meanings.

Examples :

" The lion is the beast to fight ;
He leaps along the plain,
And if you run with all your might,
He runs with all his *mane*."

" Ben Battle was a soldier bold
And used to war's alarms,
A cannon-ball shot off his legs
So he laid down his *arms*."

" I am indeed, sir, a surgeon to old shoes :
When they are in great danger, I *recover* them."

19

FIGURES BASED ON ASSOCIATION
OF IDEAS

METONYMY.	TRANSFERRED EPITHET.
SYNECDOCHE.	ANTONOMASIA.

> " Sceptre and Crown
> Must tumble down,
> And in the dust be equal made
> With the poor crooked scythe and spade."

We associate sceptre and crown with one who rules, a spade and scythe with a peasant. The literal meaning of these lines may be expressed thus :—" Kings and peasants are made equal in the grave."

Metonymy is a figure of speech in which we use something associated with the idea we wish to express instead of the literal expression of that idea.

Examples :

Gray hairs are honourable.

He took *silk* (*i.e.* a barrister became a K.C. or Q.C.).

Give every man thine *ear*, but few thy *voice*.

Synecdoche is a figure of speech in which we use a part for the whole or the whole for a part. The part used should always be so significant that the synecdoche is easily seen.

Examples :

He had two hundred *hands* in his factory.

He was the *bread*-winner in the house (bread stands for food in general).

In **Transferred Epithet** we apply an adjective, which is properly associated with one idea, **to** another.

Examples :

The ploughman homeward plods his *weary* **way.**

The prisoner was lodged in the *condemned* cell.

In **Antonomasia** the name of an outstanding character in literature or history is substituted for the quality or qualities which is or are associated with that person.

Examples :

He was a Judas to his party.

Some village-Hampden, that with dauntless **breast**
  The little tyrant of his fields withstood,
Some mute inglorious Milton here may rest,
  Some Cromwell, guiltless of his country's blood."

FIGURES BASED ON ARRANGEMENT

CLIMAX	INVERSION.
ANTICLIMAX.	RHETORICAL QUESTION.
	EXCLAMATION.

In **Climax** (Gr., *a ladder*) ideas are expressed in ascending order of importance, the most important thus being placed last.

Examples :

I came ; I saw ; I conquered.

The cloud-capp'd towers, the gorgeous palaces,
The solemn temples, the great globe itself,
Yea, all which it inherit, shall dissolve.

Anticlimax is not a reversal of climax. The ideas are stated in ascending order of importance, as in climax, but the last idea is of much less importance or dignity. Thus humour often results from this arrangement.

Examples :

Some have for Wits, then poets past,
Turn'd Critics next, and prov'd plain *Fools* at best.

If parts allure thee, think how Bacon shin'd,
The wisest, brightest, *meanest* of mankind.

Inversion occurs when we change the normal order of the parts of a statement. (In English, it is subject, predicate and object.)

Examples :

Great is Diana of the Ephesians.

To them his heart, his love, his griefs were given.

Rhetorical Question (Interrogation)

Be careful not to confuse this with the ordinary question, as one who frames an ordinary question expects an answer. The Rhetorical Question is really a statement put in the form of a question for the sake of emphasis.

Examples :

Can the Ethiopian change his skin or the leopard his spots ?

What female heart can gold despise ?
What cat's averse to fish ?

Exclamation, indicated by an exclamation mark, is used to indicate strong emotion, not fully or accurately described.

Examples :

Dear God ! the very houses seem asleep ;
And all that mighty heart is lying still !

Look on my works, ye mighty, and despair !

MISCELLANEOUS FIGURES

APOSTROPHE.	CIRCUMLOCUTION.
HYPERBOLE.	INNUENDO.
EUPHEMISM.	IRONY.

In **Apostrophe** a writer or speaker addresses an inanimate object as if it were alive, or an absent person as if he were present. An exclamation mark is used.

Examples :

Milton ! thou shouldst be living at this hour.

O Music ! sphere-descended maid,
Friend of pleasure, Wisdom's aid !

In **Hyperbole** (Gr., *exaggeration*) for the sake of emphasising his meaning, a writer or speaker purposely exaggerates his statement. There is no desire or intention to create a false impression.

Examples :

Hell grew darker at their frown.

I lov'd Ophelia. Forty thousand brothers
Could not, with all their quantity of love,
Make up my sum.

In **Euphemism** we soften an expression which contains some harsh or disagreeable news or meaning.

Examples :

He passed away.

He is a stranger to the truth.

He is guilty of taking what is not his own.

Circumlocution (Latin, *circum*—about ; *loquor*—I speak) or **Periphrasis** consists in stating something in a roundabout way. It is frequently used in Euphemism and also for the purpose of humour.

Examples :

My better half (for wife).

    And the cups
That cheer but not inebriate (tea).

In **Innuendo (Insinuation)** the writer hints or suggests his meaning and does not convey it openly and directly.

Example :

Saint Peter sat by the celestial gate :
His keys were rusty, and the lock was dull,
So little trouble had been given of late.

Irony is present when a writer or speaker states the opposite of the meaning he intends. The words are not expected to be taken in their literal meaning. When the words are spoken, the tone of the speaker will usually give a clue to his intention.

Example : Mark Antony's repetition in his funeral oration—

" Brutus is an honourable man "

is ironical *after* he has won over the mob, and knows that it is now against Brutus.

EXERCISES ON FIGURES OF SPEECH AND LITERARY DEVICES

Name the figures of speech or literary devices illustrated in the following:—

1. From silver spouts the grateful liquors glide,
   While China's earth receives the smoking tide.
2. Bright as the sun, her eyes the gazer's strike,
   And, like the sun, they shine on all alike.
3. As it will be the right of all, so it will be the duty of some, definitely to prepare for a separation, amicably if they can, violently if they must.
4. The stubborn spear-men still made good
   Their dark impenetrable wood,
   Each slipping where his comrade stood,
   The instant that he fell.
5. So little done, so much to do.
6. I have a rendezvous with Death,
   At some disputed barricade.
7. The barge she sat in, like a burnish'd throne,
   Burn'd on the water ; the poop was beaten gold,
   Purple the sails, and so perfumed, that
   The winds were love-sick with them.
8. Let us sit and mock the good housewife
   Fortune from her wheel, that her gifts may
   Henceforth be bestowed equally.
9. All the world's a stage,
   And all the men and women merely players.

10. Rich honesty dwells like a miser, sir, in a poorhouse ;
    as your pearl in your foul oyster.

11. O, for a horse with wings !

12. Now is it Rome indeed, and room enough.

13. Thou art the ruins of the noblest man
    That ever lived in the tide of times.

14. O judgement ! thou art fled to brutish beasts,
    And men have lost their reason.

15. Nae man can tether time or tide.

16. A voice so thrilling ne'er was heard
    In spring-time from the Cuckoo-bird,
    Breaking the silence of the seas
    Among the farthest Hebrides.

17. Go ! lovely Rose !
    Tell her, that wastes her time and me,
    That now she knows,
    When I resemble her to thee,
    How sweet and fair she seems to be.

18. Argument for a week, laughter for a month, and a
    good jest for ever.

19. The redcoats soon filled the village square.

20. The thundering line of battle stands,
    And in the air Death moans and sings.

21. He receives comfort like cold porridge.

22. Are we downhearted ?

23. God's finger touched him and he slept.

24. Was there a man dismayed ?

25. He was a rake among scholars and a scholar among
    rakes.

26. When well-apparelled April on the heel
    Of limping winter treads.

27. There were gentlemen and there were seamen in
    the navy of Charles the Second. But the seamen were
    not gentlemen, and the gentlemen were not seamen.

28. Man is the hunter ; woman is his game.
29.   I will drink
     Life to the lees.
30. If from society we learn to live,
    'Tis solitude should teach us how to die.
31. And the sentinel stars set their watch in the sky
32. Sapping a solemn creed with solemn sneer.
33. The holy time is quiet as a nun
    Breathless with adoration.
34. The Wedding-Guest stood still,
    And listens like a three years' child.
35. The lark becomes a sightless song.
36. Have I not had to wrestle with my lot ?
37. And the mute silence hist along.
38. Laughter, holding both his sides.

CHAPTER XVI

HOW TO READ

A well-known professor used to tell his students how he kept his daughter from reading fairy tales until she was nearly twelve, when she took the law into her own hands and for years read nothing else. It might have been worse. She might have been discouraged from reading of any kind. You, it is hoped, are encouraged to read even if you do read a certain amount of rubbish in the shape of silly sentiment or hair-raising adventure. If among the rubbish you find a certain amount of what is good, you will in time learn to respect and value what has been written by those who are wiser, wittier and more tolerant than the rest of us. In time you will learn to value books as a storehouse of information on every subject in which you are interested. From them you will add to your knowledge of what is happening all around you and develop and satisfy your powers of imagination. To your surprise, you will learn that what you thought and felt had never been experienced or understood before, has been expressed far more clearly and vividly than you can ever hope to do. Others have had pet dogs and cats and described them delightfully, others have longed to see strange places, and realising their ambition, are able to deepen and widen your own secret thoughts by stories in prose and verse. When you begin to realise how much reading can do for you, you will feel that you wish to get the most out of your reading, and it is then that a little advice may be helpful on How to Read.

To make sure that you have got the best out of a book, ask yourself the following questions :—

1. Have you been able to follow the thread of the story ?
2. Can you retell the story briefly or give the main ideas in an orderly fashion without omitting any important facts ?
3. What has the author tried to do : (a) tell a story, (b) interest you in characters, (c) explain his own feelings or opinions ?
4. Do you understand his subject better, whether it dealt with some way of living, a country and its people or human nature ?
5. Was the purpose of the author worth-while ? Is any part of the book specially pleasing or irritating ? If so, why ?
6. Does the writer use any devices, e.g. metre, description, conflict, humour, that have impressed you ?

In answering these questions, do not assume that you must always praise a book, though it is just as bad to do nothing but find fault. *Don't* praise a book because others do, but remember that to dislike a book because others like it is not in itself praiseworthy. At first you will find it difficult to explain your likes and dislikes to others but with practice you will learn how to tell not only what is good from what is bad, but what is much more difficult, the best from the second best.

READING PROSE

The forms of prose to be considered are :

I. Short Story.
II. Novel.
III. Essay.

I.—A **Short Story** is of course to be read right through, but when you begin to think it over, you will find that it divides naturally into three parts :

(a) The **Introduction,** which tells you of the chief characters and when and where the story takes place.

(b) The **Crisis,** or Turning Point, is the second part of the story and it puts before you the difficulties with which the hero has to deal, how they arise, and the various characters affected by them.

(c) The **Climax,** which tells you what the hero does and what comes out of his action. According to whether the result is good or bad, the ending is what is often called " happy " or " unhappy."

The following exercises will help to bring out the full meaning of the story when you have read it and are thinking it over :—

1. Divide the story into **Introduction, Crisis** and **Climax,** giving in a paragraph a brief summary of each.

2. What do we learn of the story, the characters and the setting (scene and time of the action) from the **Introduction ?** Which arouses your interest most ?

3. What difficulties face the hero in the problem before him ?

4. What does the hero do ? Could he have decided in a better way, or is it the only thing he could do in view of his nature or any other circumstances ?

5. What is the result of the action of the hero ?

6. Write down any references by which you have learned something of the characters, the place and the time of the story.

7. Have you enjoyed the story ? If so, is it because it is exciting, strange and romantic, like real life or otherwise ?

Here is an example of what you might do. *The Two Drovers* is a well-known story by Sir Walter Scott to be found in many collections of short stories :—

1. THE TWO DROVERS.

   (a) The story begins with a description of Highland drovers in the eighteenth century shortly after the '45 rebellion, and tells of their lives and characters. It describes Robin Oig, with details of his appearance, general popularity and his hidden but intense family pride. A prophecy is made, which we feel will come true, that during his journey he will slay an Englishman.

   (b) He meets and travels with his close friend, Harry Wakefield, a genial English drover. They cross the Borders into England, but Wakefield quarrels with him over grazing rights at a resting place in Yorkshire. Later, at the inn, Robin tries to make up the quarrel, but Wakefield, his anger increased by the taunts of his friends, challenges him to a fight. Robin, unskilled in fighting with his fists, is badly beaten. Wakefield now feels sorry, but Robin, his pride aroused. threatens revenge.

(c) He regains his dagger from a fellow Scot **and**
refusing all aid, returns to the inn.   Refusing
Wakefield's offer of friendship, he challenges him
to fight and strikes him dead with a single blow.
He offers no resistance to the officers of the law
but surrenders with the words, " Death pays all
debts ; it will pay for that too."

Here the story really ends, but Scott, who was
himself a lawyer and interested in the legal side of the
case, adds an account of the trial where Robin Oig,
despite the sympathy of the judge, was by the law
of the land condemned to death.

2. Introduction makes it clear that Robin was a brave
   man to whom his good name was very precious.

3. The real interest of the story is in the character of
   Robin.   You know early in the story that he will
   commit a murder and, very shortly afterwards, who is
   to be the victim.   You read on because you wish to
   know how such a man will come to kill his dearest friend.

4. Robin Oig's pride is such that only death can wipe
   out the insult which affects not only him but the
   honour of his family.

5. The result of his action is the death of his friend and
   of Robin himself.   You may regret what happens but
   you feel that it is the just solution.

6. You learn something of the character of the Highlander—so different from that of the Englishman, or
   even the Lowland Scot—with its strong sense of pride
   and its superstitions.   In contrast you learn something
   of the English character with its qualities, both good
   and bad.   There is an interesting description of the
   life of the drovers, an English inn and of an English
   Court of Justice.

7. The interest of the story is in the contrasts of national
   character in the years after the Jacobite rebellion.

EXERCISE I

(Most of these exercises are based on well-known stories but may be applied to any others you are reading.)

1. **What do we learn of the appearance and character of the dealer in Markheim by R. L. Stevenson, from the following quotations ?—**

   (a) Some of my customers are ignorant and I touch a dividend on my superior knowledge.

   (b) The little, pale round-shouldered dealer stood almost on tip-toe looking over the top of his gold spectacles.

   (c) The dealer . . . thus ran on in his dry, rasping voice.

   (d) I in love ! I never had the time, nor have I the time to-day for all this nonsense.

   (e) His thin blonde hair falling over his eyes.

   (f) The dealer struggled like a hen.

2. **The Pit and the Pendulum, by E. A. Poe.** Explain the plot in detail and show how your interest is maintained to the end.

3. Name any story in which you learn a great deal about the time, place, customs, etc., which form the background of the story. State briefly what you learn.

4. Name any story (one for each) in which you found the plot (a) far-fetched, (b) impossible, (c) unconvincing, and explain why you have come to these conclusions.

5. Make a list of the characters in any short story in two columns according as they are for or against the hero. Write a sentence or two on each to show what part they take in the story.

6. Select any short story in which there is much dialogue and show what it tells you of the plot or the characters.

II.—A **Novel** is a long story and tells of the relations or behaviour of a number of people. The action may last a short time or extend over a life-time and may be confined to a village or extend over several continents. From it you learn something of the author's idea of what life means and you will find that where one writer will see pathos, another sees only humour, and what is gently treated by one is attacked bitterly by another. So that when you have read a novel, you should know something of the plot, characters, setting and the author's way of looking at life. The following exercises will help you when you are thinking over what you have read :—

1. Make a summary of the story without omitting any important facts.

2. Gather information about the main characters by considering what they say and do, what others say about them, and what the author himself says. The following plan is useful :—

Character	Qualities	Illustrations	Chapter

3. What have you learned of the setting? (Descriptions of places, customs, dress, language, etc.)

4. Select your favourite passages and explain why you like them. Refer to the author's use of humour, pathos, vivid writing, satire, etc.

EXERCISE II

1. Write a summary of the story of your favourite novel. Make sure that your summary brings out what you have enjoyed.

2. What do we learn of the appearance and character of John Silver from the following quotations from " Treasure Island " :—

   (a) He was very tall and strong, with a face as big as a ham—plain and pale, but intelligent and smiling.

   (b) The man's a perfect trump.

   (c) All the crew respected and even obeyed him.

   (d) Silver twice buried his knife up to the hilt in that defenceless body.

   (e) Did any of you gentlemen want to have it out with me ?

   (f) It's us must break the treaty when the time comes.

   (g) I never was feared of Flint in his life, and by the Powers I'll face him dead.

   (h) John Silver, you're a prodigious villain and imposter ?

3. In what novels do the following characters play a part? Describe one of them fully, and tell briefly the part he plays in the story.

   A miser, a Jew, a cripple, a giant, a Highland robber, an archer, a pirate, an American boy.

4. Name the characters referred to in the following questions. Name the novels (with names of authors) in which they may be found.

   (a) Who had his savings stolen but found a greater interest and happiness in a baby ?

   (b) Who was drowned with her brother in a flood ?

20

   (c) Who discovered a plot while hiding in an apple barrel ?

   (d) Who experienced a change of heart at Christmas ?

   (e) Who made his first appearance in a combat in armour much too big for him ?

  (f) Who was pursued through the Highlands on a charge of murder of which he was innocent ?

   (g) Who distinguished himself at a football match during his first day at school ?

   (h) Who shocked the Master of a Workhouse by asking for more ?

5. Take any historical novel you have read and tell what interested you in the manners, customs, dress, etc., of the period described.

6. Describe any humorous incident or character from any novel you have read. Show what you found amusing.

III.—The **Essay** you read in school is generally a short one by some modern author but very often you read one of the longer essays of Macaulay. These modern essays generally treat of what may seem a trivial subject. The great essayists of the eighteenth and nineteenth centuries, such as Addison and Lamb, generally have a more important subject. You may apply the same method of study to both types for both are short and express the direct thoughts of the author on some subject which has engaged his interest.

Structure of the Essay

  (1) The Beginning, which may be—

    (a) A quotation.

    (b) A definition of the title.

     (*c*) An anecdote.

     (*d*) A general statement of the subject.

(2) The Middle or main section of the essay.

(3) The End.

     (*a*) A quotation.

     (*b*) A summary.

     (*c*) A general statement.

To test your reading of an essay, work out the following exercises :—

1. Brief statement of the subject or theme.
2. Brief summary of the ideas of the essay. This may often be built up from the topic sentences of paragraphs. Pay special attention to the first and last paragraphs.
3. Note the kind and arrangement of sentence commonly used and any unusual words.
4. What do you learn of the likes and dislikes of the writer ?
5. Note references to illustrate humour, pathos, etc.

Let us apply the method to Addison's essay, *Sir Roger at Church* :—

1. The essay gives a description of a service in a country church.
2. The writer describes the value of Sunday and of church-going to country people. He describes the successful attempts of Sir Roger de Coverley to improve the appearance of the church and arouse the interest of the congregation. He describes his behaviour in church and his careful watch over the congregation. He notes that in some churches the quarrels between the squire and the parson have a bad effect on the congregation.

3. The sentences are simple and clear. The words are simple, with at times an old-fashioned quality.

4. The writer is mainly concerned with the value of religion in teaching ignorant people how to behave properly inside and outside the church.

5. There is a quiet humour running through the essay, especially in his description of the behaviour of Sir Roger.

The following method may be applied to a longer essay :—

THE TRIAL OF THE BISHOPS (*Narratives from Macaulay. Macmillan*).

Introduction, pp. 1-5.

1. After the Restoration of Charles II, what acts were passed against Nonconformists ?

2. What was the immediate purpose of James II's Declaration of Indulgence ?   What was his real aim ?

3. Why did the Bishops sign the petition against the Declaration ?

4. The trial of the Bishops was part of a struggle against the claim of the King to " do no wrong." Explain this statement.

Pp. 5-11.

1. Why did James II delay appearance of the Bishops at the Council ?

2. Name three Bishops who supported the King's Declaration of Indulgence.

3. What question did the Archbishop decline to answer in the Council Chamber and what reason did he give for his refusal ?

4. What privilege did the Bishops claim as peers of the realm ?

5. What serious step did James take when the Bishops refused to surrender their rights ?

6. What " coincidence " cheered them on Black Friday ?

7. How did the Government " add insult to injury " during their imprisonment ?

8. Write down four words from the book that describe the behaviour of the Bishops in the Tower.

9. How did the Bishops prove their loyalty to the King while under his displeasure ?

10. Explain these terms :—

Diocese, extant, chicanery, casuist, criminate, recognisance.

Pp. 11-16.

1. What mistake did the common people make when the Bishops left Westminster Hall in freedom ?

2. Why was Cartwright unpopular with the crowd ?

3. What precautions did the King take to prevent a disturbance ?

4. How did the Grenadier Guards show their sympathy with the Bishops ?

5. What steps did the King take to ensure that the jury would return the verdict he desired ?

6. Name the four judges.

7. Why did the Government find difficulty in obtaining Advocates ?

8. Make a list of the lawyers who acted for the Bishops.

9. Who was " junior counsel " for the Bishops ? Write out some words and phrases which Macaulay uses to show his qualifications.

10. Explain these terms :—

Importunate, nullity, advocates, forensic, Attorney General.

Pp. 17-23.

1. What was Michael Arnold's dilemma as a juryman ?

2. Write out the sentence which gives the actual charge against the Bishops.

3. What was the first point to be proved ?
4. What evidence did Blathwayt give ?
5. How did Pemberton turn this evidence against the King ?
6. What was the second point of the charge to be raised ?
7. Why did it seem impossible for the King's Counsel to prove it ?
8. Why was Finch for some hours " the most unpopular man in the country " ?
9. What was the Lord President's evidence ?
10. Explain :—Dissemble, equivocated, apostate, an implied engagement, alleged libel.

Pp. 23-29.

1. What was the third and last point of the charge to be raised ?
2. Why was this the most important ?
3. State briefly Somers' four arguments proving that the petition was not (1) false, (2) malicious, (3) seditious, (4) a libel.
4. Give briefly the verdicts of each of the four Judges.
5. What precautions were taken to prevent any communication between the jury and the outside world while the verdict was under consideration ?
6. Which of the Jurymen held out longest against the Bishops ?
7. What argument was used to convince him ?
8. Describe how the news of the acquittal was received and passed on.
9. Describe briefly the scene outside the hall after the acquittal.
10. Explain :—Constitutional, acrimony, venal, prerogative, sacerdotal garb.

EXERCISE III

1. **Give a list of essays, one for each topic, naming the author, which deal with the following. State briefly how the author treats his subject.**

   Gardens, sport, school stories, food, holidays.

2. **Select essays which make use of the methods given above for the beginning and end of the essays.**

3. **Tell what you have learned of the author of any collection of essays you have read. Deal with appearance, life, dress, habits, likes, dislikes.**

4. **Name any essay you have enjoyed because of the humorous treatment of the subject. Explain why you found it humorous and refer freely to the essay for illustrations.**

5. **Name two essays which deal with the same subject, e.g. Travel. Select the one you prefer and give your reasons.**

6. **Who is your favourite essayist? Name some of his essays and tell what you find enjoyable in them.**

READING POETRY

Many of you find so many strange things in poetry that you dislike it without trying very hard to understand it. There are so many things that you find unusual. The people in poems seem unreal ; they talk in a strange old-fashioned language at times ; words are omitted, or the order of words is inverted. You feel that poetry is a tiresome and unsatisfactory way of saying things and you are not very sure what it means. Here again, however, if you persevere, you will have your reward in the pleasure that poetry can give to those who appreciate it. You will find that poetry can and does express itself in vivid and concise language, and that the poet makes you feel things in a way that the writer of prose cannot. You will find that his words can stir your imagination not by disguising facts but by revealing their true meaning. There are no short cuts to such an appreciation of poetry but it is possible to give you some guidance in your reading. Remember, however, that your opinion of a poem should be honest and based entirely on how it affects you. There are many forms of poetry, but you should start with the simpler kinds, such as

 I. **Narrative Poem**.

 II. **Ballad** (special type of Narrative Poem).

 III. **Lyric**.

I.—Test your reading of any **Narrative Poem** by means of the following exercises, remembering that a Narrative, a Ballad and a Lyric can be generally divided up into three parts, like the prose forms you have studied in this chapter. (See p. 300.)

1. Make a summary of the poem in your own words in three paragraphs corresponding to Introduction, Crisis and Climax, as already explained.

2. Make sure of the meaning of any unusual words or phrases.

3. Enumerate the chief characters, if any, and tell what you have learned of each. In dealing with a long Narrative Poem such as *The Ancient Mariner* or Scott's *Marmion*, the method explained in the study of the novel (see p. 304) will be found useful.

4. Pick out any words, lines or phrases which seem specially good and suitable and learn them.

5. Write down and name any Figures of Speech and explain their effect in the poem.

6. Give the metre, rhyme scheme and stanza form. How do they add to the appeal of the poem ?

7. State what feeling the poem arouses in you and, if you can, explain why.

8. What do you learn of the setting of the poem ?

(For an application of the method, see treatment of *The Wife of Usher's Well* and *The Solitary Reaper*.)

The following type of exercise may be applied to a longer narrative poem :—

LADY OF THE LAKE.

Canto I

Stanzas 1-10.

1. In what part of Scotland does the story begin ?
2. Name all living things in stanza 3.
3. What did the last huntsman do after his horse had died ?
4. Explain :—

   Stag, copse, linn, mettle, scourge and steel, brake, quarry.

Stanzas 10-20.

1. Describe the view the huntsman saw from the top of the precipice.
2. Where did he think he would spend the night ?
3. How did he come to meet Ellen ?
4. Describe briefly the Lady of the Lake.
5. Explain :—

   Pinnacle, insulated, turret, pagoda, mosque, minaret, cupola, nymph.

Stanzas 20-30.

1. Briefly describe the huntsman.
2. How did Ellen know a stranger would arrive ?
3. What preparation had been made for his arrival !
4. Describe Ellen's home.
5. What was the Huntsman's name ?
6. Explain :—

    Marshall, ptarmigan, frigate, portico, tapestry, rite.

Stanzas 30-35.

1. What was Fitz-James' nightmarish dream ?
2. How did Fitz-James regard the Douglas Family ?
3. Explain :—

    Symphony, pibroch, cadence, spontaneous, orisons.

EXERCISE IV

1. **Name a poem which deals with each of the following and give a brief summary of *one* of them :—**

    A charge of cavalry ; a shipwreck ; a field of flowers ; a plague of rats ; an escape.

2. **Tell the story of the following poems :—**

    The Revenge, John Gilpin's Ride, The Ancient Mariner, The Jackdaw of Rheims, The Battle of the Baltic.

3. **What do we learn of the appearance and character of Young Lochinvar from the following ?—**

    (*a*) So faithful in love and so dauntless in war.

    (*b*) He swam the Esk river where ford there was none.

    (*c*) So boldly he entered the Netherby hall.
    Among bride's-men and kinsmen and brothers and all.

(*d*)   T'were better by far
      To have matched our fair Ellen to young
        Lochinvar.

(*e*) So light to the croupe the fair lady he swung,
      So light to the saddle before her he sprung!

4. Name *Three* poems which describe the sea. Pick out
   quotations which suggest the sight or the sound or the
   movement of the sea.

5. Who is your favourite character in poetry? Select
   suitable quotations or allusions which refer to
   him and use them as topic sentences to write short
   paragraphs about him.

6. Select *Six* lines of poetry which seem to you specially
   beautiful for any reason. Explain why you like them.

II.—The **Ballad** is a form of narrative poetry
written in the early days of our nation and has in
consequence certain features peculiar to itself.
It tells you generally some well-known story and
reveals the thoughts, emotions and superstitions of
the people who were living when the action of the
story took place. The main interest, you will find,
is in sudden and violent action. The hearers,
then—for the ballad was heard, not read—like
many schoolboys now, had little time for description
or comment. You will easily know most ballads
by the four-lined stanza, known as the ballad
stanza, a trick of using certain adjectives to describe
certain types of people, a frequent use of dialogue
and repetition and at times a refrain, in which no
doubt the audience joined. To the tests already
given for the ordinary Narrative Poem, add the
following :—

   1. If there is dialogue, what use does it serve?

2. Note the influence of supernatural beings, if any.

3. Give examples of any of the following features of the poem : refrain, epithet, repetition.

Example:

THE WIFE OF USHER'S WELL.

1. (a) **Introduction** : In the introduction you are told how the wife of Usher's Well, despite her wealth, sends her three sons to sea, where shortly afterwards they are drowned. In her grief and impatience, she calls down a curse upon the sea and all who sail on it by wishing for perpetual storms until her sons are restored to her.

(b) **Crisis** : In response to her wild curse, her sons return home but from no place in this world. In her joy she makes merry till nightfall and when they retire to bed, watches over them.

(c) **Climax** : At the first sign of morning, the sons leave their home to return to the grave for they dare not stay, although they know that their mother, in her grief, will go mad. They must suffer the torture of leaving all they have loved in life.

2. There are some unusual dialect words, e.g. fashes, channerin'.

3. From the poem we picture the mother as greedy, strong-willed, and rebellious against God's judgement. Note such references as " I wish the winds may never cease," etc.

4. Note such lines as " the channerin' worm doth chide."

5. There is frequent use of Alliteration, e.g. " cock doth craw."

6. The metre is the ballad stanza and is simple and direct

7. The Wife of Usher's Well, by her selfish love and defiance of God, brought suffering upon herself and her sons.

8. There is much dialogue, which quickens the interest.

9. There is a superstitious belief in the return of spirits from the dead.

10. Note the use of adjectives " stout and stalwart," and repetition—

> " They hadna been a week, a week
> But barely three."

EXERCISE V

1. Name ballads which deal with the following subjects and write one sentence about each :—

   Fairies, death, unhappy love, treachery, a fight.

2. Name *Four* Border ballads, state briefly the themes and give the historical incidents on which they are based.

3. Name *Four* modern ballads and show how they compare with the old ballads.

4. What feature of the ballad (language, metre, dialogue, supernatural beings) are found in *The Ancient Mariner* ?

5. Write a brief summary of the following ballads :—

   Chevy Chase, Sir Patrick Spens, Thomas the Rhymer, Rosabelle, Lord Ullin's Daughter, The Twa Corbies.

6. Select *Five* ballads in which there is a refrain. What feelings are expressed in the refrain ?

III.—**The Lyric** : In a Narrative Poem you may put up with the poetry for the sake of the story and even come to enjoy it, but the Lyric is pure poetry which you must enjoy for its own sake or not at all. In a lyric the poet sets out to express certain deep feelings and to arouse in you these same feelings by his use and arrangement of words. You must probe deeply to find out why you like a poem, and what it is that appeals to your ear, or your reason, or your imagination. You will find that the sounds, thoughts and mental pictures of the poem all play their part, though at first you may be somewhat vague as to the reason for the attraction of the poem. At all cost avoid any empty talk of " beautiful " ideas or even " beautiful " words. Remember that the lyric has a well-defined structure in most cases, and that, to understand how it is made, will add to your enjoyment of it. With this warning in mind, you may approach the study of the Lyric.

Like the short story it consists of three sections :—

(a) The **Introduction**, in which the motive or cause of the poem is stated.

(b) A **Middle Part**, in which the feelings and thoughts aroused directly by, or through association with, the motive are expressed.

(c) A **Conclusion**, which reveals the mood of the author as his feelings gradually calm down and he is left with a final impression.

Apply the following tests to your knowledge of any lyric you have read :—

1. Make a summary of the ideas of the poem consisting of three short paragraphs, making clear :
   (a) The cause or theme or motive of the poem.
   (b) The feelings aroused in the poet.
   (c) The final mood of the poet.

2. Pick out any words, lines or phrases which seem specially good and suitable and learn them.

3. Write down and name any figures of speech and explain their effect in the poem.

4. Give the metre, rhyme scheme and stanza form. How do they add to the appeal of the poem ?

5. State what feeling the poem arouses in you, and, if you can, explain why.

6. What do you learn of the setting of the poem ?

EXAMPLE :

THE SOLITARY REAPER.

1. (*a*) The first stanza tells how the poet stops to listen to a Highland girl singing as she works in the field

   (*b*) He compares the effect of her singing in its beauty and mystery to the effect of the song of a nightingale on weary travellers in the desert or of the song of the cuckoo in the quiet Hebrides. He wonders what the song may mean, whether it tells of the commonplace or strange.

   (*c*) In the last stanza he tells how the effect of the song remains with him long after he no longer hears it.

2. Note such references as " Breaking the silence . . . Hebrides," " Of old unhappy . . . ago."

3. The language is simple, the order of the words normal, and there is an absence of figures of speech.

4. The poet uses a stanza of eight lines rhyming *a b a b c c d d*, the metre being iambic tetrameter.

5. There is a deep sense of the beauty and appeal of simple ordinary things which is emphasised by associating them with what is universally accepted as beautiful, such as the songs of the nightingale and the cuckoo ; or with the romantic, such as " old unhappy far-off things."

6. The setting is simple with its picture of the field and hillside in the autumn.

EXERCISE VI

1. **What impressions have the following poems made upon you ?**

   Daffodils, To the Cuckoo, Leisure, The Village Blacksmith, Full Fathom Five.

2. **Name poems which deal with the following topics :—**

   Children, birds, the sea, liberty, love of one's country.

3. **Name *Five* modern poems which deal with the following topics :—**

   War, love of the countryside, trees, simple things, city life.

   Summarise the poems.

4. **Name *Five* lyrics of Burns which reveal his humour, love of country life, patriotism, independence, love of animals.**

5. **Compare and contrast the poems on the skylark by Wordsworth and Shelley.**

6. **Name *Five* lyrics which are intended to be sung. What do you think makes them suitable for singing ? Consider such things as simple ideas, simple regular metre, swinging movement, musical words.**

READING A PLAY

So far as you are concerned, a play is generally intended for class study, and is therefore less likely to suffer from silent reading than fiction or even poetry. It is necessary, however, for you to remember that a play is intended for acting and in Shakespeare's time no other treatment was possible. Many modern plays you will find are intended for reading also, but, at all times, make it a rule to read a play aloud, changing the voice as far as possible to suit each change of character. Treated thus, dialogue will never be found dull or difficult.

In forming your estimate of a play, remember that the plot rises in action to the crisis or turning point and then falls in action to the solution or final stage. Here again, as in the novel, you must study the characters as they are, and in their relations to one another. Shakespeare's plays are generally in blank verse though many modern plays are written in prose. You will find that the dramatist uses certain devices to develop the plot and the characters, such as contrast, comic relief, and what is called dramatic irony. (See Chapter XVII.)

You may find the following method of approach useful.

1. Make a brief summary of the plot, scene by scene.

2. Construct a plot diagram to show the chief incidents in the play.

3. Gather information about the main characters by considering what they say and do, and what others say about them. (See under " The Novel.")

4. Describe the sub-plot if any, show its relation to the main plot and note what characters are common to both.

5. Is the play a tragedy or a comedy ? Illustrate by reference to plot, characters, language.

6. Describe the language, figures of speech and the metre.

Plot Diagram of Julius Caesar

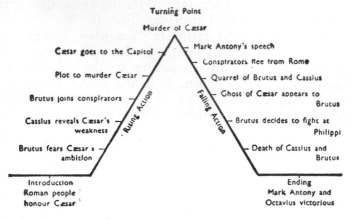

Turning Point
Murder of Cæsar

Cæsar goes to the Capitol — Mark Antony's speech
Plot to murder Cæsar — Conspirators flee from Rome
— Quarrel of Brutus and Cassius
Brutus joins conspirators — Ghost of Cæsar appears to Brutus
Cassius reveals Cæsar's weakness — Brutus decides to fight at Philippi
Brutus fears Cæsar's ambition — Death of Cassius and Brutus

Rising Action   Falling Action

Introduction
Roman people
honour Cæsar

Ending
Mark Antony and
Octavius victorious

QUESTIONNAIRE FOR "AS YOU LIKE IT. Act 1. *Scene* 1.

1. What complaint does Orlando make against his brother Oliver ?

2. How does Oliver set Charles against Orlando ?

3. Why was Rosalind not banished along with her father ?

4. Put into your own words Oliver's tribute to Orlando's character.

5. Give the meaning of the following :—Taught their manage ; mines my gentility with my education ; give me the poor allottery my father left me by testament ; fleet the time carelessly ; requite ; emulator.

6. "What prodigal portion have I spent." Explain this reference.

7. Explain these metaphors :—Nothing remains but that I kindle the boy thither ; I will physic your rankness.

Scene 2.

1. Why was Rosalind sad ?
2. What news did Le Beau bring ?
3. " I would thou hadst been son to some man else." Why did Duke Frederick say this to Orlando ?
4. " You have wrestled well and overthrown more than your enemies." Who said this and what does the last clause mean ?
5. What line tells us that Celia's disposition was not like her father's ?
6. Explain the following :—Yet he looks successfully ; Hercules be thy speed ; a quintain ; usurping ; the duke is humorous.

Scene 3.

1. What reasons does Duke Frederick give for banishing Rosalind ?
2. Where do Rosalind and Celia decide to go ? What are their plans for the journey and who is to accompany them ?
3. Explain the change of meaning in the words in italics :—My father hated his father *dearly* ; we *stay'd* her for your sake ; you *cousin* (Duke Fred. to Rosalind).
4. What do the following words mean ? Purgation ; irrevocable ; umber ; martial ; assay'd.

EXERCISE VII

1. **What aspects of the character of Bottom the Weaver are revealed by the following ?**
    (a) My chief humour is for a tyrant ; I could play Ercles rarely. (Bottom is prepared to play all parts).
    (b) Thou are as wise as thou art beautiful. (To Bottom, wearing an ass's head).

(c) The shallowest thickskin of that barren sort (said by Puck).

(d) I have a reasonable good ear in music. Let's have the tongs and bones (Titania invites him to hear fairy music).

(e) He hath simply the best wit of any handicraft man in Athens (said by one of his friends).

2. What does the first scene of " Julius Caesar " or of " As You Like It " tell you of the chief characters and the plot?

3. Show how the actions of Portia, Rosalind and Mark Antony affect the other characters in the plays to which they belong.

4. Write a brief summary of the following sub-plots, tell what characters are in each, and show the connection with the main plot :—

(a) Story of the Rings . . . *The Merchant of Venice.*

(b) Pyramus and Thisbe . . . A *Midsummer Night's Dream.*

5. Write out in two columns the characters on one side and those who are opposed to them in " As You Like It," " Julius Caesar," " The Merchant of Venice."

6. What scene do you consider to be the turning point of " The Merchant of Venice " ? Show its effect on the chief characters.

HOME READING

Whatever Home Reading was, or was supposed to be, there is no doubt that nowadays you are seldom asked to read any book at home which is dull or uninteresting. The trouble is that you like the books and could enjoy them if it were not that you know that your knowledge will later be tested. What should be a pleasure becomes a task and in consequence becomes distasteful. You feel that you cannot relax. You must always be watching for what is important and so Home Reading becomes merely a piece of tedious preparation.

In the pages following, you will find a set of tests based on well-known novels which may help to solve the problem for you, if you use them as suggested. Read the story for its own sake without any thought of examination. Then, and only then, study it with the help of the Questionnaire which is an attempt to direct your attention to what is important in the story. It is hoped that you will find a certain pleasure in locating quotations and in gathering material to answer questions on the plot, characters and other importants aspect of the story. But remember to read the story first before you look at the Questionnaire.

Note.—In annotation you are expected to tell who is the speaker, the person spoken to, and the occasion when it was said.

Some Examples of Home Reading Tests.

(1) OLIVER TWIST.

1. Annotate :—

   (a) Please, sir, I want some more.

   (b) Hello, my covey ! What's the row ?

   (c) What's your name, you hardened scoundrel ?

   (d) Once fill his mind with the idea that he has been a thief ; and he's ours.

   (e) Coals, candles and house rent free, —— oh, Mrs. ——, what an angel you are !

   (*f*) Hush, my dear! It is he sure enough. **Come away.**

   (*g*) The laudanum has taken effect at last. I may be too late even now.

   (*h*) We have not so much dust as that in London.

   (*i*) Here is a stain upon the hat of a gentleman in company, that I'll take clean out, before he can order me a pint of ale.

   (*j*) Do my hi's deceive me or is that little Holiver?

2. (*a*) Describe the scene in the workhouse when Oliver asked for more.

   (*b*) Describe the fight between Oliver and Noah Claypole and what led up to it.

   (*c*) Write an account of the " games " that Fagin played with his boys. What do you think was the purpose of them?

   (*d*) Describe the robbery in which Oliver was shot.

3. (*a*) Tell what you know of the interview of Mr. Bumble and Mrs. Corney, in which he proposed.

   (*b*) Describe the strange interview between Nancy and Rose Maylie.

   (*c*) Describe the last interview of Nancy and Bill Sykes.

   (*d*) Describe the interview between Monks and Mr. Brownlow.

4. Write an account of :—

   (*a*) The Artful Dodger in Court.

   (*b*) Bill Sikes' escape over the roofs.

5. Write a character sketch dealing with appearance, dress, qualities and part in the story of the following :—

   The Artful Dodger, Mr. Bumble, Fagin, Mr. Brownlow.

(2) CRANFORD.

1. Annotate :—

   (a) I must say I don't think they are by any means equal to Dr. Johnson.

   (b) But why does not this Lord Mauleverer do something for the man who saved his life ?

   (c) The most proper place in the world for his arm to be in.

   (d) And how came Miss Matilda not to marry him ?

   (e) I don't believe frogs will agree with him.

   (f) I had very pretty hair, my dear, and not a bad mouth.

   (g) Have you done enough, sir ?

   (h) My father took him into every house in the parish. He was so proud of him.

   (i) When I cough, open the door. I'll not be a minute.

   (j) Ye'll have been in Edinburgh, maybe ?

2. (a) Give some account of the quarrel between Miss Jenkyns and Captain Brown.

   (b) Tell how Peter Brown came to quarrel with his father.

3. (a) Describe the events leading up to the death of Captain Brown.

   (b) Describe a dinner in the house of Miss Jenkyns.

   (c) Tell in your own words the narrow escape of Mrs. Forrester's lace collar.

4. (a) Give an account of the visit to the old bachelor, Mr. Holbrook.

   (b) Describe the party given by Miss Betty Barker.

   (c) Tell what you know of the party given in honour of Lady Glenmire.

5. Describe the appearance, dress and manners of Captain Brown, Mr. Holbrook, Miss Matty Jenkyns, Lady Glenmire.

(3) Tom Brown's Schooldays.

1. Annotate :—
   (a) Blood, blood, Joe's head's broke.
   (b) And so here's Rugby, sir, at last and you'll be in plenty of time for dinner at the Schoolhouse as I tell'd you.
   (c) Well, he's a plucky youngster and will make a player.
   (d) Doctor's study d'rectly you come in—that's the orders.
   (e) You'll never get rid of that fellow till you lick him.
   (f) Confound you——what's that for ?
   (g) Just run and tell East to come and back me.
   (h) Where are your manners ? You'll stare my mother out of countenance.
   (i) I daresay now I've lost the match by this nonsense.
   (j) Ah ! You've heard all about it, sir, I see.

2. Describe :—
   (a) Tom's first journey to Rugby.
   (b) Tom's first football match.
   (c) Tom's first interview with the doctor.
   (d) Tom's last match at Rugby.
   (e) Tom's fight with Slogger Williams.
   (f) The fight with Bully Flashman.

3. (a) What points in the " Fagging System " do you think were good and what were bad ?
   (b) In what ways did the behaviour of the boys at Rugby differ from that of modern schoolboys ?

(c) Name three boys who did not behave like the normal schoolboy at Rugby. Quote one incident about each boy to illustrate your answer.

4. Give one incident to illustrate each of the qualities ascribed to the following people :—

   (a) East (loyal, courageous, quick of foot, mischievous, humorous).

   (b) Flashman (cruel, cowardly, cunning, treacherous).

   (c) Arthur (gentle, religious, courageous, studious).

   (d) Martin (untidy, fond of birds and animals, interested in science, odd).

   (e) Dr. Arnold (kind, firm, just, wise, learned).

(4) IVANHOE.

1. Annotate :—

   (a) The swine turned Norman to my comfort ! expound that to me.

   (b) The unbelieving dog kennels in the cell next your holiness.

   (c) Beware ! beware ! Sir Disinherited !

   (d) It were not fit I should do so where my society might be held a disgrace to my protectress.

   (e) To bid you prepare yourselves for death.

   (f) He will not die, my father, he will not die unless we abandon him.

   (g) Wilfred of Ivanhoe ! prisoner and perish !—The life of every man in the castle shall answer it, if a hair of his head be singed.

   (h) Daughter of an accursed race ! arise and follow me.

   (i) For what art thou cast down, mad priest ?

   (j) This is indeed the judgement of God.

2. Describe the banquet in the hall of Cedric the Saxon, noting the chief persons present and the conversation that took place.

3. Describe the part played by the Disinherited Knight on the first day of the tournament at Ashby de la Zouche.

4. Tell what you know of the behaviour of the Black Knight on the second day at Ashby de la Zouche.

5. Narrate what happened in the cell of the Holy Clerk of Copmanhurst.

6. Describe the attack on the castle of Front-de-Bœuf. Deal particularly with the part played by Locksley and his outlaws.

7. Describe the fight between Wilfred of Ivanhoe and the Templar for the life of Rebecca, with the events leading up to it.

8. What part is played in the story by (a) Prince John, (b) The Templar, (c) The Lady Rowena ?

(5) SILAS MARNER.

1. Annotate :—

(a) I remember now—the knife wasn't in my pocket.

(b) Besides, whenever I fall, I'm warranted to fall on my legs.

(c) Now then, Master—what's this you've got to say—as you've been robbed ?

(d) It's worse than breaking the horse's knees—he's been staked and killed.

(e) Men's stomachs are made so comical, they want a change.

(f) It'll be fine fun to see how you'll master your husband and never raise your voice above the singing o' the kettle all the while.

    (*g*) I'm come for the doctor—I want the doctor.

    (*h*) If she makes me a bit o' trouble I can bear it.

    (*i*) Yes, child, nobody could behave better. He's his mother's lad.

    (*j*) I can't feel as I've got any father but one.

2. Describe fully any one of the following scenes :—

    (*a*) How Silas Marner came to leave Lantern Yard.

    (*b*) How Dunstan Cass stole the gold.

    (*c*) How Effie came to the cottage at the Stone-Pits.

    (*d*) How Godfrey Cass tried to recover his daughter.

3. Give some account of the sports and amusements of the people at Raveloe.

4. Discuss the simplicity, commonsense and humour of the country people and gentry as revealed at the Rainbow Inn and at the Red House.

5. Illustrate by reference or quotation the qualities ascribed to each of the following people :—

    (*a*) Godfrey (recklessness, extravagance, weakness of will, selfishness, kindness, generosity).

    (*b*) Dolly (kindness, cheerfulness, simplicity, good sense, unselfishness, industry).

    (*c*) Silas Marner (gentleness, independence, honesty, patience, quietness, humility).

    (*d*) Nancy (neatness, beauty, thoughtfulness, stubbornness, kindness, sense of duty).

6. How far is it true to say that the good people are rewarded and the bad people are punished in *Silas Marner* ?

(6) Kidnapped.

1. By whom, to whom, and when was this said ?—

    (*a*) Be soople, in things immaterial.

(b) I thought not and yet ye have a kind of gliff of Mr. Alexander.

(c) "And O, man," he cried, in a kind of ecstasy, "am I no a bonny fighter?"

(d) There's many would like to see him girning in a tow.

(e) And what seek ye at Aucharn?

(f) "Jouk in here among the trees," said a voice, close by.

(g) Hang or drown!

(h) Very well, then, I'll carry ye.

(i) There is naething there that I ken, but heath, and crows, and Campbells.

(j) Body of me! ye have mair music in your sporran than I have in my head!

(k) Are ye to lie in your warm bed and think upon us, when the wind gowls in the chimney and the rain tirls on the roof?

(l) There has never yet been a King Thomson, or his fame at least has never come my way.

2. Which of the following adventures interested you most, and why?—

(a) The adventure on the unfinished stair at Shaws.

(b) The fight in the round-house.

(c) The experience on the isle of Earraid.

(d) The murder of Red Fox.

(e) The "birstling" on the rock in Glencoe.

(f) The flight across the heather.

3. Describe the following incidents :—

(a) The departure of the emigrant ship.

(b) The gambling scene in Cluny's cage.

(c) The quarrel between David and Alan.

(*d*) The piping duel between Alan Breck and Robin Oig Macgregor.

(*e*) The conversation between Alan Breck and Ebenezer Balfour.

4. Describe the following :—

    (*a*) The house of Shaws.

    (*b*) The crew of the Covenant.

    (*c*) Cluny's cage.

    (*d*) The dress and personal appearance of Alan Breck.

5. Give a brief character sketch (appearance, dress, qualities and part played in the story) of the following :—

    (*a*) Ebenezer Balfour.

    (*b*) Ransome.

    (*c*) Elias Hoseason.

    (*d*) Mr. Rankeillor.

6. Contrast the Highland and Lowland temperaments as typified by Alan and David, giving the good and bad points of each and stating which of the two you prefer.

Oral Composition

Note.—Choose one or more of the themes indicated in the above questionnaires and be prepared to talk on them, with the minimum of notes, before the class. Remember that your classmates may " heckle " you at the end of your talk.

CHAPTER XVII

COMMON LITERARY TERMS

Alexandrine : A line consisting of six iambic feet, so called from French poems on Alexander the Great or from the French poet, Alexandre Paris, *e.g.*

" With pangs | unfelt | before | unpit | ied and | alone. |

Allegory : A story told by means of a sustained metaphor or a series of metaphors, which has two or more meanings, one of which is explicit, the other being implicit, *e.g.*

Pilgrim's Progress, Faerie Queene.

Alliteration : Consists of a repetition of the same sound. (Usually a consonant or consonants but may be a vowel : the sound may comprise a letter, letters or syllables.) This repetition is most frequently found at the beginnings of words and may occur throughout a stanza or sentence, *e.g.*

" Whereat, with blade, with bloody blameful blade,
He bravely broach'd his boiling bloody breast."

Antecedent : The noun or pronoun in a clause to which the relative pronoun in the following adjective clause is related, *e.g.*

" This is the *book* which you gave me."

Anachronism : The post-dating or ante-dating of the existence of any thing, *e.g.*

" As cannons overcharged with double cracks."

Archaism : A word or phrase which belongs to an earlier period and is no longer in common use, *e.g.*

" Nathless, wot, varlet."

Assimilation (Latin *ad + similis*) : Occurs when a sound is changed through the influence of a neighbouring sound, *e.g.* oppose is derived from Latin *ob*—against, and *pono*, I place. The sound *b* of the prefix is influenced by the following *p* and for ease in pronunciation the word becomes oppose.

Assonance : A term generally applied to the similarity of vowel sounds, *e.g.*

" Blunder, number."

Ballad : Originally a song sung to dancing ; now a simple song or, more commonly, a simple narrative poem dealing with a well-known subject and written in the ballad metre, *e.g.*

Sir Patrick Spens, The Wife of Usher's Well.

A common ballad stanza :—

Annan Water's wading deep,
And my Love Annie's wound'rous bonny ;
And I am loath she shall wet her feet,
Because I love her best of ony.

Blank Verse : Any unrhymed verse, but generally applied to verse of unrhymed iambic pentameter, *e.g.*

" Will all great Neptune's ocean wash this blood
  Clean from my hand ? No ; this my hand will
    rather
  The multitudinous seas incarnadine."

Burlesque : A ludicrous imitation of a work, generally a drama or part of a drama, for the purpose of ridicule, *e.g.*

Bottom's play in *A Midsummer Night's Dream.*

Cæsura : " Cutting." A break or pause in the metre, generally about the middle, common in the longer metres, *e.g.*

" But do not use it oft, let me entreat you."

Catalectic : The name applied to the metre of a line when the unaccented syllable of the last foot is missing ; if two are missing, the line is called hypercatalectic, *e.g.*

" But rapture | and beauty | they cannot | recall." |

Cognate Object : A noun or pronoun which contains the same meaning as the verb which it follows, *e.g.*

" I have fought the good fight."

Colloquialism : A word or phrase used in ordinary conversation or in written dialogue, but not in dignified speech or in ordinary writing, *e.g.*

" This looks quite alright."

Complement : The word or words required to complete the sense after a verb of incomplete predication, *e.g.*

" They made him their *leader.*"

Conceit : A far-fetched or strained simile or metaphor, *e.g.*

" But thou thereon didst only breathe,
And sent'st it back to me ;
Since when it grows, and smells, I swear,
Not of itself, but thee ! "

Dialect : The term applied to the form of language peculiar to any province or district of a country, *e.g.*

Loon (Aberdeenshire—a boy).
Jannock (Lancashire—excellent).

Dramatic Irony : This occurs when in a play a character makes a remark which is supposed to have only a surface meaning to others on the stage, but which has an underlying meaning for the audience, who are in the secret beforehand, *e.g.* in *The Twelfth Night*, Viola, when dressed as a youth Cesario, is asked by Olivia if she is a comedian. " No," she replies, " —and yet I swear I am not that I play." The audience appreciates the underlying meaning of the remark as they know of her disguise, but Olivia is not in the secret.

Elegy : A mournful, plaintive and generally reflective poem, usually a lament for the dead or a longing for what is absent, *e.g.*

Gray's *Elegy* ; Milton's *Lycidas*.

Elision : The omission of a vowel or syllable in pronunciation, especially when it immediately precedes another vowel, *e.g.*

" All pains the immortal spirit must endure.
Scan. All pains | th' immor | tal spir | it must | endure." |

Euphemism : The substitution of a pleasing expression for a coarse or harsh expression, *e.g.*

" Your explanation convinces me that you are a stranger to the truth."

22

Euphony : Pleasantness or smoothness of sound, *e.g.*

" The moan of doves in immemorial elms,
And murmuring of innumerable bees."

Inflection : The change in the termination of words to denote changes in declension or conjugation, *e.g.*

Boy, boys ; talk, talked.

Irony : A mode of speech in which the meaning is contrary to the words as the speaker pretends to adopt another's point of view for the purpose of ridicule, *e.g.*

" Verily ye are the people and wisdom shall die with you."

Lyric : Originally a poem to be sung to the music of the lyre. It may be defined as a poem directly expressing the thoughts or feelings of the poet, *e.g.*

Wordsworth's *Daffodils.*
Keats's *Ode to a Nightingale.*

Onomatopœia : Formation of words or names suggested by sounds peculiar to the action or object named, *e.g.*

" Quack-quack, cuckoo, swish.
By zig-zag paths and juts of pointed rock."

Parenthesis (a placing of one thing beside another) : Is a word, phrase or sentence put into another sentence already grammatically complete without the addition. The words that make up the parenthesis are marked off from the rest of the sentence by commas, brackets or dashes, *e.g.*

The result, as you know, is uncertain.

When you get to the house (*The Laurels*, 9 Park Circus), ask for Mr. Brown.

When you reach the corner—and that will take you a full half-hour—turn sharply right.

Parody : An imitation of a serious work where the style is the same but the theme, in order to arouse ridicule, is ludicrously different.

Plot Divisions : These are Rising Action, Turning Point and Falling Action.

(*a*) Rising Action consists of a series of incidents which form the complication or entangling of the plot (sometimes called Introduction or Exposition).

(*b*) Turning point is the decisive incident of the plot (sometimes called the Crisis).

(*c*) Falling Action consists of a series of incidents which form the resolution or disentangling of the plot. It ends in the Catastrophe, which is, in tragedy, the death of the chief character and, in comedy, is a happy ending, usually the marriage of hero and heroine and the defeat of those opposed to them.

Poetic Licence : A liberty allowed to poets but not to prose writers in the use of archaisms, ellipses and distortion of facts, *e.g.*

" Youth's a stuff will not endure."

Rhetorical Question : A question put not to elicit information but to emphasize a statement of the opposite meaning, *e.g.*

" Shall not the Judge of all the world do right ? "

Slang : The mode of speech peculiar to one class of society, educated or uneducated, but not accepted as standard language. It is often applied to the terms peculiar to a trade or profession, *e.g.*

Take the count ; show the white feather.

Soliloquy (speaking alone or to oneself) : When an actor, alone on the stage, speaks to himself, (the audience overhearing him voicing his thoughts) his words are a soliloquy. Soliloquies were much used by Shakespeare but, like stage-whispers and asides, are now regarded as artificial in modern realistic drama.

Spenserian Stanza : A stanza consisting of nine lines, rhyming *a b a b b c b c c*, the first eight being iambic pentameters and the last an alexandrine. First used by Spenser in *The Faerie Queene.*

See Chapter on " Prosody."

Split Infinitive : The term applied to the insertion of an adverb or adverbial phrase between the " to " and the verb of the infinitive, *e.g.*

I want you to in every possible way assist me.

Syntax : That part of grammar which deals with the arrangement and relations of words in a sentence.

Vers Libre : " Free Verse." Verse which follows no definite rules of prosody and is generally un-rhymed, *e.g.*

" This is the dead land
This is cactus land
Here the stone images
Are raised."

CHAPTER XVIII

HOW TO USE A LIBRARY

Your study of English will, it is hoped, help to create an interest in books and a desire to make full use of them. School and public libraries furnish you with the opportunity if you are willing to take advantage of it. Nowadays most secondary schools have a school library which may still, in some of the older schools, consist of a few bookcases in one of the English classrooms, but is generally housed in a special room on open shelves and often fitted out as a reading room also. Public libraries usually have a Juvenile Department where the books are displayed for your inspection and you are at liberty to borrow them for reading at home or in the library reading room.

Most of the pupils in a secondary school, except perhaps those in the very lowest forms, are allowed to become members of the school library and may borrow books on certain days. In some schools, one or more of the English periods in the school time table are taken up with work in the library. To become a member of a public library, it is necessary, since you are not a ratepayer, to have an application form (to be obtained by request at the public library) completed by your parent if he is a ratepayer ; if not, by a ratepayer who knows you. Return your completed form to the librarian and within a day or two you will receive a Borrower's Card, which allows you to borrow one book at a time, usually for a period of fourteen days. When you join a library, read carefully the rules and regulations regarding the issue of books and note the penalties you may incur by breaking them.

At first the arrangement of books in the library may seem very complicated. The following hints and a very little thought should enable you to grasp where and how books are arranged on the shelves, how to find out if a certain book, or a book by a certain author, or a book on a certain subject is in the library. The key to this information is the **Library Catalogue.**

Types of Library Catalogues

(*a*) **Book Catalogue.**—In this kind of catalogue, each name (book, author, subject) is entered at least once. It is convenient for reference, but since each addition to the library makes it out of date it must be constantly revised or it is soon misleading.

(*b*) **Loose-Leaf Catalogue.**—In this catalogue, each name is given one page or leaf. It can be added to indefinitely, but it is not convenient to handle nor does it stand up to constant use.

(*c*) **Card Catalogue.**—This consists of a number of cards arranged in boxes called **Trays,** one card for each name. At intervals there are projecting cards called " **Guide Cards** " with the letters of the alphabet or numbers (see Methods of Cataloguing) to indicate the limits of your search, *e.g.*

Guide Card **A** will be followed by all names beginning with A.

Guide Card **Ce—Cu** will be followed by all cards with names between these limits.

Methods of Cataloguing

When you are in search of a book, you generally know the title of the book, or the name of the author, or the name of an author whose books you like, or you are seeking information about a certain subject. Catalogues are planned to assist you by using one or more of these facts and employ one or more of the following systems :—

(*a*) **Alphabetical order of titles,** omitting " A," " An," " The " *e.g.*

Cruise of the " Cachalot "—under C.

The Hill under H.

(*b*) **Alphabetical order of surname or pen-name,** *e.g.*

Sir Walter Scott—under Scott.

Lord Tweedsmuir—under Buchan (John).

(*c*) **Class order of subjects** (with an index in which the subjects are arranged alphabetically).

Where this system is used in School or Juvenile Departments of Public Libraries it is generally a simplified form of the Dewey or Decimal System, introduced by Melvil Dewey, an American librarian, in 1876. This is the system adopted by most adult libraries. A brief explanation of a modified form of this system is given later (p. 346).

Notes :—

1. Methods (*a*) and (*b*) are often combined for fiction, *e.g. Treasure Island* may be found under " T " or " S " (R. L. Stevenson).

2. Methods (*b*) and (*c*) are often combined for non-fiction, *e.g. Historical Essays* (Lord Macaulay) may be found in the Class of History and under " M."

3. Works of fiction which deal with a certain subject are often found after other books on that subject and marked " F," *e.g.* *A Tale of Two Cities* (Charles Dickens) may be found under " T " or " D " or **French Revolution.**

4. Some libraries issue a catalogue which combines all three methods.

5. To find *Kidnapped* or *Little Women*, or a story by Percy Westerman or Charles Kingsley, look up in Alphabetical order. To find a book on Aeroplanes or Exploration look up class number in subject index and then locate it in the class list.

In many libraries you will have access to the shelves where the books are arranged according to the method of cataloguing. Non-fiction shelves often have the names of the subjects above the shelves. You select your book and have it entered on your borrower's card with the date on which it is returnable. Your card is retained until you return the book. In some libraries, where access to the shelves is not permitted, you must fill in the name of the book, the author's name and class number, if any, on a slip provided. If the book is in, the librarian brings it to you. The method of entering the book is then carried out.

Book Index

If you wish to select certain information from a book, consult the Index, which is usually at the end of the book. It deals with the chief topics of the book in alphabetical order and gives the pages on which they appear. Here are some extracts from indices :—

Rabbits, 52, 473–476.

Bridges, 170–211 ; designs and parts, 174–5 ; double, 174 ; history, 171 ; materials and stresses, 175–182 ; Waterloo, 171–4 ; types, 182–210.

Education, 27, 36, 173, 388 ; college, 369 ; a failure ; impracticable, 362 ; stupidities about, 413 ; technical, 422.

At times you will find a reference in the Index of this nature, *e.g.*

Clutch (*see* Motor Engine).
Corsican Adventurer (*see* Napoleon).
Christianity (*see* Religion).

This is called a **Cross Reference** and means that all information on the subject mentioned is found in the index under the second heading.

Some common abbreviations in a catalogue :—

B.—Biography.
bibl.—Bibliography, *i.e.* List of books.
col. ill.—Coloured Illustrations.
D.—Drama.
ed.—Edited, Editor.
F.—Fiction.
ill.—Illustrations.
mus.—Music.
P.—Poetry.
trans.—Translated, Translator.
V.—Volume(s).

Dewey System (*Modified*)

Books are divided into ten **Classes** which are given a number, to which, for convenience, oo is added :—

Number	Class
0(oo)	General, *e.g.* Encyclopaedias, News-papers, etc.
1(oo)	Philosophy, *e.g.* Character training.
2(oo)	Religion, *e.g.* Mohammedanism.
3(oo)	Social Science, *e.g.* Education.
4(oo)	Language, *e.g.* French.
5(oo)	Science, *e.g.* Chemistry.
6(oo)	Useful Arts, *e.g.* Engineering.
7(oo)	Fine Arts, *e.g.* Architecture. (Amusements, Sports).
8(oo)	Literature, *e.g.* German.
9(oo)	History (Geography), *e.g.* Scottish.

Each Class is divided into ten **Divisions :—**

Number	Division
80(o)	Literature.
81(o)	American.
82(o)	English.
83(o)	German.
84(o)	French.
85(o)	Italian.
86(o)	Spanish.
87(o)	Latin.
88(o)	Greek.
89(o)	Minor Languages.

Each Division is divided into ten **Sections** :—

Number	Section
820	English.
821	Poetry.
822	Drama.
823	Fiction.
824	Essays.
825	Oratory.
826	Letters.
827	Satire, Humour.
828	Miscellany.
829	Anglo-Saxon Literature.

Each Section is divided into ten **Sub-Sections** by means of a decimal point :—

Number	Sub-Section
823	Fiction.
823·1	Early English.
823·2	Pre-Elizabethan.
823·3	Elizabethan.
823·4	Post-Elizabethan.
823·5	Queen Anne.
823·6	Later 18th Century.
823·7	Early 19th Century.
823·8	Victorian.
823·9	Early 20th Century.

Each Sub-Section may be further divided into ten **Sub-Sub-Sections** :—

Number	Sub-Sub-Section
823·8	Victorian.
823·81	Bronte.
823·82	Thackeray.
823·83	Dickens.

823·84   Lytton.
823·85   Kingsley.
823·86   Disraeli.
823·87   Reade.
823·88   Trollope.
823·89   G. Eliot.

Note.—In some catalogues the second decimal is replaced by the initial letter of the author's name, *e.g.* a novel of Thackeray will appear as $\dfrac{823\cdot8}{T}$.

Each digit of the number, starting from the hundred digit, gives some information. It is sufficient if you memorize the classes and the single division given above.

You have now sufficient information to enable you to use a library with confidence. In conclusion, remember that books suffer if exposed to rain, if bulky objects are used to mark the place, if pages are turned down for the same reason, if they are defaced by writing, if one book is supported on another open one, if books are left to rest on the fore edges of the pages. In short, take as much care of them as you ought to do of your own.

EXERCISES

I. **Use the Library Encyclopaedia to prepare a talk (10 minutes) on** the following :—

1. History of the Boys' Brigade or Girl Guides.
2. The structure of a steam or petrol engine.
3. A collection of birds' eggs.
4. The story of the film industry.
5. The life story of Charles Dickens, G. A. Henty, Louise M. Alcott, Sir Isaac Newton, Marconi.
6. A short account of your native town (or nearest town given in the Encyclopaedia).

7. Native butterflies.
8. The history of football.
9. Postage stamps.
10. African explorers.

II. (a) **Name the Classes of books with the following numbers :—**
343, 721, 914, 636, 516.

(b) **State the class digits of books dealing with the following subjects :—**
Buddhism, Indian Mutiny, Nelson, Television, Cricket, Stamp collecting, Pearl-fishing, A guide to Pictures, Self Help, Modern Inventions.

III. **In what classes will the following books appear ?**

As You Like It.	*Models any Boy can Build.*
Dictionary of Careers.	*How to Think Clearly.*
Tales of a Grandfather.	*Home Mechanic Encyclopaedia.*
Peter the Whaler.	
Essays of Elia.	
The Boy's Book of Astronomy.	*Pets and How to Keep Them.*
The Heart of a Continent.	*New Testament Stories.*

IV. **Under what letter (alphabetical catalogue) will you find the following ?**

The Cruise of the Midge.	*Sir Thomas Browne.*
T. O. Paget and Others.	*A Plucky Schoolgirl.*
Alfred, Lord Tennyson.	*An Outline of Modern Knowledge.*
The Boyhood of a Naturalist.	*Professor Huxley.*
Mackay of Uganda.	*Harper's Handy Book for Girls*, Paget (A. P.), ed.

V. **Find out the Cross References for the following :—**
e.g. M'Neill, *see* Sapper.
Samuel Langhorne Clemens, Elia, Mohammedan Bible, Werewolf, Apocrypha, A.L.O.E., England, Petroleum, Rails and Sleepers, Cine-photography.

INDEX

Licence, poetic, **339.**
Lyric, 317, **338.**

M

Marks, quotation, **136.**
Melody, word, 276.
Metaphor, 285.
Metonymy, 290.
Metre, anapaestic, **267.**
    ,,   dactylic, 271.
    ,,   iambic, 270.
    ,,   trochaic, 270.
Mood, 50.

N

Neologism (coinage), **200.**
Noun, 23.
    ,,   case, 28.
    ,,   kinds, 23.
    ,,   gender, 25.
    ,,   number, 26.
    ,,   plurals, 27.
    ,,   clause, 79.
Novel, reading a, 300.

O

Object, adverbial, 18, 30.
    ,,   cognate, 30, 49, **336.**
    ,,   direct, 14, 46.
    ,,   indirect, 16, **46.**
    ,,   retained, 49.
Obsolete terms, 199.
Octave, 275.
Old English element, **252.**
Onomatopoeia, 277, **338.**

P

Parable, 287.
Paradox, 288.
Parenthesis, **338.**
Parody, 339.
Participles, 62.
Period, uses of, **114.**
Personification, 286.
Phrase defined, 7.
Phrases idiomatic, **100.**
Play, reading a, 320.
Plot, divisions of, 339.
Plurals, formation of, **27.**
Poetry, reading, 312.
Predicate defined, 10.
    ,,   extension of, **16.**
Prefix, defined, 252.
Prefixes, English (or Teutonic), 256.
    ,,   Greek, 256.
    ,,   Latin, 256.
Preposition, 68.
Pronoun, 33.
Pun, **289.**

R

Redundancy, 203.
Rhetorical question, 292, **339.**
Rhyme, 268.
    ,,   middle, 269.
Rhythm, 267.
Romance element, 255.
Root defined, 251.

S

Scandinavian element, 255.
Scansion, 271.
Semicolon, uses of, 117.
Sentence, 7.
    ,,   complex, 78.
    ,,   compound, 77.
    ,,   compound-complex, 88
    ,,   simple, 8.
Short story, reading a, 300.
Simile, 284.
Slang, 199, 340.
Soliloquy, 340.
Sonnet, 275.
Speech, direct, 136.
    ,,   indirect, 138.
Stanzas, 273-5.
Subject defined, 10.
    ,,   enlargement of, **13.**
Suffix defined, 252.
Suffixes, English, 257.
    ,,   other, 258.
Syllable, 267.
Synecdoche, 290.
Syntax, 340.
Synonyms, 98.
Synthesis, 126.
System, Dewey, **346.**

T

Tense, defined, 52.
    ,,   sequence of, 56, **189.**
    ,,   tables of, 53.
Terms, technical, 199.
    ,,   vulgar, 199.

V

Verbs, 44.
    ,,   active, 53.
    ,,   auxiliary, 47.
    ,,   factitive, 17, **48.**
    ,,   finite, 50.
    ,,   infinitive, 59.
    ,,   principal, 47.
    ,,   strong, 57.
    ,,   transitive, 45.
Verbs of incomplete predication, **46.**
Verse, blank, 270, 335.
Vers, libre, 340.